PEOPLES of the COAST

George Woodcock

PEOPLES of the COAST
The Indians of the Pacific Northwest

Indiana University Press
Bloomington and London

Library of Congress Cataloging in Publication Data

Woodcock, George, 1912-
    Peoples of the coast.

    Bibliography: p. 4
    Includes index.
    1. Indians of North America — Northwest coast of
North America.   I. Title.
E78.N78W72   979.5'004'97   77-6964
ISBN 0-253-34344-5

Manufactured in Canada

Contents

The Haida village of Skidegate in 1887.

The Peoples of the Coast

Organized into great cities like Tenochtitlan and Chan Chan or into great feudal states like the empires of the Incas and the Mayas, the Indians of Central and South America left durable monuments that still stand solid and perplexing in the massive landscapes from which they rose. But the Indians of North America, peoples of villages and wandering clans, were rarely builders of any consequence, and if they had vanished before travellers arrived from Europe we would be reconstructing dubiously accurate sketches of their cultures from the fragments of stone tools and bone ornaments that might have survived the lapse into soil of their very modest and temporary habitations.

Only one of the North American groups who survived out of prehistory had something of the monumental impulse, though even they gave it expression mostly in such perishable materials as wood and textiles. These were the fishing Indians inhabiting the coasts of present-day British Columbia and southern Alaska, who built their settlements of great wooden houses, among which clustered tall and massively carved heraldic poles celebrating the megalomaniac concern with prestige that dominated this richest of primitive cultures. These Indians, entirely unagrarian in their way of existence, are perhaps unique in having created an abundant material culture of considerable social complexity and artistic achievement entirely on the basis of a food-gathering economy, founded on fishing, hunting, and the utilization of the wild products of land and sea.

The Indians of the Pacific Northwest were few in numbers. The most generous estimate of the region's population when Spanish mariners and English traders arrived in the late eighteenth century is less than a hundred thousand, as compared with the millions who were subjects of Moctezuma in the Valley of Mexico or of Atahualpa in Peru. An exceptionally successful and sophisticated food-gathering economy such as they operated might provide a relatively high culture for small numbers of people; it could never support the large settled peasantries who sustained the great empires of Central and South America.

Not only were the Indian peoples of the Pacific Coast few in numbers. They were also politically and linguistically disunited. Along the Pacific Coast between the points where Seattle and Skagway now stand, no less than six sharply distinct languages, with considerable local dialect variations, were spoken: Tlingit and Haida, Tsimshian and Kwakiutl, Nootka and Salish. Even these language groups had no unity of political organization; they were scattered in independent villages between whom at most there might be temporary alliances, and the villages themselves were divided by the complex prestige rivalries of kinship groups. The linguis-

7

tic groups did not even form clearly defined cultural provinces. There was the example of the Bella Coola, a Salish-speaking enclave, who in terms of art and ceremonial were far closer to the Kwakiutl groups surrounding them than they were to their Salish-speaking brethren who lived around the shores of the Gulf of Georgia and Puget Sound. And there were the riparian groups of Tsimshian-speakers, the Nishka of the Nass River and the Gitksan of the Skeena, whose largely inland way of life had created among them social and ceremonial patterns that were often nearer to those of non-Tsimshian inland peoples than they were to those of the salt-water true Tsimshian.

Yet these few people, living in a linguistic and political chaos, accentuated by the sharp fracturing of the land with deep fjords and high coastal mountains, evolved a vital culture, homogeneous in spirit yet marvellously varied in its detailed manifestations, which produced elaborate dramatic ceremonials related to religious beliefs and social prestige systems, and an art more rich than any that flourished in pre-European America north of the Valley of Mexico.

It was a culture that flourished into the times of men who today still cling precariously to the last years of their lives, and it was indeed stimulated by the early stages of its peoples' contacts with European traders and mariners; barely eighty years ago the great anthropologist, Franz Boas, witnessed and recorded the last hectic flowering of its rituals. But today, in the 1970s, the artifacts of this greatest of all the primitive cultures are scattered in the museums of the world, and most of the great heraldic poles that once stood in veritable groves among the beachside villages of British Columbia and Alaska have either been shipped away or have rotted into the ground.

It is true that the culture of the Coast Indians does not now seem quite as moribund as it did when I first reached the Pacific Coast more than a quarter of a century ago, in 1949. Then, the rich cultural life of the Indian peoples of the region, their winter ceremonials, their spirit dances and their potlatches (at that time illegal according to Canadian laws) seemed barely to linger among a few obstinate adherents in the more isolated coastal inlets and inland along the Skeena River. The poles rotted in deserted Haida villages on the remoter islands of the Queen Charlottes; and even in the distant Gitksan villages of the upper Skeena — where the poles still stand in the inhabited settlements and the last of them was actually raised under the old customs in 1950, the year of my first visit to that region — the situation was not really much better. I found about eighty poles, scattered in five villages, and some of them were remarkable works, richly carved with animal crests and human figures; but many were prostrate and decaying in the tall grasses on the neglected verges of listless communities, and those that still stood or leaned — weathered, paintless, and neglected under the grey northern sky — only seemed to emphasize the death of the past they represented.

Now there is a new spirit in many of the Coast Indian villages. Since the law forbidding potlatches has been repealed, there has been a renaissance of traditional ceremonies, usually somewhat adapted to modern circumstances. Among the Kwakiutl and the Gitksan especially, potlatches have revived and new poles are being raised to validate family titles. Among the Salish, spirit dances have once again taken on the character of mass events; a year ago I attended one on Vancouver Island where between seven and eight hundred people had gathered in the long houses around the great central fires to watch the initiates perform their individual dances. And the traditional arts of wood carving, painting, and weaving, together with the arts acquired since European contact, like argillite carving and silverwork, have shown a quite remarkable renewal, notably among the Kwakiutl, among some of the younger Haida, and especially among the Gitksan where the historic poles I saw decaying so long ago have been salvaged and repaired, or have been reproduced by skilled carvers. At Hazelton the reconstructed traditional village of 'Ksan serves both as a museum to house the ceremonial regalia still in the possession of local lineages and also as a centre where some of the most remarkable modern Indian wood carving is being done. The culture is at least not dead.

Where and how that largely vanished native culture of the Pacific Northwest came into being is inevitably a matter of conjecture, though, as we shall see, clues to its origins have become quite numerous in recent years; and as a result of recent archaeological discoveries, one can speculate on a past of several thousand years, during which techniques of living and the elements of distinctive artistic styles were developed along lines consistent with the Coast Indian culture as it has been known since the first Europeans encountered the Indians and left records of them about two hundred years ago, in the 1770s. Moreover, the Indian peoples of the Pacific, with their almost obsessive concern over the proper inheritance of titular rights, were much more historically minded than most primitive peoples, and they maintained reliable oral traditions extending back over many generations, so that we can also assume that the way of life the early explorers encountered must have existed unchanged for at least two or three centuries preceding their arrival.

In the introductory chapters to this book I shall reconstruct, as far as the available archaeological evidence allows, a picture of prehistoric Coast Indian life, in which the evidence of surviving artifacts will be subjected to a process that one can only call "informed conjecture," a process inevitable where archaeological evidence is not supported by written records, a process in which "It may have been like this" is often transformed by some flash of conviction into "It must have been like this."

There is other evidence, even less substantial than that acquired by excavation, yet too impressive to be ignored, which seems to take the record of the Indian cultures back beyond the time when the earliest petroglyphs were pecked on seashore rocks along the coasts of Alaska and British Columbia, back even before the day when the earliest of the excavated sites on North American soil was first inhabited, back to the ancestral lands of Asia. I refer to the remarkable resemblances between shamanistic practices and concepts among the Coast Indians and among Siberian and other Central Asian peoples in a long arc reaching into ancient Tibet, and to the hardly less striking resemblances between certain very early Chinese art forms and those of the Haida and other Coast peoples. This evidence of an art and a tradition more ancient and more travelled than its existing relics suggest, will also be discussed at length in the opening chapters.

But anything in the way of a full and immediate account of the Coast Indian culture inevitably belongs to the period when they first established contact with people who had means more durable than mere oral traditions to record the details of a culture on which they looked with the curious eyes of outsiders. Although even the slightest of trading contacts necessarily had some effect on the coastal way of life, if only by increasing the availability of iron tools, it is fortunate that for almost a century after the first encounter on the Pacific Coast, the Europeans who dealt with the Indians were mainly traders who had no interest in changing their basic way of life. Indeed, the main effect of early post-

A Kwakiutl wedding party. The square box drum held by the musician on the right of the picture is a typical Pacific Coast instrument.

contact trading on the Pacific Coast was a feverish intensification of some of the unique elements of the indigenous culture, such as the potlatch feasts, the carving and erection of heraldic poles, and the winter secret society ceremonials, so that it could be argued that the culture actually reached its greatest complexity under the stimulus of alien contacts. To be sure, that somewhat bizarre expansion of a culture was the prelude to an equally rapid collapse, accentuated by the sharp fall in population among the seaboard settlements due to the ravages of smallpox, venereal diseases, and other white men's scourges. But it meant that at least the first of the great anthropologists to reach the Coast, Franz Boas, was able at the end of the last century to observe the culture very near to its prime, and that the pioneer photographer, Edward Curtis, was able to make a visual record before its decline had reached an advanced stage.

This fact is particularly fortunate, since the early explorers were too concerned with matters of their own (such as charting unknown shores, sorting out the territorial issues between Spaniards and British, and exploring the possibilities of trade) to gain more than a superficial view of Indian life, except in a few rare cases when circumstances forced them into the heart of it — as happened to John Jewitt who from 1803 to 1805 was the prisoner of the celebrated Nootka chief, Maquinna.

The first Europeans actually to make contact with the Indians of the Pacific Northwest left no record because they do not appear to have survived the experience; they were a party of Russian sailors, who on 17 July 1741 landed at Sitka Sound from the *St. Paul,* one of Bering's ships, in search of water; they were never heard of again. Juan Perez, the Spanish commander of the *Santiago,* which arrived off Vancouver Island on 8 August 1774, was the first voyager to describe the Coast peoples, but he wrote from a very superficial acquaintance, since he never landed to look at their villages and merely traded cautiously from his ship.

James Cook, entering Nootka Sound almost four years later, on 29 March 1778, was the first European to walk through a Coast Indian village and live to record it. In later chapters I shall quote more fully from his account, but in the present context it is most appropriate to note the inner distance from which he observed these people, aware mainly of their strangeness, unwilling or perhaps unable as a rational eighteenth century man to make the leap of empathetic understanding.

Cook tells how he was welcomed by three canoes of Nootka chiefs who cast eagle's down on the water and delivered long orations to the sound of rattles carved in the shape of birds. The Nootka impressed Cook by their dirt, their phlegmatic appearance, and above all by the fantastic wooden masks which they wore for ceremonial occasions. His comment was that of a reasonable man faced by the appearance of gross unreason: "If travellers or voyagers in an ignorant or credulous age, when many unnatural and marvellous things were supposed to exist, had seen a number of people decorated in this manner, they would readily have believed, and in their relations would have attempted to make others believe, that there existed a race of beings partaking of the nature of man and beast."

Yet, like others among the early explorers, Cook was not without admiration for the achievements of the Coast Indians, and he remarked especially on the houses where he found many families living in compartments divided off by mats and planks. Captain John Meares, a British trader who arrived in 1788, described one such large gabled house, supported by great carved posts, in which he claimed — almost certainly with exaggeration — that a clan of eight hundred people lived. Yet one cannot be entirely sure that he was wrong, for a few years later the methodical Simon Fraser paced the sides of a Salish house near the present site of Vancouver and found that it was fifteen hundred feet long and ninety feet wide. And Alexander Mackenzie, coming overland down the Bella Coola River in 1793, was impressed by the workmanship of the wooden houses he found in the valley, built of cedar boards so neatly jointed that they seemed of one piece; Mackenzie appears to have been the first European to view the art of the Coast Indians with at least a hint of the appreciation we now feel for it, since he added that the Bella Coola houses "were painted with hieroglyphs and figures of different animals and with a degree of correctness which was not to be expected of such an uncultivated people."

But few of these early explorers, even when they admired the buildings and were curious about the art of the Coast Indians, realized the complexity of the culture as it was later revealed when the British, American, and Russian traders, and later the missionaries, established extended contact with the various peoples of this long coastline and its numerous islands. And even the traders and the missionaries looked with visions limited by their special interests, so that it was not until the anthropologists appeared that a relatively objective view of the Indian cultures and of their complexities was established. Only the early pioneers among the anthropologists saw the culture in full flower. Their successors had to rely on the memories of older Indians or on the traditions that have lingered through oral transmission in villages still occupying ancient sites. During recent years, with the revival of their culture, a growing number of Indians have become interested not merely in reviving their own traditional ceremonials, but also in helping to complete the record of their own past as trained anthropologists with special insights and advantages.

It is likely that our knowledge of the Indian cultures as they existed before contact with Europeans will always be incomplete, for the very first contacts began the process of acculturation by introducing unfamiliar trade goods and stimulating the hunting of furs to acquire wealth that could be applied to ceremonial purposes; and even the first missionaries, though they arrived a generation before Franz Boas, encountered a culture that had been greatly influenced not only by the effects of prolonged trading but also by alien diseases, by the introduction of alcohol, and by the inhibition of native warfare and the introduction of new concepts of land ownership following the imposition of colonial government. The law forbidding such ceremonies as the potlatch and the Salish spirit dances, introduced in 1884 as a sequel to British Columbia's entry into Confederation, was another factor in changing Coast Indian life and in introducing a further complication for the investigator, since what ceremonials did take place were likely to be conducted without strangers being informed, and Indians became understandably reluctant to talk about their heritage. Undoubtedly such reticence is in part responsible for the varying accounts and divergent theories one encounters among anthropologists regarding customs central to the Coast Indian way of life, and particularly the potlatch. Few of the non-native researchers have spoken fluently any of the Coast Indian languages. Most have relied on interpreter-informants, who have varied in their breadth of knowledge and in their inclination to reveal the whole truth, and have usually been influenced by the unwillingness, often encountered among peoples with traditions of formality in behaviour, to leave questions unanswered; it is polite to make some reply even if one does not know the true answer and has to draw a little on fancy.

But if one accepts such obvious gaps in our knowledge and takes into account such different interpretations of what is known, the amount of information that has been gathered regarding the Coast Indians is still abundant enough to do honour to the complexity of their culture, and it is certainly sufficient to draw a full and fascinating portrait of the culture at its height, in all its aspects, which is what this book sets out to do. I do not propose to enter the more recondite disputes between anthropologists; in the rare cases where different opinions seem important in affecting the larger pattern of interpretation, I shall state the varying points of view and shall argue from the viewpoint which my own observation of the people and their surviving culture — an observation extending over almost thirty years — leads me to regard as the most credible.

Since the Coast Indian culture was indeed so rich and complex, some form of chart is needed to

Whether or not the Coast Indians originally used sails is a matter of dispute. But soon after their encounter with Europeans they were using sails made of matting, as seen in these Kwakiutl canoes.

inform the reader of the kind of territory he will be entering, and so I complete this introduction with a general sketch to outline at least the perimeters of the coastal way of life at the time of first contact with the European explorers and maritime traders.

It was a life sustained by an extraordinary abundance of the raw materials needed for survival, an abundance such as no other nonagrarian culture has enjoyed. Famine was virtually unknown among the peoples who pursued it. The protected channels between Yakutat Bay and Puget Sound were populated from spring to autumn by successive waves of salmon migrating on their final spawning runs; from the runs of oolichan, or candlefish, the Indians obtained vast supplies of fish oil; sea otters — now almost extinct — were among the common fur-bearing animals; seals and sea lions were numerous, and the Nootka and the Makah hunted the whale in epic canoe expeditions. If, in some rare season of misfortune, fishing was scanty, there were enormous clam beds and other kinds of shellfish to provide emergency food, while seaweeds of various kinds were used extensively and the giant kelp provided cables and strong fishing lines, and served in many other ways. Finally, the dense rain forests sheltered much game and gave a wealth of vegetable foods, including abundant berries which were dried for winter

13

Even utilitarian objects were quite elaborately carved, as in the case of this Haida halibut hook which is made of wood with a bone barb.

use. Most important, they furnished an inexhaustible supply of gigantic trees, some of which, like the red and yellow cedars, provided not only easily workable wood but also fibrous barks that could be shredded and woven into blankets, mats, and garments.

On such materials the Coast peoples based an elaborate and lavish existence. Their tools were limited in utility; they were familiar with copper and used it for personal ornaments and for the ceremonial shields which were among their paraphernalia of chiefly dignity, and they obtained a little iron — perhaps from Asia by indirect trading through the Aleutians — even before the Europeans arrived; but for the most part they used stone and jade for their implements until iron began to appear on a large scale at the end of the eighteenth century with the arrival of British and American sea traders. But within the limits imposed by the nature of such implements, they had evolved surprisingly sophisticated techniques. As well as the great gabled houses of split cedar planks which aroused such admiration among the early explorers, they constructed canoes large enough, particularly in the case of the great Haida craft, to carry sixty or seventy people on sea journeys of hundreds of miles; they wove richly designed textiles not only from cedar bark but also from the wool of the mountain goat and the hair of small dogs which they reared especially for this purpose; from wood they made intricately carved and coloured masks, diadems, storage boxes, thrones, rattles, ritual objects, and feast dishes; and from the horn of mountain sheep they made exquisitely wrought festival spoons. Even such utilitarian objects as the hooks with which they caught halibut and the clubs with which they killed their fish were often carved with designs that were believed to increase their potency.

Thanks to the abundance of salmon and other fish, extensively preserved by drying and smoking, the life of the Coast Indians never became that unceasing daily pursuit of food that is the fate of so many hunting and gathering cultures. Long periods of relaxation were made possible by sound techniques of food preservation, and this allowed the year to be divided functionally into two parts. The summer could be devoted to fishing, hunting, and generally laying in stores, and the autumn became the time of trading journeys. The first storms of winter signalled the departure from such mundane tasks; and this season, when the spirits were supposed to emerge from their fastnesses and seek the haunts of men, was given over to the supernaturally-oriented life of art and ritual. Everywhere up and down the Coast, during the dark rainy months between November and March, the men carved and painted, and made boxes, cooking vessels, and boats, while the women wove blankets and baskets and made garments of cedar fibres and furs. There was, in these tasks, a significant division between the sexes, not only in function but also in the use of form. The men worked in a symbolic and quasi-representational style, in which distortion was allowed and even encouraged for aesthetic reasons; its forms were based on the natural shapes of beasts and beings who were linked by legend with the well-being of each clan and lineage. The women's designs, on the other hand, were secular and entirely geometrical, with the sole exception of the ceremonial Chilkat blankets woven by the Tlingit in Alaska (though there is reason to suppose that they originated among the Tsimshian to the south) and worn by the high chiefs of the northern peoples; these, however, were woven with the help of pattern boards painted by male artists, so that in fact the symbolic designs were always originated by men, who presumably were alone able to interpret them in terms of myth and genealogy.

But the artistic activities of the Coast Indians, though we now treasure their products for the formal qualities of high art, were ancillary to the social and cult ceremonials which dominated the winter months on the Coast. These fell into two divergent categories. Among the Salish groups to the south of the area, the principal ceremonies were connected with personal spirit quests, and although the spirit dancers might form themselves into societies, the individual character of each experience was and is treasured and emphasized. Among the northern groups, the extreme sense of lineage property meant that even spiritual functions were inherited and had to be validated, like secular titles, by gifts and public witnessing; so that although a quasi-religious order prevailed during these months, and people assumed winter names related to their functions in the secret societies, in fact spiritual rank usually tended to parallel secular rank.

The northern secret societies — of which the Hamatsa, or cannibal society, ranked the highest — appear to have originated among the Kwakiutl, who carried them to their greatest degree of elaboration. From the Kwakiutl they spread to the other northern peoples, by purchase, conquest, or marriage. They were paralleled in modified form among the Tsimshian, the Tlingit, the Haida, and the Bella Coola, and even — in variations that sometimes amounted to caricature — among Athapaskan hunters of the mountainous interior of the region, like the Carriers and the Chilcotin.

Among the Kwakiutl the change from the summer life of mundane affairs to the winter life of spiritual initiation was, as we shall later see in more detail, carried so far that the rule of the clan chiefs lapsed; and the societies, led by the powerful Hamatsa (whose initiates mimed the eating of desiccated corpses and even on occasion of freshly killed slaves), assumed the direction of village life from the moment when ritual whistles announced the approach of supernatural beings

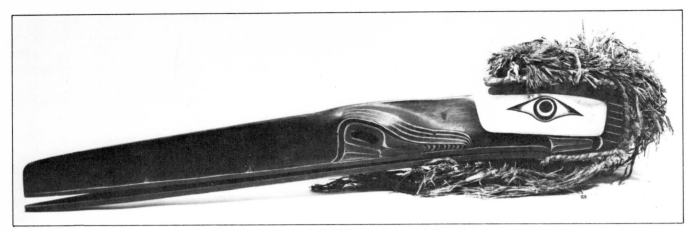

Gigantic masks were worn at Kwakiutl winter ceremonials. This Hokhokw bird mask is over five feet long.

in the woods beyond the houses. The secret societies were custodians of the origin myths of the various lineages and the intermediaries through whom, during winter, the supernatural world was brought directly into the affairs of men, as the dancers spinning around the fires in the great houses manipulated their ingenious and terrifying masks in the flickering half-light to mime the formidable presences of spirits with whom they were held to be in close communion. The power of the secret societies varied from group to group and became weaker on the peripheries of the cultural area. Among the Haida — who probably acquired the rights to the ceremonials fairly late, towards the end of the seventeenth century — the secular chiefs managed to keep control of the societies entirely in their hands, so that in their villages no even nominal shift in the basis of authority occurred during the winter; while among the Salish, the more complex secret society observances were only carried on by groups like the Vancouver Island Comox, whose territories bordered on those of the Kwakiutl.

A ceremonial perhaps even more dramatically characteristic of the Coast culture was the potlatch, the great giving feast which illustrated admirably the close link between the social life of the Coast Indians and the extraordinary abundance of their environment. In describing the potlatch, it is necessary to re-emphasize the high development of the idea of clan or lineage property as distinct from personal property. Winter villages and summer camps might be widely scattered, but in the intervening vastnesses the fishing waters, clam beaches, and hunting and berry-picking grounds were all traditionally attached as property to various clans or extended family groups. Such rights were ancient, deriving from mythical ancestors and rarely relinquished, so that lineages often possessed rights over sites far distant from their existing villages, from which their forefathers had moved so long ago that no one — even in a society with complex oral traditions — could remember the event. Such rights were always owned collectively, though the clan or house chief might appear as titular possessor; it was understood that their produce would be so distributed that no living member of the lineage would be allowed to starve through ill-fortune, sickness, or plain ineptitude. Yet parallel to such collective ownership of the means of production, with its built-in insurances against misfortune, there had developed a degree of private ownership of tangible chattels and intangible rights based on the surplus productivity of a society functioning in the midst of natural abundance.

Among tangible chattels, slaves were perhaps the most important. Slaves might be bondsmen for debts contracted and not paid in a society highly conscious of the obligations related to property. More often they were prisoners taken in the raiding wars along the Coast; such prisoners were not absorbed into the victorious tribe by adoption, as happened so often among the Plains Indians, but became the absolute property of their captors and could be used or sold or killed or liberated as their owners wished. It has been estimated — probably with some exaggeration — that in some northern villages as many as a third of the inhabitants were slaves, mostly Salish from around Puget Sound and the Gulf of Georgia, captured in raiding expeditions by fiercer tribes like the Haida and the Kwakiutl.

Canoes, blankets, and carved dishes were also important items of property, while engraved sheets of copper acquired immense prestige, which meant exchange value (sometimes ranging up to sixteen thousand blankets for a single copper), through being sold from chief to chief at ever-increasing prices. These "coppers" were even given individual names and the most costly gained a fame far outside their owners' villages, which made ambitious chiefs willing to pay all they owned and to run into debt for the glory of possessing them. The greatest glory came from being willing to destroy a copper in potlatch competition with other chiefs; the rival who could not destroy a copper of equivalent value was deeply shamed.

Intangible property among the Coast Indians was in some ways the most valuable property of all, since on its innumerable manifestations depended a man's standing in society; or rather, his seating, since it was where he sat at a potlatch or during a winter ceremonial and the order in which he received gifts that determined his rank and thus deeply affected his honour. Such intangible properties included the rights to names, dances, and songs, to family crests, to membership of certain secret societies, and even to the names of pet dogs. Such rights were rigidly guarded and could be acquired only through inheritance, marriage, gift, purchase, victory in war, or murder.

But rights were inseparable from the obligations that custom attached to them. Possession without validation was pointless, and validation involved the liberal outlay of material property. A chief of the Kwakiutl or more northerly peoples could only dance the dances that supernatural beings had given to his ancestors, or assume his hereditary title, or give his son a prestigious name, or celebrate the puberty of his daughter, or raise a totem pole to record his greatness and his family's legends interpreted in appropriate crests, after he had validated his pretensions by a potlatch feast. At this feast, which might take years of preparation if the chief's obligations were large, the guests would arrive dancing their personal dances and singing their songs on the prows of the great ceremonial canoes. And the host chief would not merely feed his guests extravagantly, sometimes for many days on end; he also gave away as many material goods as he had been able to amass or borrow from his fellow clansmen, matching the gifts to the rank of the recipients. The more he distributed, the greater his prestige; the greater also the shame of his guests if, at their own later potlatches, they failed to give even more magnificently. For, especially in the post-contact years when possessions became more abundant, competition was a feature of the potlatch system, and in this way it became a substitute for physical combat when growing European power on the

Coast put an end to the raids which passed for warfare; but the terms of warfare and its rhetoric of hostility and contempt were transferred to the potlatch. The host chief would boast (either personally or through a kinsman who acted as orator) of his own generosity; and he would taunt his guests with their meanness, while his clansmen sang songs insulting the visitors and sometimes even exhibited carved wooden caricatures of them. Guests would be subjected to tests which they had to pass if they were not to lose face, such as drinking in a single draught an immense wooden ladleful of oolichan oil.

Yet, though a chief might temporarily beggar himself by a particularly lavish potlatch, he usually gained not merely prestige but also eventual profit, since a mechanism of economic adjustment was provided by the fact that, for the sake of their own good names, his guests would be obliged to return his gifts with increase whenever they held their own potlatches. Some anthropologists, notably Ruth Benedict, have seen the potlatch as combining the elements of usury and insurance, as well as that of conspicuous spending, in a primitive anticipation of capitalism, but the intangible aspects of the occasion should not be forgotten; it was pride far more than the desire for profit that was being satisfied, and the occasion was always — except in the rare "play potlatches" of the Bella Coola and some Kwakiutl groups — related to the validation of some potent ancestral right.

The occasions when pride was clearly in the ascendant over profit were those in which a chief anxious to show his special superiority and to shame his rivals most effectively would destroy his goods instead of giving them. I have already referred to the destruction of coppers; even more spectacular in terms of prestigious waste were the so-called grease feasts, when the fires within the houses would be fed with great quantities of oolichan grease and valuable canoes were dragged in to augment the flames, while, to preserve their own prestige, the guests refused to abandon their seats as the flames scorched and blistered them. Occasionally at such feasts the house itself would be allowed to burn as part of the grand gesture; and very often slaves, who were mere chattels without rights, were immolated at key points in the festivities.

Such destruction of property must not be seen as an act of genuine renunciation like the burning of his house by a Doukhobor who wishes to show his contempt for material goods. The Coast Indians had the highest respect for material wealth, and for this reason the chief who destroyed it gained enormous respect; the rival whom he challenged to match his achievement, and who failed, would lose so much face — and so shame his lineage — that suicide might become his only escape from social ruin.

At first glance, it seems as though in every way the potlatches expressed and aggravated a desire for individual self-glorification rare among primitive peoples. Yet it should cautiously be remembered that the chief was only the temporary bearer of names and privileges belonging to the lineages, whose prestige was collectively enhanced by his actions — a fact recognized by his kinsmen who would eagerly share in his efforts to gather goods for the potlatch so that the honour of the house and the clan should be sustained. A lack of individualism as we understand it is suggested by the fact that, while still alive, chiefs would relinquish titles and even secret society roles to their recognized heirs, who in the northern tribes with matrilineal systems of inheritance were likely to be not their natural sons, but the sons of their sisters.

The potlatch and similar customs spread down the whole Pacific coast from the Aleutians to the Columbia estuary, and they were imitated by inland tribes as far as the foothills of the

Rockies. No ceremonial act in this whole region was recognized unless it had been validated by giving; and even the commoners, dancing their spirit dances among the Salish, would celebrate their initiatory performances by distributing gifts among the witnesses. They still do, as I have experienced by receiving gifts as a spectator, and therefore a witness, in a Vancouver Island long house.

Outside the main pattern of winter ceremonials, in which the whole village shared as participants or spectators, there were at least two ways in which contact was maintained with the supernatural world. One was by means of ritual acts performed on behalf of the clan or village, usually by a chief of high rank, which ensured success in some enterprise essential to the economic well-being of the groups. Such occasions were the ceremonies connected with the catching of the first salmon or — among the Nootka — with the departure of a whale-hunting expedition. But there was a whole realm of supernaturally-oriented activity that stood outside the ordinary structure of the group; it was the activity of the shamans, who were usually socially humble people but who acquired influence and inspired fear because of their special powers of clairvoyance, healing, and cursing. It is in shamanism that we find perhaps the most ancient roots of the Coast Indian culture, those linking it with its undoubted origins in east-central Asia.

The spread of rites up and down the Coast was a manifestation of the constant intercourse that went on among these peoples, in spite of their linguistic differences. War and trade were other means by which the various groups came into contact. Since the Coast tribes had no effective military organizations like the Iroquois or the Plains Indians, their warfare — at least until the introduction of firearms — was probably not very deadly in its actual effects. It consisted mainly of night raids, and most of the slaves on the Coast were captives acquired on such occasions; those of high rank were usually ransomed and had to give feasts to wipe out the shame of bondage. Almost certainly, trading was a more regular and important form of sustained contact than war. Through the Chinook of the Columbia Valley, whose dialect became the basis of a trading pidgin still occasionally used by older Indians, abalone shells were brought up from Oregon to decorate the diadems of the northern chiefs. From Alaska, the Tlingit exported native copper to the south, and the canoes of both the Haida and the Nootka were widely traded to peoples in whose territory the giant cedars needed for such large craft did not grow. The Tsimshian, who lived around the present site of Prince Rupert, became the middlemen between the northerly and southerly currents of trade, and thanks to their strategic control over the great runs of oolichan up the Nass and Skeena, they controlled the main part of the trade in fish oil. These two facts made them the great pre-European merchants of the Coast, and even after the establishment of Hudson's Bay Company posts, the Tsimshian traders — among whom women were regarded as particularly adept bargainers — pressed far inland by canoe and up paths through the forest that can still be traced and which were called "grease trails" because of the oolichan oil that was still the most travelled of all commodities. Such trading intercourse furthered the exchange — often by hard barter — of immaterial commodities like dances, rituals, and art forms.

But there were other important and still not fully understood links among the various tribal groups. Down the whole Alaskan panhandle and through British Columbia as far south as the northern Kwakiutl subtribe of the Bella Bella, as well as inland among the hunting Carriers, there existed a system of "phratries," as some eth-

Here the bear crest is displayed on the frontlet of a Tsimshian chief's head-dress *(above)* and on a Tsimshian chief's bird rattle *(below)*.

nologists termed them, that overran geographical and linguistic barriers. The clans and house families in all the villages of this region were grouped into exogamous and matrilineally-organized groups, varying from two in number among the Tlingit and Haida to four among the Tsimshian. The origin myths of the phratries suggest that some of the linguistic groups that now appear homogeneous were divided in ancestry: some of their clans appear to have reached the Coast by one river system and the rest by another. The demands and privileges of the phratric groups seemed to outweigh the somewhat fragile loyalties that existed within villages composed of various clans. A Tlingit of the Eagle phratry could not marry and probably could not enslave a Haida Eagle and was tacitly expected to avoid him in battle. A man outside his territory might expect hospitality and protection from his Eagle or Raven brethren in another tribe, even though he might not speak their language. The fact that the southerly Salish were not included in the phratric freemasonry may be one of the reasons why they were the main victims of northern slave raids.

But if the presumably ancestral bonds of such groups were often deep and wide ranging, conventional political links among the Coast peoples were light and loose. As I have suggested, none of the language groups was a true political entity; they had no systems of common government; and though food-gathering areas might be owned by particular lineages, there was no way in which a whole people, defined linguistically, could own an actual territory in the same way as a modern nation owns a country. Thus, while raids were carried out for plunder or to revenge injuries, wars for land were rare, and if there were Medicis — great patrons of the arts — among the local chiefs, there seem to have been no Bonapartes.

The villages, in fact, were virtually autonomous and rarely acted together. Within the villages each house had its own chief, and several houses would together form a clan in which the house chief with the most prestigious titles, duly glorified by generous potlatches, would assume a somewhat nebulous leadership. Similarly, the leading chief of the most prestigious clan would be the first man in the village, but his position was one of prestige rather than power in the conventional political sense. Only among the Tsimshian did a kind of hereditary village chieftainship with some degree of authority exist. The higher chiefs among that people formed a superior caste, sometimes called "royal" by European observers, whose status was higher than the normal Coast gradations of nobles (who owned validated titles), commoners (usually younger sons or nephews and their descendants) who had no tangible property that would enable them to claim titles available in their lineages, and slaves who had no rights except possibly — and even this is by no means certain — within some of the less prestigious winter secret societies. Such social gradations affected the pattern of marriage, already limited by the exogamous rules of the phratric system (which decreed that a man should take a wife from outside his own phratry). To marry someone whose ranking at a potlatch was markedly lower than one's own was regarded as a loss of face, and for a free man or woman to marry a slave was unthinkable. As a result, among the Tsimshian "royal caste" especially, the choice of eligible spouses was highly restricted.

On this elaborately ceremonious culture, with its curious combinations of aesthetic sensibility and megalomaniac pride, the effects of contact with Europeans could not be other than complex. They were, as we have seen, both stimulating and destructive; they inspired an unparalleled fever of creativity which eventually collapsed into an apathy so intense that for whole generations it seemed as though not only the culture of the Coast but also the peoples who had produced it would die out.

Here again, a brief overview of the various ways in which the contact affected the Indian peoples will provide a framework for a later more detailed discussion of the changes that took place in the culture from the late eighteenth century onwards.

Russian fur traders began to reach Alaska and make contact with the Tlingit as early as the 1760s and it was during the next decade that the first Spanish and British mariners arrived. Apart from its significance as an incident in his explorations, James Cook's visit in 1778 was important because the sea otter skins acquired by members of the expedition were traded at great profit in China, and the news of these transactions stimulated an interest in the region which led to the appearance of the British and American sea traders during the 1780s and in later decades.

Until the Fraser Valley gold rush of 1858, the main concern of the Europeans who came to the region now divided between British Columbia and the American states of Alaska and Washington was still the fur trade. The North West Company, and later the Hudson's Bay Company by which it was absorbed in 1821, replaced the earlier individual sea traders like Captains Meares, Portlock, and Dixon (to whom we owe some of the earliest accounts of Coast Indian life); but although they set up trading establishments that were somewhat grandiosely called "forts" throughout the present territories of British Columbia, Washington, and Oregon, and although they assured their own safety by a rough kind of *lex talionis*, demanding an Indian life for every white life, the companies made little effort to infringe on native customs, since they relied on the good will of the Indians to maintain their trade. A similar policy of virtual noninterference was followed by the Russian-Alaskan Company, whose representatives were more than once forced into desperate self-defence because of the aggressiveness of the Tlingit, who thought the foreigners were interfering with their own local trading privileges. Not until some years after the Colony of British Columbia was founded in 1858, followed by the American acquisition of Alaska in 1867, was any kind of political interference in the Indian way of life attempted.

Nevertheless, the technological changes that even such a limited degree of interference brought about were immense in their social implications. The musket caused raids on other villages to be more deadly and led to considerable shifts in the relative strengths of various Indian groups. The introduction of an abundance of iron for making into tools was less important for the changes in basic technique that it brought about than for the elaboration of design and the increased production it allowed, since the Indians retained — and retain to this day — virtually the same kinds of adze and finishing knife which they had already refined in stone and jade. The degree of elaboration can easily be seen by comparing the artifacts which Cook acquired in 1778 — and which fortunately are still preserved by the British Museum — and those which form the greater part of modern museum collections and were, for the most part, made less than a hundred years ago, at least a century after the first explorers reached the Coast. These masks and rattles made after contact with Europeans are not only more ingenious in the details of design and more smooth in finish; they are also bolder and more expressionistic in their general approach, as though facility of production encouraged the artists to push hard on the bounds of creation. One has the same reaction on comparing the drawings of the rather simple carved Nootka house posts, which illustrate Cook's *Voyages*, and Kwakiutl and Gitksan poles carved during the past century; the former have a grand

classic simplicity, but in the latter one feels a change of temper as well as of technique, and undoubtedly the reaction is accurate, for the greater ability of the Indian artist to produce more artifacts in a short time was paralleled by the greater ability of his patrons — acquiring large quantities of European-made goods through trading furs — not only to commission more poles, masks, and other ritual paraphernalia but also to pay for the feasts in which they would be validated or used. Perhaps for the first time among the Coast Indians, virtuoso artists like the Haida sculptor, Charles Edenshaw, appeared and gained celebrity. Their names are still remembered with respect.

It was in this period, from the middle of the nineteenth century onward, that the great free-standing heraldic poles — most commonly called "totem" poles because of the animal crests they display — became familiar features of the Coast villages. Some anthropologists, notably Marius Barbeau, have argued that the practice of carving poles of any kind was entirely a product of contact with Europeans, but there is too much contradictory evidence to accept such a hypothesis without reservations. There is no doubt, from the evidence of Cook, Mackenzie, and other eighteenth century travellers, that the upright posts both within and outside the great gabled houses must have been carved for centuries with figures representing the mythical ancestry of the resident chiefs. It is equally certain that mortuary poles, with recesses at the top to hold the remains of celebrated chiefs, were being made long before the Europeans arrived; indeed, it seems likely that the earliest of all kinds of potlatch was that at which the dead chief's remains were enshrined in his pole, and his heir assumed the ancestral name and the power and prestige accompanying it, all validated by the appropriate feasting and giving.

Yet there is reason to grant that Barbeau was

Ancestral memory. A pole on
the upper Skeena River.

These poles used to stand in the deserted Haida village of Ninstints on Anthony Island. In 1957 they were moved to the University of British Columbia.

24

at least partially right and that the great free-standing crest-bearing poles, sometimes sixty feet high and ostentatiously displaying chiefly claims to titles, legends, and spiritual guardians, were mostly carved in the age of prosperity that followed the first encounters between the Indians and the traders — the American "Boston Men" and the British "King George Men" — who came after Cook. The celebrated and vanished grove of poles at Skidegate in the Queen Charlottes appears to have been carved entirely in the 1870s and 1880s; the equally celebrated Kwakiutl poles at Alert Bay, some of which still stand, were probably carved between 1880 and 1900, after which the craft of carving as well as the culture it represented began to decline very rapidly on the actual coast and more slowly elsewhere. Fine poles were still being carved by the isolated Gitksan on the Skeena in the 1920s, though the best examples of this people's work — like the famous "Hole in the Sky" pole which still stands at Kitwancool — were probably carved in the 1890s.

The hectic stimulation of cultural life that produced the great poles and other artifacts, through which we are mainly familiar with the Coast Indian culture, was linked closely with the influences that caused the break-up of the native social order, which also must be sketched out to demonstrate the rapidly changing character during historical times of the culture we are representing. Here, perhaps, the most influential circumstance was the coincidence of a period of unprecedented and precarious prosperity with the steady decline in population, which was another consequence of contact with Europeans.

The story is a dismal one, though it will not be surprising to those familiar with the general history of European contacts with peoples without immunity from the sicknesses of the old world. Smallpox was first introduced during the 1770s by the Spanish explorers; in the nineteenth cen-

tury there were recurrent epidemics which wiped out whole communities and left few parts of the Coast untouched. An epidemic of influenza sweeping through the Indian villages was recorded as early as the 1830s, and in 1918 the Spanish influenza was as devastating as smallpox had been in earlier generations. Tuberculosis played its part, while the spread of venereal diseases among the Coast peoples was encouraged by the enthusiasm with which the Indians in the mid-nineteenth century welcomed the commercial possibilities of prostitution. During the gold rush period of the late 1850s and the 1860s, the northern people brought canoe loads of women — mostly slaves — hundreds of miles to Victoria in order to take advantage of this new means of acquiring trade goods for potlatches; as a result, syphilis and gonorrhoea became endemic in many northern communities.

The effects of this massive impact of alien sicknesses were strongly evident among the Haida. The native population of the Queen Charlottes was probably 6,000 in 1835. By 1885 it had shrunk to 800, and by 1915 — the low ebb so far as the Haida were concerned — the remnant of that proud and powerful people was a mere 588 individuals, less than a tenth of their former numbers. The decrease in other groups was not quite so dramatic, yet the entire native population of the Coast appears to have fallen, over the eight years after 1835, from about 50,000 down to 13,000, while the 1835 figure — based on rough counts by Hudson's Bay Company officers — may well represent an already diminished population in comparison with pre-contact times when the Coast peoples probably numbered between 60,000 and 70,000 individuals.

The combination of temporarily growing prosperity and a sharply diminishing population produced a situation that could not help but lead to the break-up of the old social order. Suc-

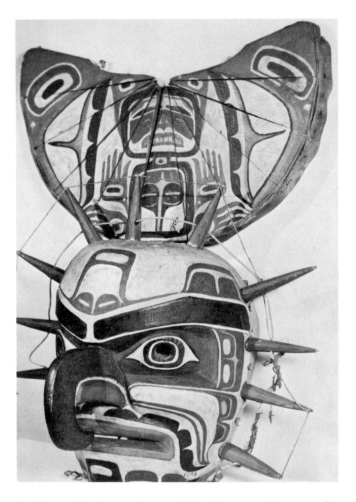

This sun mask *(above)* whose rays can change into a killer whale's tail is a fine example of the ingenuity of Kwakiutl transformation masks.

cessive deaths often meant that titles that had formerly been contained within a fairly rigid pattern of succession were open for competition within the whole lineage. Prestige began to stem less from prowess and ancestry than from the adeptness in trading that would bring an abundance of potlatch goods. Any commoner who had been lucky in hunting became an aspirant to chiefly rank, owing to his real if remote relationship to deceased titled ones, and younger sons of younger sons justified with lavish potlatches their appropriation of lineage titles that were not being used. The Kwakiutl even invented, during the period of high prosperity, a special title of Eagle which only had significance in the context of potlatching activities; an Eagle was a man who had acquired great wealth and who was given consideration within the community because of his willingness to dispense it generously, but he

had no chiefly rank or obligations and no traditional role in the village or the lineage. With such innovations, the traditional order, which had never been very cohesive, moved rapidly towards disintegration. At the same time, the wildly growing extravagance of potlatch ceremonies involved the chiefs in a tightening network of mutual obligations that often led to disputes and petty warfare. Shamed chiefs, now that they had firearms, often found it easy to kill their triumphant rivals, and vendettas ensued. Other chiefs tried to win property or titles by conquest; and under the pressing need to gain new means of wealth, the slave trade on the Coast actually increased in the mid-nineteenth century, despite the efforts of both British (later Canadian) and American colonial authorities to stamp it out. Once the slaves were freed, some of them entered in their turn on the round of property gathering and potlatching, though the stigma of having once been in bondage clung to them, as it does to their descendants in more traditional villages, even in the later twentieth century.

The upsurge of prosperity, ceremonial activity, and artistic creativeness came to an end in most parts of the Coast towards the turn of the century, when a growing economic shortage complicated the effects of epidemic sickness. The almost total extermination of the sea otter brought an end to the early prosperity based on the fur trade, while the establishment of fish canneries on the best salmon rivers, and the demand for tinned fish in North America and western Europe, led to a drastic reduction in the availability of native staple foods; the Indians of British Columbia (except for a few hunting bands in the far northeast) signed no treaties with the federal government, and when white fishermen and canners appeared, the native people found that although they had been granted reservations comprising the sites of their winter and summer villages, their traditional fishing and hunting rights over certain waters and certain areas of land were unregarded by the white intruders.

Sickness, malnutrition, and the sense of being made to feel alien in their own country resulted in a widespread breakdown of morale among the Coast Indians of British Columbia and Alaska. By the first decade of the twentieth century these formerly proud people, who had gained such an extraordinary mastery over their environment and had created one of the greatest of human art traditions, began to regard them-selves and to be regarded by others as a doomed group of peoples (anthropologists writing even during the 1930s had little doubt that they would soon die out), and this pessimistic resignation made their hold on their cultural heritage grow progressively weaker. It also made them less capable of resisting the efforts of alien governments to deprive them of their traditional land-use rights and the attempts of missionaries — with a few laudable exceptions — to destroy, as symbols of paganism, all the most vital manifestations of the native way of life.

Some of the missionaries (like the celebrated William Duncan who founded the so-called Holy City of Metlakatla) herded their converts into new mission villages, where, away from the contamination of heathen custom, they sought to turn the Indians into pious and industrious Victorian workingmen. Others concentrated on attacking the winter ceremonials and the secret societies, or on inciting the Indians to burn their own poles, under the mistaken impression that these monuments were worshipped as idols; in this way almost all the remarkable poles of the Nishka were destroyed in the villages along the Nass River, as well as most of the poles belonging to the clans of coastal Tsimshian who had relocated their villages around the Hudson's Bay Company's Fort Simpson during the 1840s. But in Canada — where most of the Coast Indians lived — the worst attack on the traditional way of life, engineered mainly by the missionaries, was the legal prohibition of the potlatch by Sir John A. Macdonald's government in 1884, the year before he destroyed the Métis culture of the prairies by sending in the army that defeated Gabriel Dumont's guerrilla fighters in the battle of Batoche. Highly respected Indian chiefs, particularly among the Kwakiutl, were imprisoned for defying the ban, and much indignation was aroused when the Mounted Police seized and transferred to the National Museum in Ottawa the ceremonial regalia of the lineages who had participated in forbidden potlatches. It took seventy years before the potlatch — and the Salish spirit dances that had been proscribed at the same time — were freed of legal prohibition. There were certain rather plausible arguments against the potlatch which enlisted even some of the more piously Christian Indians into the campaign for its prohibition: such ceremonies encouraged waste and indebtedness at a time when the Indians were becoming steadily poorer, and they often ended in violence. Yet the potlatch had been a central institution in the traditional society of the Coast, serving to validate the ranking system and giving a bond of unity in an otherwise loosely linked social order. Where the authorities succeeded in abolishing it, communal life immediately lost much of its significance and cohesion.

Fortunately the inlet-bitten coast and the densely forested inland country along the Skeena River and its tributaries sheltered many small Indian communities to which access was difficult in winter, particularly in the days before the airplane became a factor in coastal transport. In such places the potlatches continued, often curiously modified by the fact that the Indians now lived in at least commercial contact with a mass production society. As the weaving of the splendid Chilkat blankets of mountain goats' wool declined, their place was taken by red or blue Hudson's Bay Company blankets with elaborate designs carried out in pearl buttons. And the traditional items of potlatch giving — blankets of cedar fibre, canoes, carved feast dishes, slaves, etc. — were replaced by manufactured items. At one celebrated Kwakiutl potlatch scores of mirrored dressing tables and hundreds of enamel baths were given away; at another, among the Tsimshian, a chief climaxed his feast by ordering his nephews to slash open more than a thousand sacks of flour and spill their contents into the sea; cash, in notes and silver, was also given freely at potlatches.

The worst period for the Coast peoples was from the end of the nineteenth century down to the 1930s, when the decline in population drew to an end. Since then, the birth rate has increased and the death rate fallen steadily, with the result that the natural increase among Indians in British Columbia is now three times that among the rest of the local population; if the present trend continues, the pre-contact population should be matched before the end of the 1980s. The civil disabilities that Indians once suffered have been taken away. They are now full Canadian or American citizens and can take part in elections in the country of their residence; by the 1970s, a Coast Indian was a member of the British Columbia provincial cabinet. Indians are no longer treated insultingly as minors when they wish to buy liquor, and they are allowed to carry on any of their traditional ceremonials without hindrance. An Indian organization, the Native Brotherhood of British Columbia, acts as a kind of trade union protecting the interests of Indian commercial fishermen, and various Indian groups have been active in pressing land claims based on customary possession and use, a problem still far from settlement. Although some Indians are prosperous, the general level of income and formal education is lower than that of the Coast population in general; the incidence of sicknesses like tuberculosis is higher; and it is a sign of a sense of deep alienation from the majority culture, particularly among young Indians, that the proportion of the native population committed to provincial jails for relatively minor offences is much higher than that of the local population in general.

Yet, in balance, it seems that we may be nearing the end of the tragic period when the Indian of the Pacific Coast is seen as a poor disease-ridden, feckless and despised ward of the state.

As with the Eskimo, the recent wide recognition of the imaginative quality of Coast Indian art at its best has brought the Indians an unfamiliar degree of esteem, which — added to the revival of old ceremonials — has helped them to recover self-respect.

At the same time, the Indian life as it was lived before the white man came is obviously beyond revival. The ambient world has changed too much. The arrival of the salmon is no longer the magical coming of a friendly people to be appeased with ceremonial. The winter ceremonials may be held again in modified form, but nobody really believes any longer that the spirit whistles announce the arrival of "Cannibal from the North End of the World" and his supernatural companions. Although potlatches are now held quite frequently, no chief's days are dominated by the obsessive preparation for such events — or ruined by the failure to meet the obligations they impose. Many of the objects made by Coast Indians during the present revival of their arts, fine though they may be in quality, are intended not for traditional ceremonial use but for the pleasure of non-Indian collectors or museum visitors. Native herbalists and shamans still practise; and their knowledge of herbs, manipulation and the psychology of their people often bring about quite remarkable cures, but they no longer enjoy a monopoly of medical practice, and their clients are always ready to try the rival shamanism of modern medicine. And the concepts of romantic love, introduced through school studies, the cinema, and television, have eroded the old exogamous marriage rules, so that traditional marriages with the appropriate ceremonials have become progressively rarer and the rate of intermarriage with non-Indians has increased steadily during recent decades.

Perhaps, however, the most important reason why the old culture can never be revived

Kwakiutl house frames showing construction. Note how the adze cuts were used as decorative fluting.

in a completely authentic way lies in the total change in socio-economic conditions. The whole complex of social, ceremonial, and artistic life on the Pacific Coast was based materially on the migrations of salmon and spiritually on an animistic view of the universe. It was also closely tied to an elaborate social structure and to what — despite the apparent individualism expressed in institutions like the potlatch — was essentially a communitarian way of existence, in which the extended household group shared in whatever the clan produced, even if for reasons of prestige the chief's share might be the greater.

The basic infrastructure has been knocked out of this way of life. Indians no longer depend principally on the salmon runs for their food; they depend, like other western Canadians, on money earned through employment or through welfare services. And except in a commercial sense, if they happen to be fishermen, the salmon run is no longer the event on which their year's cycle, with all its ceremonials and its succession of necessary food-gathering activities, is centred. Except for the small areas of land in their reservations, the Coast Indians no longer hold property in common according to their lineages; they are, far more than in the classic days of the potlatch, individual proprietors who earn their livings in competition with each other and with their white neighbours.

Moreover, in modifying the Indian view of the universe, the influence of the missionaries has been profound and irreversible. Although many individuals and some whole groups still appear to believe in the reality of possession by spirits, this faith no longer runs through the whole of existence so that a man acquires his manual as well as his magical skills through the influence of supernatural guardians; the encounter with and placation of the spirits no longer dominates a whole season of the Indian year. Most of the Coast Indians are now members of one of the churches that have proselytized in the region during the past century: Anglicans, Catholics, Methodists, Presbyterians, with a few Pentecostals and Salvation Army followers. Even when native religious cults have arisen during the generations since contact with Europeans (like the Indian Shaker Church, which is still strong among the Salish, and the various "prophet" movements), they have been profoundly influenced by Christian doctrine, placing far greater stress on a supreme being than any of the local peoples did in pre-contact days, and envisaging a redeemer and redemption through faith in him. The local languages re-

main, but language is usually the most obstinately retained element in any culture changing radically in response to outside influences, and it can be adapted to almost any alteration in the social or the economic pattern.

But if one cannot look at the way of life of Coast Indians in the later 1970s and take it as a reliable guide to their way of life in the 1770s (or, for that matter, in the 1870s), there is one body of evidence that stands apart from the clues presented by the archaeologists and from the necessarily imperfect records of traders, missionaries, and anthropologists. It is the records of the tangible objects, which — provided they are preserved from physical decay — remain unchanging, whereas oral traditions change over time and oral accounts given to outsiders change in the very process of transmission. The artifacts of a people have always been the most reliable evidence of their way of life, more reliable than the written or printed records of even a literate civilization. And when the culture of that people is represented by a high art tradition, as in the case of the Coast Indians, it is among that art's products that we find ourselves most closely in contact with their intellectual and spiritual life. It is for this reason that in the chapters which follow I shall stay close to the concrete realities of Coast Indian art, regarding the carvers and other master craftsmen as its most notable chroniclers. Just as Ruskin found the spirit of a great and vanished European age still living in the stones of Venice, so the modern historian can find the spirit of the great primitive cultures still surviving in their artifacts of wood and bone and textile. For art defies the death of cultures.

Part I

A dancer of the Hamatsa Society.

CHAPTER ONE

Before History: Archaeology's Questions

Until very recently the prehistory of the Coast Indians of British Columbia and Alaska had been only lightly studied, and it was generally believed that the culture which Russian, Spanish and British mariners encountered in the latter part of the eighteenth century had probably developed during a very few centuries before the first contact with Europeans. There were a number of negative factors encouraging such an assumption. The Coast Indians never made pottery, and so the sherds that in many other cultures were found so enlightening by archaeologists, in the way they marked cultural continuities and changes, have not been discovered in their village sites. The major Indian artifacts were made of perishable materials such as wood, and their preservation was not considered important by their makers or possessors until post-contact times, so that the oldest works of art known to have belonged to the historic culture are probably the curios which the survivors of James Cook's visit of 1778 took back with them to London for safekeeping in the British Museum.

There were, indeed, some rather mysterious relics in stone, which took two principal forms. First were the petroglyphs cut into coastal boulders and cliffsides, usually round about the tide line but sometimes on much higher ground, and evidently linked with shamanistic practices.

Then there were the small sculptures which people kept turning up in the Fraser Valley and at odd spots on the coast, usually either seated anthropomorphic figures or zoomorphic vessels, which also appeared to have some link with magical rites. But the Indians who were living when such relics were discovered disclaimed any knowledge of the purposes for which petroglyphs or portable sculptures were carved or of the peoples who carved them, and for this reason it was long taken for granted that there was no continuity between these unknown prehistoric cultures, whose relics appeared to be mostly of stone, and the historic culture whose most impressive products were carved out of wood. What tended to be forgotten was, first of all, that the Coast Indians known to history did in fact continue to carve in stone, so that even before the Haida began to make argillite carvings for merchants and travellers, they were cutting tobacco mortars, ceremonial clubs and other objects out of local stone for their own use; these objects tended to be overlooked until quite recently since they were neither so numerous nor quite so spectacular as the poles, masks and rattles of painted wood. At the same time, the stone carvings dug by chance out of the earth were in fact comparatively few in number, and it is reasonable to suppose that among the people who made them — as among the historic peoples — artifacts of perishable materials were also more numerous and perhaps more spectacular than those of stone.

Any effective answer to such problems had to wait until an energetic attempt was made to establish the prehistory of the Pacific Coast by scientifically conducted excavations. And the archaeologists, with their digging tools and their precise measurements of levels and carbon datings, only appeared in force a couple of generations after the anthropologists had made their enquiries, that penetrated no further, in chronological terms, than the reliable backward vision of oral tradition, which is never deeper than a few generations — at most two or three centuries.

There was a brief and somewhat peremptory beginning in archaeology at the turn of the century, between 1897 and 1902, when Harlan I. Smith accompanied the Jessup North Pacific Expedition, organized by the American Museum of Natural History. Smith performed some excavations, particularly of shell middens, examined and recorded local collections of what were then regarded as Indian curios, and salvaged a fair number of artifacts, while he drew attention to a series of important prehistoric sites which he had no time to investigate. But he did very little in the special direction that now seems so important in the context of Coast Indian prehistory — the establishment of a chronology of cultures, which was not to be attempted seriously for almost half a century. In fact, very little was done in the field of Pacific Coast archaeology after Smith's departure until the appearance of that remarkable, self-effacing man, Charles E. Borden, who in the past thirty years has completely changed our views of the early millennia of the Coast Indian cultures. Borden was not by training a professional archaeologist; he was an expert in German language and literature whose academic career led him to the University of British Columbia, where he developed a double passion for the science of archaeology and the culture of the local native peoples. He became a scientific amateur in the grand Victorian manner, the manner of Darwin and Wallace. It was in 1946 that he began his excavations in the Fraser Valley, and for almost twenty years he was virtually the only practising archaeologist, amateur or professional, in the region — so strong a hold did the anthropologists then retain over our knowledge of the local Indian cultures. Summer after summer, Borden led groups of enthusiasts on scientifically conducted digs in various parts of the province, from the Skeena down to the Fraser, and from 1950 onwards he availed himself fully of the newly developed carbon 14 dating techniques to establish the chronologies of the sites and subcultures he investigated. It was appropriate that Borden should be given the opportunity to work on the Milliken site, which was discovered at Yale in 1958, for this has turned out to be the oldest yet known locality of human settlement in British Columbia. The first men who used it arrived no less than nine thousand years ago; they may possibly have arrived as early as twelve thousand years ago. Furthermore, the site presented stratified evidence of millennia of successive and possibly continuous occupations from its first use almost down to the present day.

The Milliken site opened unexpected vistas of a cultural evolution that might have taken place on the British Columbia coast itself rather than by importation, and a series of further discoveries in various parts of the province reinforced the lesson of the relative antiquity of human occupation and technological development west of the Rockies. Finds at Glacier Bay in Alaska date back at least ten thousand years; in the Haida archipelago of the Queen Charlottes, the site at Skoglund's Landing may well have been first occupied more than eight thousand

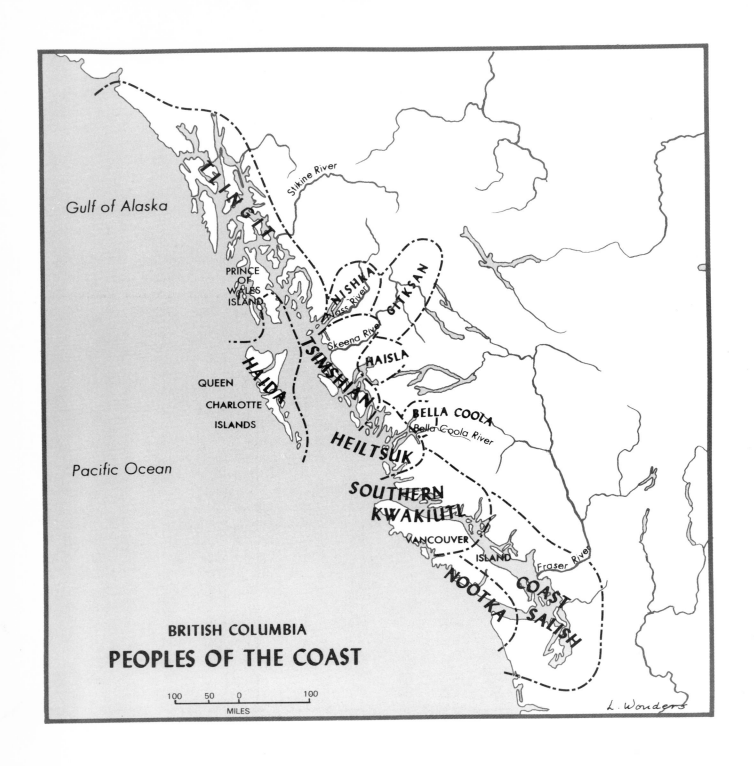

Gulf of Alaska

TLINGIT

Stikine River

PRINCE
OF
WALES
ISLAND

NISHKA

Nass River

GITKSAN

Skeena River

HAISLA

HAIDA

QUEEN

CHARLOTTE

ISLANDS

TSIMSHIAN

BELLA COOLA

Bella Coola River

Pacific Ocean

HEILTSUK

SOUTHERN

KWAKIUTL

VANCOUVER

ISLAND

Fraser River

NOOTKA

COAST

SALISH

BRITISH COLUMBIA

PEOPLES OF THE COAST

100   50   0   100

MILES

L. Wonders

years ago; several datings between eight and five thousand years ago showed up in the area now occupied by the Kwakiutl, and sites four thousand years old were found in the Tsimshian region around the mouth of the Skeena. All these datings suggested that man first penetrated into the region as the great icefield began to retreat round about 9000 B.C., at the end of the last great glaciation period on the Pacific Coast. So far, no evidence has emerged to suggest that there was any human occupation before that time.

The earlier sites yielded the paleolithic remains of primitive fishing and hunting cultures, which used crude tools flaked from pebbles and harpoons headed with points of bone or deer antlers. There may well have been two different groups probing in as the ice melted — hunters moving down the Fraser Canyon to occupy the Milliken site quite far inland up the river, and water-borne fishermen occupying sites on the coast, like Namu in Kwakiutl territory, which it is difficult to believe anyone could have reached except by water or could have survived in without some kind of craft for fishing and hunting marine animals. This means, of course, that among the earliest settlers on the Pacific Coast were people who had mastered the woodworking techniques necessary to make at least small dugout canoes — unless one entertains the rather less likely possibility that in the sheltered but shoaly waters around Namu the people travelled on and fished from some kind of narrow raft like that which is still used on the rivers of Fiji.

So, in the beginning, we see rather darkly an influx of early Stone Age men, who used rough tools and yet were able to live from hunting and fishing. The climate appears to have been warmer and drier on the Coast in those early millennia than it became after about 1000 B.C., when the familiarly cool and humid climate of modern British Columbia first began to move in. This meant, on the one hand, that the vegetation was not as lush and generous as it has been over the three most recent millennia and that the rain forest, which in historic times covered almost the whole of the coastal slopes and the offshore islands, was not so dominant a feature of the ecology. On the other hand, it also meant that less elaborate clothing and less solidly weatherproof houses were needed. We can assume reasonably that the first inhabitants had not yet begun that evolution in woodworking techniques which created the massive dwellings and splendid carving of the Coast Indians known to history, and that they were as yet unaware of the techniques of weaving or of the uses to be made of the barks of cedar and other trees. Like later peoples on the Coast, they had no agriculture and no domestic animals except the dog, whose remains have been found in Namu sites dating back eight thousand years; it must have accompanied the ancestors of these early settlers when they crossed the land bridge over the Bering Sea on their way to populate a manless continent.

How directly the first people whose remains we have found were related to the present inhabitants of the Coast, there is little evidence to determine. We do know of sites inhabited over thousands of years by people whose progress is charted in the changing patterns of stone and horn implements and weapons. Yet, as the history of such multilayered sites as Byblos in Lebanon seems to suggest, continuity of occupation is no guarantee of continuity of lineage or culture; an inhabited site usually has advantages that might lead to its being taken over by invaders or occupied by later streams of migrants after the group that first settled there has vanished. Certainly, on the Pacific Coast, the variety of physical types among excavated skeletal remains suggests a mingling over the millennia of people with different origins; as we shall see later, the traditions of the Indians themselves seem to bear out this assumption.

It is when apparent continuities of technique begin to appear that the pursuit of prehistory becomes acutely interesting. A prime example is the Salish village at Musqueam, near the mouth of the north branch of the Fraser River and not far away from the University of British Columbia. It was the people of Musqueam whose bellicosity made Simon Fraser turn back in 1808 up the river that bears his name, instead of sailing out into the Gulf of Georgia, and the descendants of the people that Fraser encountered occupy to this day a reservation on the site of their ancient village. Recent finds among the mire of a water-logged midden suggest that their ancestors have been using the same village site for several thousand years. Excavations in the midden turned up not only the stone and bone artifacts that usually survive over long periods, but also wooden dishes and pieces of basketry and matting, which in technique and design show a cultural continuity with historic artifacts that leaves little doubt of the Salish having lived on this spot continuously for millennia, prospering because of the rich flow of salmon and other migratory fish into the river's mouth and the abundance of marine animals who followed the great fish migrations.

These early Musqueam relics are linked with the emergence on the Coast, about the beginning of the first millennium B.C., of a technically progressive culture (particularly associated with Locarno Beach on Burrard Inlet) that resembles in many ways the neolithic cultures of Europe. There had been time for ingenuity and leisure to express themselves in the perfecting of tools and weapons made from nonmetallic substances. The pebble tools had been replaced by elaborately chipped arrowheads and, later, by ground slate projectile points and knives adapted for a variety of purposes. The uses of bone and antler artifacts were even more varied. Not only were there weapons of hunting, and doubtless some-times of warfare, like harpoon heads, fleshing knives, and daggers, but there were also awls of various kinds and sewing needles used in making skin garments, as well as netting needles which suggest that the people of this intermediate period (perhaps the ancestors of the modern Indians who live on the ancient sites) already made the nets of nettle fibres which the fishermen of the Coast were using far into historical times. Small adzes were being made of stone and bone, while the sharpened beaver's teeth — which later carvers used to etch in the finer details of their masks and poles — were already in use. These transitional people may not have had the tools needed for major woodworking efforts, like building large communal dwellings and carving massive canoes like those of the historic Haida and Kwakiutl, but they had the means to make small dugout canoes, to hew dishes and bowls, and to carry out simple carving of the kind one sees on comparatively recent Salish grave posts, which bear conventionalized and roughly executed anthropomorphic images.

Certainly, by this period, the urges towards artistic creation and personal adornment were finding expression. The women were already wearing that characteristic West Coast ornament, the labret, which long afterwards so disconcerted the early European explorers; it consisted of a grooved disc of stone, bone, or some other rigid material, inserted into a hole in the lower lip, which protruded in a kind of shelf of flesh, considered highly becoming by the local peoples (and therefore reserved for aristocratic ladies) and very ugly by strangers. There were also necklaces of bone and slate beads and animal teeth, and even what appear to have been finger rings made of bone.

Very striking also is the evidence, which shows up at a number of these sites, of the beginnings of a tradition of carving which dates back for at least three thousand years. Most of the

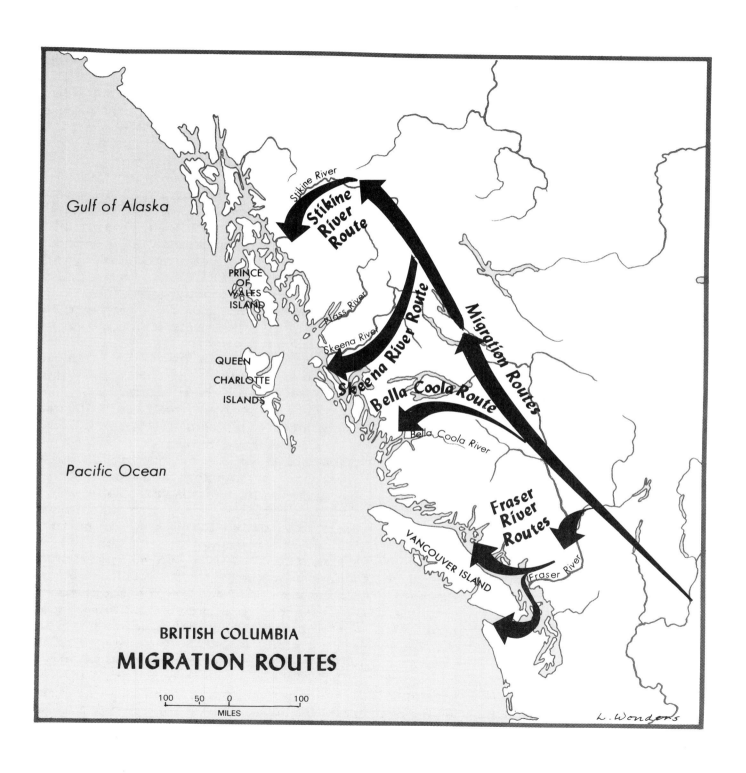

Gulf of Alaska

Stikine River

Stikine River Route

PRINCE OF WALES ISLAND

Nass River

Skeena River

QUEEN

CHARLOTTE

ISLANDS

Skeena River Route

Bella Coola Route

Migration Routes

Bella Coola River

Pacific Ocean

Fraser River Routes

VANCOUVER ISLAND

Fraser River

BRITISH COLUMBIA

MIGRATION ROUTES

100   50   0   100

MILES

L. Wonders

examples evoke the magical tradition within which these people enjoyed their mental and physical being. A piece of antler bone is shaped into the rough effigy of a killer whale; and one questions whether its presence means that the killer whale clans, with their appropriate crests, were already in existence so long ago. Or was this little carving, shaped so that it could be held in the hand, perhaps a charm used by a prehistoric sea mammal hunter? — which would suggest that, at this early period, the whale hunting followed historically by the Nootka on the ocean coast of Vancouver Island was originally practised also by the people of the sheltered Gulf of Georgia, if not in pursuit of the large true whales, then of the giant dolphin known as the killer whale or blackfish. The end of a deer bone found on a beach of Burrard Inlet is meticulously carved into a tiny human skull, an inch and a half high; it was clearly used as a shaman's charm, since similar miniatures have figured among the apparatus of Coast Indian medicine men in recent times, and also among the apparatus of Siberian shamans and Tibetan Bon wizards. And an *atlatl*, or spear-throwing device, from the same site is carved in the form of a human head, wearing what appears to be a conical basketry hat of a type still being worn by Indians along the Coast in the late nineteenth century.

At this point we are drawing very near to the technological leaps — perhaps associated with an invading group pushing down the Fraser Valley from the inland plateaus — that carry us into something that appears to have been close to the Coast Indian culture as it was first encountered by Perez and Cook two hundred years ago. These occur in the so-called Marpole culture, which flourished between 400 B.C. and about 450 A.D. It is named after the community of Marpole on the north branch of the Fraser, very near the southernmost end of Granville Street in Vancouver and several miles inland from the village of Mus-

queam. The rich finds at this and other sites of the same culture suggest the flourishing, round about the beginning of the Christian Era, of a way of life much more ample in its resources and much more ceremonially elaborate and more socially complex than anything that had previously existed on the Coast. Tools and techniques had at last been developed that enabled Indian groups on the Coast to take full advantage of the abundance of food and material for housing, clothing, and winter entertainment that existed in the waters and on the land around them.

The Marpole people possessed, in fact, what Charles E. Borden has called "the basic triad of tools" associated with the monumental woodworking tradition of the Coast Indian culture at its highest point: large wedges of antler and wood that would split the trunks of cedar into broad planks; hand hammers of basalt and other tough stones, shaped in pestle form to provide a kind of phallic handle; and sharp-edged finishing adzes made of finely polished blades of nephritic jade. Having such tools, the Marpole people were able to construct the great plank houses, whose foundation holes and cold hearths have been found on landlocked beaches that once faced out to the waves but have long since been isolated by the steadily accumulating alluvium of the Fraser Delta, which has been pushing the sea westward at the rate of about ten feet annually for at least the last two thousand years. Along the beaches in front of the great houses, the long canoes which the new tools had made would be drawn up and protected from the sun by coverings of rush and cedar mats.

These canoes, and the great variety of harpoons and other fishing and hunting gear which the Marpole people created, enabled them to diversify their sources of food and to accumulate the surplus of goods which subsidized the ceremonial life and provided the seasonal leisure to develop the arts appropriate to it. Seals, sea

A prehistoric stone club from the Hazelton area. The phallic handle is typical of clubs found in this area.

lions, and the Fraser River sturgeon, which grew to a length of twenty feet, were caught in great numbers, and there was an abundance of the different species of salmon in their appropriate seasons, while by now the art of preserving fish by smoking and drying had evidently been developed, providing the basis for winter stores. Molluscs were collected on the wide beaches and sandbanks, and waterfowl were taken in the great marshes whose remnants still survive along the shores of the Fraser Delta. Nor had these early people dissociated themselves as much as later Coast tribes from the hunting culture that lay in their past, for they killed large numbers of deer and elk and made the antlers into the barbed harpoons they used in fishing and on their sea hunts.

The elaborate trading networks that existed up and down the Pacific Coast two millennia ago are suggested by the materials not native to the Fraser Delta region that have been discovered in the Marpole sites, the most impressive of them being native copper, used for personal ornaments (and at the time of first contact with the Europeans still being traded down the coast from the Copper River in Alaska), clear obsidian blades from the Oregon interior, and dentalium shells fished off the west coast of Vancouver Island. Ornaments of copper, shell, and worked stone were buried in a few of the graves dug on the lee side of the village middens, and this — along with the fact that some skulls were already being deformed in a manner that later became habitual among the Salish — suggests that a social hierarchy already existed on the Coast two thousand years ago. Hoards of material wealth, like the cache of more than twenty thousand shale beads discovered at Marpole, indicate that large quantities of nonutilitarian property were accumulated by the people of this ancient riparian society, perhaps for trading, but perhaps also for giving away at feasts resembling the potlatch of historical times.

There are many indications that the Marpole

people were already versatile craftsmen. They were certainly weavers, since decorated stone and bone spindle whorls, closely resembling those of historical times, have been found in the villages of this era. Evidently they were already using the wool of the mountain goat, still found in the mountains overlooking the Fraser Valley, and breeding the now extinct little dogs, that were kept by the Salish up to early historical times, so that their fine curly hair could be woven into the blankets worn by people of high status; the existence of such fine weaving, as distinct from coarser textiles woven from cedar fibre, is a further indication that a society sharply divided by rank already existed on the Coast two thousand years ago. It is true that no actual wool fabrics from this time have yet been found, nor have fragments of cedar blankets or of mats or baskets belonging specifically to the Marpole culture, but the fact that such artifacts survived from the earlier and more primitive culture, represented by the water-logged midden at Musqueam, makes it virtually impossible that such types of manufacture were not, by 400 B.C., incorporated into the regular daily life of the Coast peoples.

So much has obviously perished that we can envisage only in a fragmentary fashion the level of artistic achievement attained on the Coast by the last century B.C. No wooden artifacts survive in village sites of the Marpole period, and therefore we have little idea of the skill these people developed in the making of large carvings or of their ability in painting, another art widely practised in later periods on the Coast. Yet it seems likely that even in this early period the houses and wooden utensils were decorated with carving — though perhaps less elaborately than in historical times — for the tools found in Marpole period middens include not only the large stone adzes and antler wedges used for rough carpentry, but also small, fine-edged jade adzes, tiny chisels of nephrite, sharpened beavers' teeth, and fine-edged fragments of quartz used for working the sharper details.

With such a range of tools, the Marpole peoples were able to work not only perishable wood but also such durable substances as horn and stone. Fragments of antler were carved into animal and human forms. Soft stones, like steatite and soapstone, were also carved, into anthropomorphic images and into the curious figures which are characteristic of this period of Coast Indian prehistory on eastern Vancouver Island and in the lower mainland of British Columbia — seated humanoid figures with bowls lodged between their knees, which evidently had a ceremonial and probably a shamanistic function. One such bowl at Marpole was found on top of a cairn containing a human skeleton, and it is likely that the buried man was the shaman to whom it had belonged. The stone figures of the Marpole phase vary in nature, some of them being roughly carved and quite massive (up to a human figure more than twenty-one inches high) and others being small and carved with expressive detail, though never quite so felicitously conceived as the man-bowls from a slightly later period, discovered higher in the Fraser Valley and along the Thompson River in the area now inhabited by the inland bands related to the Coast Salish.

Recent discoveries, and comparative studies of stone artifacts in British Columbia and Alaska — like that which resulted in Wilson Duff's epoch-making exhibition, Images Stone B.C. (which began its national circuit at the Victoria Art Gallery early in 1975) — have shown the falsity of past theories of the isolation in time and place of the early stone-carving culture of the Fraser Valley. Discoveries far to the north suggest that a stone-carving culture flourished not long afterwards in the area of the Nass and the Skeena rivers, and stone continued to be carved, particularly among the northern groups of Indians, well into historic times. There appears to have been a similar continuity in another form of stoneworking: the petroglyphs pecked and scored out of the surface of boulders, cliffs, and rock outcrops down the whole length of the coast from Alaska to the Columbia River. Carbon 14 dating of organic materials found in deposits covering some of the early petroglyphs suggests that they were made about the beginning of the Christian Era, but the carving on coastal rocks continued well into historical times, for some of them portray sailing ships and horses, and one represents the S.S. *Beaver*, which did not begin to ply the coastal waters until 1836.

The sense of a long continuity, which one gains from studying the prehistoric portable stone carvings and fixed petroglyphs of the Alaskan and British Columbian coasts, has a significance beyond itself. In historic times, when stone carving continued to be practised in different forms from those of prehistory, and often — as in the case of the commercially motivated argillite carvings from the nineteenth century Queen Charlotte Islands — for rather different purposes, the carving in wood was always in quantity greater and in quality more varied and, at its best, more satisfying. It is fair to assume that the easier craft (if equally difficult art) of wood carving was even in the past more widespread, and that stone carving was less frequent and done mainly for ceremonial uses. In other words, although the Coast Indian wood carvings that survive into the late twentieth century are rarely more than two centuries old, we can assume that the first such artifacts brought to Europe by James Cook's companions were in fact the refined products of a tradition of craftsmanship in both stone and wood at least two thousand years old, uniting the ancient carvers of man-bowl figures with the men who created the great poles of the Haida and Nishka and

Gitksan during the final nineteenth century blossoming of the Coast Indian culture. Later I shall return to the stone figures and petroglyphs of Coast Indian prehistory to consider what they have to tell us of the less material aspects of the region's early cultures.

There remain a few other aspects of the archaeological evidence that deserve to be considered. As will be evident by now, I have devoted a great deal of space to the Marpole culture of the Fraser estuary not only because its sites were so rich in remains, but also because its people seem to have developed, at least two millennia ago, an existence economically abundant and socially complex when compared with other high primitive cultures, including those that have survived into our world. Such a people must have been at once industrious and ceremonious, accustomed to comfort yet willing to endure the voluntary trials that are aspects of growing up and initiation in all such societies. They had their artists and their shamans, their chiefs and their common people, but a warrior class seems to have been absent from among them, since unlike the later cultures on the Coast — particularly those of the north — they had many weapons designed for killing the wild creatures on whose death they depended for survival, but few that seem to have been designed specifically for killing men. They appear, in other words, to have been an unusually pacific people — as, indeed, the Salish who still occupy their lands undoubtedly were — in comparison with the Kwakiutl and the Haida and the Tlingit in historic times.

During the centuries that followed the waning of the Marpole culture around 400 A.D., other people and other influences seem to have moved into the Fraser Valley, until the situation stabilized round about 1200 A.D. with the culture particularly associated in the minds of archaeologists with the old village of Stselax on the

Musqueam reserve near Vancouver, which all the available evidence suggests has been inhabited continuously for more than seven hundred years. The period from 1200 to Simon Fraser's arrival in 1808 seems to have been one of extraordinary cultural stability — even stagnation. The people of this period retained the techniques developed during the Marpole culture a thousand years before, without greatly changing the shapes or the variety of tools, so that it is fair to assume that the large dugout canoes, capable of travelling hundreds of miles in sheltered waters, and the big plank houses several hundred feet long, which the early European visitors saw at the beginning of the nineteenth century in Musqueam and other lower mainland villages, were similar to those created and used by the men of Marpole.

Yet in two important respects the Stselax culture differed from that of Marpole. Mortuary practices changed from burial in the local midden to the custom — continued well into the nineteenth century — of wrapping dead people in mats or blankets and depositing them in grave houses outside the village or even in canoes perched in trees; only the shamans were still buried in the ancient way, but in their cases the burial was a good distance outside the village. This quite radical change of practice suggests the influence of some group moving in from outside the area, probably from the north. The other remarkable difference is the striking scarcity of personal ornaments and the entire absence of stone carvings among the remains of this late Fraser Valley phase. Combined with technological stagnation, this poverty in artistic creation suggests that the Fraser Valley culture, as it was first seen by Europeans almost two hundred years ago, had in fact regressed somewhat since the dynamic times of the Marpole culture two thousand years ago.

Our knowledge of the cultural sequences in the Fraser Delta, and up the Fraser Valley to the canyon, where the great river plunges down out of the mountains into the alluvial plain, is much greater than our knowledge of prehistoric developments on other parts of the Coast, mainly because the sites have been more accessible and the proximity of two local universities (University of British Columbia and Simon Fraser) has made available considerable teams of archaeological workers, who have naturally enough tended to carry their earliest investigations as closely as possible to their academic bases.

It is only, in fact, during the past ten years that pilot excavations in the area of the northern cultures have begun to establish scales of antiquity in places now inhabited by peoples like the Haida, the Tsimshian, and the Bella Coola, that are similar in extent to those already established in the Fraser Valley. But there is still much empty space in the intervening periods to be filled in, and it is not at all clear in any satisfactory detail how the cultures north of the region now inhabited by the Salish proceeded from their early Stone Age to the degree of civilization first encountered by Europeans at the end of the eighteenth century.

Yet even the slight evidence we possess makes it clear that many centuries ago the impetus of development moved away from the region of the Marpole culture towards the region where the territories of the Haida, Tsimshian, and the northern Kwakiutl groups faced each other across the waters of Hecate Strait and Queen Charlotte Sound. The shift probably took place around the middle of the first millennium A.D., with the result that by the end of the eighteenth century, the northern cultures had been developing steadily in social and artistic complexity for perhaps a millennium, while in the Salish area there had been relative cultural stagnation.

This leaves us with the interesting problem of

whether the historic Salish culture, as Vancouver and Simon Fraser first saw it almost two hundred years ago, with its comparative simplicity and passivity, was nearer than the more elaborate and aggressive northern cultures to an original common coastal way of life out of which they all developed. Philip Drucker, one of the more important anthropologists to deal with this question, has suggested that there must have been a kind of primal culture founded by an early Mongoloid fishing and hunting people, who came across the Bering Strait land bridge from northeastern Asia and made their way down the coast towards California at the end of the Ice Age, about ten thousand years ago. He believes that both the Aleuts and the Alaskan Eskimos are descended from this original migration, and that among the Coast peoples, the Nootka and the Kwakiutl (who both belong to the Wakashan language group) are isolated representatives of the same heritage. But the Coast cultures, as we have known them in historical times, he believes to have developed as a result of the mingling of this original strain with two later streams of migrants who found their way south from the mountainous hinterland where they had already established themselves as hunting peoples — the Haida, Tsimshian, and Tlingit descending the northern rivers, and the Salish coming down the Fraser.

There is little strictly archaeological evidence that supports or disproves this line of speculation, and to test it and establish clearer ideas of the origins and development of the cultures, we have to move into other areas: the languages; the legends and myths by which the various lineages explain their own origins; the evidence of beliefs and attitudes provided by the prehistoric artifacts; and, not least, the fascinating pattern of resemblances between the shamanistic beliefs and practices of the Coast Indian peoples and those of Siberia and central Asia.

CHAPTER TWO

Language and Myth: The Verbal Witness

Language and myth are closely linked; together they form the verbal heritage of a people. Among the Coast Indians they often corroborate each other, and in this way they turn supposition into evidence.

The languages these peoples speak — or at least so far as we have known them in the two centuries since the first European contact — were exceptionally varied in relation to the number of individuals involved, since there were at least six major and sharply differentiated languages and many dialects, shared among the seventy thousand people.

The northernmost group were those who spoke Tlingit. At the end of the eighteenth century their territory extended down the panhandle of Alaska from Yakutat Bay (almost 60° north) to Portland Inlet (approximately 55°), which almost exactly corresponds to the present boundary between American and Canadian territory. In this long, narrow stretch of territory, three hundred miles from north to south but bounded by the Coast mountains which from the east push very close to salt water, the Tlingit occupied the whole coastline and, with one slight exception, the offshore islands; they traded up the Stikine and the other steep coastal rivers with Athapaskan peoples who lived beyond the ranges.

The enclave in Tlingit territory was on Prince of Wales Island, territorially a part of the Alaskan offshore archipelago, whose southern end was inhabited by a people called the Kaigani. The Kaigani spoke a Haida dialect little different from the language spoken by the main group of the Haida, who occupied the whole of the Queen Charlotte Islands but had no foothold on the mainland.

On the mainland opposite the Queen Charlottes lay the territory of the group of related peoples forming the Tsimshian linguistic family. The Tsimshian proper were strictly coastal people, occupying the mainland and offshore islands from Portland Canal as far south as the north end of Princess Inlet. Many centuries had separated them from their inland relatives, the Nishka of the Nass River and the Gitksan of the Skeena; the three dialects differ enough to be regarded as languages. The Gitksan and the Nishka between them represented the farthest inland penetration of the characteristic Coast culture, whose latest blossoming actually took place among the Gitksan.

South of the Tsimshian peoples lay the territories of the various Kwakiutl groups. There were three of them, speaking very distinct dialects. The Haisla occupied a territory at the head of the Kitimat inlet, cut off from the open sea and from their fellow Kwakiutl by Tsimshian tribes occupying the coastline and the offshore islands. South of Tsimshian territory on the coast was that of the Heiltsuk, including the Xaixai, who in historical times had become a weak group, disintegrating under pressure from their fellow speakers of Heiltsuk, the Bella Bella, a somewhat aggressive people who made their first appearance in history as the hostile Indians before whose threats Alexander Mackenzie turned back in 1793. South of the Bella Bella, the Southern Kwakiutl occupied the coastal areas and also the northern tip of Vancouver Island, as well as the eastern part of the island to a little south of Campbell River.

Most of the western, ocean shore of Vancouver Island was occupied by the Nootka; and an outlying group of Nootka-speakers, the whale-hunting Makah, had established themselves across the Strait of Juan da Fuca in the neighbourhood of Cape Flattery and Neah Bay.

The remaining group — and in terms of population the largest — was the loose cluster of peoples with related languages who are generally known as the Coast Salish. They occupied southeastern Vancouver Island, the coastline of the Gulf of Georgia south from Bute Inlet down to the Strait of Juan da Fuca, the ocean coast of what is now American territory almost as far south as the Columbia River, the inland country around Puget Sound, and the Fraser Valley as far as the great canyon by which the river flows through the Coast Range. An isolated Salish-speaking group, the Bella Coola, occupied an enclave of territory on the river that bears their name and on the adjacent inlets lying between the Bella Bella and the Southern Kwakiutl.

The Bella Coola had adopted and adapted many of the cultural characteristics — including the art styles and ceremonial complexes — of their northern neighbours, and they were in every way a more sophisticated and artistically creative people than their linguistic brethren who have occupied the shores of the Gulf of Georgia in historic times. Linguistic tests, based on glottochronological criteria, suggest that the Bella Coola had been separated for many centuries from any other Salishan group; and their myths, which recount an origin in the valley where Alexander Mackenzie found them nearly two hundred years ago, tend to bear out this assumption. Even among the southern Salish peoples of the Gulf of Georgia and Puget Sound regions, there are considerable differences between the various dialects; these are sometimes so great that — as I have personally witnessed — members of Salish bands from the State of Washington, who attend ceremonials among British Columbian Salish groups like the Cowichan of Vancouver Island, are obliged to converse with their hosts mostly in English, because their ways of speaking are so far apart and because the old trading pidgin, known as Chinook, which once united all the peoples of the Coast, has faded into obsolescence and (among the young who regard it as a bastard tongue) into disrepute.

To relate any of the Coast Indian languages to other Indian tongues has been difficult, since whatever resemblances exist are not obvious, and for a long time Haida and Tlingit and Tsimshian were treated as groups on their own which must have developed in a territorial isolation so long in time that they could no longer be linked to other known languages. The extraordinary diversity of the languages made all the more surprising the apparent homogeneity of the Coast Indian culture. But if time and study have led us to appreciate the diversities that underly the cultural homogeneity, they have also led us to conclude that neither the culture nor the ethnic groups which produced and practised it were so isolated in origin as their historic distinctiveness had led those who first studied them to assume.

It was, indeed, obvious from the beginning that the coastal groups of Salish were linked to the semi-nomadic hunting tribes speaking related Salishan languages, who wandered through the southern and central interior of British Columbia as far, in the case of the Shuswap, as the Rocky Mountains. The territory of the Coast Salish peoples bordered on that of the Interior Salish on Harrison Lake and in the Fraser Canyon, and although one group followed a typical fish-oriented coastal way of life and the other a typical plateau hunting existence, they maintained trading contacts and seem to have reached fairly peaceful accommodations in the areas where their fishing grounds came together. Indeed, if one can judge from the situation in early historic times, the prehistoric lower Fraser and its estuary formed a common fishing ground for all the Salish-speaking peoples, since even the Cowichan bands from Vancouver Island had certain ancestral rights over at least the salmon runs of the Fraser. This implies that at some time in the past there must have been a colonizing expedition across the Gulf of Georgia from the river delta to establish the island villages.

By historic times all links between the Bella Coola and the other Salish-speaking groups had lapsed and even the memory of them had vanished, which suggests that many centuries ago the Chilcotin, an Athapaskan-speaking people who now occupy the headwaters of the Bella Coola River, must have separated them from their nearest fellow-Salish, the Lillooet and the Shuswap. It seems likely that the Bella Coola were originally Interior Salish, who found their way to the Coast and became acculturated through contact with the Kwakiutl, rather than Coast Salish who would have had to run the gauntlet of a series of aggressive coastal Kwakiutl groups to find a devious way up the marine inlets to the well-hidden river mouth that became the centre of the Bella Coola culture. The Bella Coola were always the smallest of the coastal groups and can never have numbered more than three thousand people even in prehistoric times, yet the distinctiveness of both their language and their special art style suggests a very long period of survival and change as a group separate and remote from the other speakers of Salish.

The other peoples whose relationship seemed evident even to early linguists were the Nootka and the various Kwakiutl groups, whose languages have obvious common elements. Assuming for this reason that they stemmed from a common progenitor language, such linguists placed Nootka and Kwakiutl in a group which they called Wakashan. Later linguists have envisaged other relationships and suggested a larger group of languages, which they call Mosan and in which they include the Salish as well as the Wakashan tongues. While the evidence for this linguistic relationship is somewhat less convincing than that for the original Wakashan grouping, the idea does seem viable in other directions, where evidence suggests that the Salish seem to have been present on the Coast at least as long as the Wakashan peoples. It is particularly notable that, while the northern Coast peoples all have striking migration myths, the Nootka, the Kwakiutl, and the Salish all possess origin myths of ancestors appearing from the sky in the territory where the tribe now lives, which shows that these three peoples came long enough ago for the collective memory of their arrival to have leached away even out of their myths. Such a conclusion fits well with the archaeological evidence that establishes a long continuous occupation of Fraser Delta Salish settlements, like Musqueam, by people whose cultural characteristics appear to have changed little and slowly over nearly three thousand years.

Recently, the languages of both the Haida and the Tlingit have been linked to the Athapaskan or Déné group of tongues, which embraces many Indian peoples in the northern interior of British Columbia and also in the Yukon and Northwest Territories, all of whom, like the

Haida and Tlingit, are matrilineal and exogamous in their clan structure. Yet glottochronological evidence apparently indicates that Haida is at least five thousand years away from any primal Déné language out of which it may have originated. Obviously the Haida and the Tlingit became distinct peoples long before they made their ways down to the coast.

The remaining northern language group, that of the Tsimshian, seems to have no relation either to the tongues of the other coastal peoples or to those of the interior Athapaskan tribes who are now their neighbours. Recently there have been suggestions that its links are with the Penutian group of tongues, spoken by people as scattered in locality as the Chinook of the lower Columbia, the Nez Percé in Idaho, and a number of small groups in California. The nearest of these groups lives at least five or six hundred miles south of the Tsimshian, and there are no myths in any of the groups that suggest a connection. But if a connection does exist, it seems likely, for reasons I shall suggest later, to be the result of a northerly rather than a southerly migration.

Yet it remains certain that the Tsimshian, whose rich and varied origin myths are a treasured part of their inheritance, remember no such migration and no connection with any groups far to the south of them. Their origin myth is, essentially, that of Temlaham, known to the Gitksan as Damelahamid.

Temlaham, according to the legends — some of which have been adopted by the Haida and the Tlingit in fairly recent generations — was the earthly paradise where men, made by the deities, lived in plenty and peace until they grew proud and, according to one of the myths, offended the powerful animal spirits by dealing irreverently with the bones of the salmon. On this occasion their punishment was the great Flood (incidentally a common enough myth

Temlaham, the earthly paradise of the Tsimshian peoples.

among Coast Indian peoples, who all have Noahs or Deucalions among their culture heroes) in which the early race of men was swallowed up and only a few of the virtuous escaped. An alternative myth (or perhaps a supplementary one indicating the ineducability of the human race) associates disaster with the mountain goats who inhabited the great and beautiful mountain of Stekyawden (which Europeans call Rocher Déboulé) that forms the most spectacular feature of the upper Skeena valley. The people of Temlaham hunted the mountain goat, which was quite permissible so long as one did so with due respect and ritual. But they also mocked and mistreated their victims, until one day the mountain goat spirits of Stekyawden decided to take their revenge. Disguised as chiefs of a neighbouring tribe, they appeared to invite the hunters of Temlaham to a great feast. The men of Temlaham accepted, and went to the mountain. Although they were surprised to notice that their hosts did not touch the feast food but instead ate grass, there was nothing to arouse their suspicions, until all at once a magical one-horned goat (whom they first imagined to be a human dancer well disguised) began to prance and posture in front of them. As he danced, a great earthquake shook the mountain, and the hunters of Temlaham were all swallowed into the opening cracks in the earth, except for a man who had once taken pity on a mistreated kid and had nurtured and released it; the kid, grown to supernatural goathood, became his rescuer.

These tales of Temlaham, as they have filtered down to us over many centuries, contain all manner of intriguing elements. The concept of the punitive flood, for example, is one of the universals of human mythology, and perhaps its greatest significance in this context is the way it shows the Coast Indians sharing with the peoples of Europe and the Middle East some of their most cherished ancestral myths. As for the theme of respect for animals, of the essential unity of all living beings, this represents an attitude that has received more acceptance in Asia than in Europe, and it reminds one of such hunter-based animal cults as that of the bear among the Ainu of Japan. Yet the fact that similar attitudes exist wherever there are animist cultures cautions us against accepting this alone as evidence of any recent connection between the peoples of Asia and those of western North America.

But in the present context, the myths' most important aspect seems to be that they locate Temlaham, in the case of the Coast Tsimshian tribes, as existing at some vaguely distant point on the upper Skeena, and in the case of the Gitksan, rather precisely on the north shore of the Skeena facing southward towards the soaring ridges of Rocher Déboulé; it lies in the rich hunting region between the Skeena and Nass rivers, through which, in early historical times, the trading route known as the Grease Trail ran, passing through the ancient and still inhabited Gitksan settlements of Kitwanga and Kitwancool. What these myths seem to establish is that, far from being an offshoot of the main Tsimshian line as the earlier anthropologists assumed, the Gitksan may at least in part be the last remnants of the original Tsimshian stock still living in the area where their culture first began to take its characteristic form, and from which they spread outward to the Nass River and to the sea.

This still means that we have to accept the earliest origin of the Tsimshian as impenetrably shadowy, as shadowy as their links with those other peoples whom the linguists have associated with them in the mysteriously far-flung Penutian group of Indian languages. It is at Temlaham that they emerge into the mythic realms of prehistory, and from which some of them departed, while the Gitksan remained on the upper Skeena to conserve the tradition with so much consistency that today, in the later twentieth century, their villages alone in British Columbia — shadowed as they still are by their clustering totem poles — have preserved in a kind of cultural amber the elusive meeting point between the indigenous past and the invading alien present.

Yet once we have established Temlaham on the north bank of the upper Skeena as the point of diffusion — if not origin — of the Tsimshian peoples, we are still faced with the fact that in the myths of both the Haida and the Tlingit, the Skeena appears as the principal route of migration from the mountainous interior. The Tlingit tell also of later groups who came down the Stikine River well over a hundred miles to the north, but the Haida talk only of the Skeena, and in both cases we have to reconcile the myths with the fact that the Tsimshian legends do not tell in any clear or specific way of alien peoples having passed through Temlaham on their way down to the coast.

Since, as we have seen, there is no linguistic

To the misty and forested inlets of the Coast migrant Indians made their way from the interior.

evidence whatever to suggest that the Tsimshian belong to the same stock as the Haida and the Tlingit, we have to assume that the two Athapaskan-speaking groups passed separately down the Skeena even before the Tsimshian first settled in Temlaham, which would fit in with the fact that the whole triangle of land between the Skeena and the Nass that comes to a blunt point at the sea near Prince Rupert has been inhabited by people of Tsimshian speech and origin through the two centuries of European contact, and also during the previous period of oral history that had crystallized out of the mythical past. Given the Tsimshian obsession with inherited titles and their consequent passion for genealogical exactitude, one can probably push back nearly another three hundred years from

the arrival of the Europeans and say with fair certainty that the Tsimshian cannot have reached the seabord after 1500 A.D., and probably got there sometime before. Tlingit legends confirm the idea that the Tsimshian came after the other two northern peoples, since they assert that they themselves once inhabited the land around the mouth of the Skeena but were expelled from it by the invading Tsimshian. The final point of major interest in the migration legends is the assertion by the Haida that when they reached the Queen Charlottes, they found them already inhabited by a people they call the Old Haida, who eventually became absorbed by the invading lineages; there is no legend of their having been exterminated or even enslaved.

The pattern that emerges from these various

legends becomes fairly clear as one puts them together. On the coast, at some point before 1000 A.D., there lived the original fishing people who had moved in after the glacial age, now divided into distinct groups: the Old Haida, the Wakashan peoples, the Salish. The Haida, it seems likely, were the first migrants from the interior to come down the Skeena and settle at its mouth. Given the changes from an interior hunting tribe, which they underwent between their arrival on the coast and the discovery by Europeans of their complex and very distinctive culture, one cannot imagine that they came less than a thousand years ago, and the actual time of descending the Skeena was probably a great deal earlier. Pressure from the Tlingit and other Athapaskan-speaking peoples in the interior hunting grounds, with their limited supplies of game, was probably the reason for their migration. After their arrival at the estuary of the Skeena, there must have been a period of adjustment to a life oriented to fishing rather than hunting, and the Haida must also have learnt to make the large canoes in which they eventually made the crossing of Hecate Strait to the Queen Charlotte Islands, which eventually became their home. Given the lack of political co-ordination that the Haida shared with all the other Coast peoples except the hierarchically inclined Tsimshian, it is likely that they sailed in small groups, each setting up its village in a convenient cove, rather than as an organized armada; but there must have been a network of information that led groups to follow each other, as the pressure on the coast increased from the more numerous Tlingit now descending the Skeena, until the good sites in the islands were entirely occupied by Haida-speakers, with whom the earlier inhabitants intermarried.

Having displaced the Haida on the lower reaches of the Skeena, the Tlingit must have experienced a similar process of adjustment, and then, when the Tsimshian in turn descended the river, moved northward into Alaska, where they were joined by other Tlingit bands who followed the Stikine down to the coast from the northern mountains and plateaus of British Columbia. Having occupied the Skeena estuary, the Tsimshian moved southward, encroaching on territory held by Kwakiutl lineages and isolating the Haisla at Kitimat, until they were finally halted by the more aggressive Heiltsuk of Bella Bella.

This, of course, is a broad and general sketch of the incursion of the three northern peoples in so far as one can reconstruct it out of the scanty evidence that language and oral tradition retrieve from the shadows of prehistory. Given the fact, that though the Coast peoples were linguistic entities they had virtually no political cohesion, what happened was undoubtedly more complex and less tidy than my simple account has suggested. There were the large movements of related groups, but there were smaller movements to complicate the intermingling of the peoples. The oral histories of every group I have mentioned tell of internal conflicts that led certain clans to abandon territories where neighbouring lineages shared their languages and traditions, and to become absorbed, even linguistically, into groups of different origin. Some anthropologists, like Marius Barbeau, even attribute the division into phratries among Tsimshian, Tlingit, and Haida to the intrusion of powerful alien lineages during fairly recent times. Barbeau's theory takes some support from the fact that a number of Haida and Tsimshian clans lay claim to inherited names that are undoubtedly Tlingit in origin and are accompanied by myths telling how they were brought from the north by fugitives. One of the historically most powerful Tsimshian lineages of the lower Skeena — led by a line of chiefs who passed on from generation to generation the name-title of "Legaic" and who were for long the most dogged opponents to Christian conversion — traced its origins to a Tlingit house. Similar vividly remembered clan myths suggest that lineages among the Gitksan on the upper Skeena originated in some cases among the Nishka and in other cases arose from the absorption of semi-nomadic groups of Athapaskan-speaking Carriers.

At least one instance of such assimilation happened in historic times, as late as the last quarter of the nineteenth century, when the remnants of the Tsetsaut, an Athapaskan-speaking tribe of hunters almost exterminated in half a century of wars with the Gitksan of Kitwancool, joined the Nishka at Kincolith in 1885 and adopted their language. A similarly well-known instance of cultural assimilation without political absorption is that of the Carrier Indian band who live beside the Hagwilget Canyon near the road from Prince George into the Skeena country. By the early nineteenth century the Hagwilget Carriers had given up their nomad hunting life to settle in a village of plank houses like their Gitksan neighbours of the upper Skeena. They potlatched in the same way as their neighbours, and as early as 1860 they were erecting poles, sometimes made by Gitksan carvers and sometimes by members of their own group. Linguistically they had remained distinct, but in every other way it was hard to tell them from their culturally dominant neighbours. Such recent instances suggest how, even outside large-scale migration, the pattern of coastal life could have changed prehistorically in small but cumulative ways, either by cultural domination or by extermination.

If the evidence of myth and language suggests that the three northern peoples arrived from the interior by migration down the Skeena and Stikine rivers, the archaeological evidence leaves no doubt that the earliest area of considerable and continual settlement on the Coast was the Fraser Valley, followed by the Fraser Delta; there are notable resemblances, suggesting links repeated over the millennia, between the cultures discovered in these two areas.

We must therefore assume — if the datings established are correct — that immediately after the end of the last ice age, men were pushing from the interior of the continent by a southerly route and reaching salt water at this point between eight and nine thousand years ago, and possibly even earlier. A migration down the Fraser Valley — with its great fish-crowded lakes (like Harrison and Pitt and Cultus and the now-vanished Sumas Lake), with its fens and sloughs rich in wildfowl, its tidal marshes, its great salmon runs — would enable an inland people to acquire, even as they moved down towards the coast, most of the techniques needed for survival there, and very soon afterwards for much more than survival. We can imagine that when these early people did reach the coast, they then turned northward and followed the receding of the ice and the warming of the climate until they reached the northern corner of the Alaskan panhandle. There, just north of Yakutat Bay, they undoubtedly encountered the Aleuts and the Eskimos who in the meantime had edged along the coast from the Bering Sea and whose permanent occupation of this region appears to have put an end, round about 6000 B.C., to further migrations from Asia. Such a meeting between northward and eastward moving peoples would explain similarities of fishing methods and implements between Aleuts, Eskimos, and Nootkas, and the presence of similar myths and art forms in their cultures, but it would also explain why, despite all these minor similarities, the peoples of the Coast possessed a culture so dramatically — but also so profoundly — unlike any other.

In summary, then, the evidence points to an early people finding their way through the Coast mountains at the Fraser Canyon between ten and twelve thousand years ago and establishing a mesolithic culture whose relics have been discovered all the way down the valley to the coast. There are no clues as to where this people came from before reaching the Fraser Canyon, but it seems likely that these early settlers reached the interior of British Columbia from the south rather than from the north. One of the peculiarities of the last ice age was that northern Alaska, the Yukon, and the valley of the Mackenzie were unglaciated, and so it was possible for nomad hunters to find their way across the north of the continent to the ice-free corridor that ran down east of the Rockies and through the Cypress Hills to the American Midwest, where there were rich pastures inhabited by the great mammals surviving from the Pleistocene age. This migration, which probably took place between twelve and fifteen thousand years ago, was followed by a northward surge of proto-Indian peoples as the ice retreated, and it is likely that the first men to settle on the Pacific Coast of North America arrived in this way, and that their push towards Alaska was merely an extension of an already established northerly impetus. (I need hardly point out the bearing of this hypothesis on the relationship between the Tsimshian language and the rather numerous related languages in Washington and Oregon states; it is simpler to assume that one component of a language group moved northward than that several components moved southward, and therefore we can assume that the Tsimshian also were northerly migrants whose ancestors had originally come southward through the ice-free corridors of the central plains.)

Moving up the shoreline and dispersing among the offshore islands, the people who had descended the Fraser Valley divided into a number of groups, or subpeoples, whose variant dialects eventually developed into the sharply different languages of Salish, Kwakiutl, Nootka, and whatever the Old Haida may have spoken. The change from hunting to fishing motivated the shift to a quasi-settled way of life, since it demanded that villages should be placed on or near the routes of the annual salmon runs. The south remained a strong centre of cultural development and innovation, and eventually of artistic production, at least until the Marpole period about two thousand years ago. Afterwards the impetus of development shifted to the north, and it must have been out of the impact between the vigorous hunting peoples of the inland plateaus (Haida, Tlingit, and Tsimshian) and the fishing people of the earlier culture — which had already invented the basic techniques for building large houses and canoes and for preserving quantities of food, and had created the first period of Coast artistry in stone and wood — that the splendid pre-European flowering of the Coast culture emerged.

From this point we must consider some even more searching questions. I have attempted a reconstruction of what happened in the ten or twelve millennia (a time, let us remember, twice as long as the entire known history of Egypt) between the arrival of the first men on the British Columbian coast and the emergence of the astounding way of coastal life that the Europeans first encountered in 1774. But except for remarking on the general acceptance of the assumption that the Coast Indian people derived from Asia, I have not speculated in any detail on their origins outside the American continent.

In terms of physiological types, there can of course be no serious doubt that the Coast Indians, like all the other pre-Columbian inhabitants of the American continent, are of East Asian origin and — since their forebears probably came over the Bering Strait or whatever land bridge existed at the height of glaciation — of

Siberian or Mongolian origin. Nobody familiar with the Mongols or the Tungus of Siberia, or the people of the warlike eastern Tibetan province of Kham, can fail to be impressed by the close resemblance in physical traits and even in behaviour between these peoples and the Indians of the Coast. There is added evidence in such factors as the prevalence of the Mongolian spot on Coast Indian infants, in the similarity of blood group frequencies between eastern Siberians and Coast Indians, and even, according to a recent medical authority, in the way earwax forms among East Asians and North American Indians. If the Coast Indians do not show the epicanthic fold ("slant eyes") commonly associated with Mongoloid stocks, this is merely an indication of the distance in time at which their migration took place; all the classic Mongoloid characteristics had not yet become established. More important than such absences, perhaps, are the links that Edward Sapir and other linguists have found between North American language groups, like Athapaskan, and the Sinic family of languages, which includes of course the Siberian and Mongolian languages as well as those of China itself.

Yet, impressively obvious as the morphological and linguistic resemblances between the Coast Indians and the peoples of Siberia and Mongolia appear to be, there are other and more illuminating ways of establishing the affinities and perhaps the relationships between the Coast Indian world, which Juan Perez first saw in the late eighteenth century, and its remote Asian parent culture many millennia ago. One is through the imagery by which, in their art, the prehistoric peoples of the Coast expressed a sense of their relation to the universe. The other is through what is perhaps the most ancient and enduring institution in Coast culture, that of shamanism, which more than any other factor confirms a link with Asia far in the past, and which may even suggest a continuing — if indirect — connection over the Bering Strait during the dark ages before history. In the following chapters I shall discuss these questions, and in penetrating such distant and echoing pathways, I hope to show the spiritual and aesthetic roots of the Coast Indian culture that was eventually revealed to us in its historic form.

Petroglyph of a sea wolf at Sproat Lake.

CHAPTER THREE

Image and Talisman: The Record in Stone Faces

The arts of the Coast Indians were so profuse in their variety of forms and uses that one tends at first to ignore the significant areas where art did not exist either in prehistoric or in historic times. Yet such areas of absence tell us almost as much about the past of these peoples as the areas in which they produced so richly and dramatically. The Coast Indians of historic times had no pottery, nor have any prehistoric sherds been discovered in excavations of their village and camp sites; in place of earthenware, wooden vessels were used, including elaborately carpentered waterproof cooking boxes, as well as baskets so closely woven of tree roots that they could be used for containing liquids. And, except for small quantities of copper (which attained a phenomenal value when beaten into the ceremonial shields, or "coppers," that played such a part in the potlatches) and even smaller quantities of iron, metal was little used until the Europeans arrived.

Such limitations tell us a great deal in a negative way about the stage at which the peoples of this region ceased to be linked with Asia and also about the period at which they separated from other North American groups (if they ever had any contact with them). There is, for example, no evidence that ceramics from ancient China, where the neolithic potters of Yang-Chao were making fine vessels well before 2000 B.C., ever reached the coastal regions of Alaska or British Columbia by trade. This tells us not only that the ancestors of the Coast Indians left Siberia before neolithic techniques of pottery making had reached that area, but also that anything more than accidental or indirect links with Asia must have ceased before the Chinese civilization developed and began to spread its cultural influences through eastern Asia. It also tells us that the Indians of the Pacific Coast had been long out of touch — if they ever were in contact — with the American Indian cultures to the far south and to the east, among which the art of pottery developed, presumably independently, many millennia after the migration of the primal Americans from Asia. Early Peruvian and Mexican pottery dates from well before the beginning of the Christian Era, and pottery was certainly being made by the New Mexican peoples and by the Mound Builders of the Ohio and Mississippi valleys in the early years of the first millennium A.D. The craft spread northward into eastern Canada, where it was being practised by the agrarian Iroquois before the time of Jacques Cartier's arrival, but it never reached the area north of the Columbia River and west of the Rockies where the Coast Indians developed their culture and in which they created their own network of trade.

Although they quickly learnt the uses of metal once the European traders made it available in quantity, the metalworking that existed

The Sechelt Image, which is about 2,000 years old, is one of the finest prehistoric Coast carvings.

among the Coast Indians at the time of first contact was so rudimentary and so rarely practised that, for all the complexity of their artistic achievement and their social and ceremonial life, we have to regard them as a Stone Age people in technological terms (a fact that should, incidentally, incline us to speculate on the possibility that some of the ancient mesolithic and neolithic cultures, of which we retain only artifacts made in durable materials, may like the Coast Indians have developed complex artistic traditions that were manifested mainly in such perishable ma-

terials as wood or weaving). Fragments of iron, used as primitive knives, were indeed already in the possession of the Tlingit, the Haida and the Nootka when the earliest European explorers reached the area, but it was obvious that they did not know how to work the material, which seems to have reached them by indirect trading through the Aleutians from Siberia. The native copper they obtained from Alaska was cold-hammered into shape with stone mallets; no smelting method of any kind was known.

The evidence relating to metalworking thus reinforces the conclusion that relations with Asia on any meaningful scale had come to an end several millennia ago, since in China the Shang had discovered the secret of bronze making before the middle of the second millennium B.C. and were already casting elaborate metal vessels more than three thousand years ago. The same applies with the great American Indian civilizations to the south in Mexico and Peru; in both these areas the arts of metalworking had been mastered, and the peoples of Peru had not only discovered how to make bronze and to alloy gold and silver, but had also developed highly sophisticated casting techniques. Of such matters nothing was known in the fishing villages of prehistoric British Columbia, though the woodworkers had developed their arts to an extraordinary degree of complexity and sophistication.

Metalworking and pottery have always been the products of agrarian societies, which have not only the stability of constant settlement in all-year villages, but also a vested interest in the actual earth that makes them inclined to investigate its uses in all directions. Food-gathering, fishing and hunting cultures like those of the Coast are concerned with the natural products of the sea and of the uncultivated forest; and the agrarian processes of digging and delving, which are essential preludes to the very idea of mining the earth for its riches, never extended among them much further than using a sharpened stick to dig out clover and cinquefoil roots and the bulbs of the blue-flowered wild camas, which formed a notable part of their diet. For them, the earth gave without the need to disturb it, and the mineral-based arts that came out of investigating its nature had no reason to develop. Yet the fact that at relatively early periods they used easily available mineral products — like free stones for their tools and their portable carvings, and clear rock surfaces for their petroglyphs — suggests that if circumstances had led them to experiment with clay and with metal ores, they might have used these materials with all the ingenuity and style that characterized their arts in general. Certainly, after their first contact with the white men, they were to produce a tradition of fine silversmiths which has continued to this day with artists like Bill Reid and Robert Davidson.

Therefore we can assume that there was never a point at which Coast Indians were in contact with primitive potters or metalworkers, and so they had no pots and only the rarest of metal objects. In the same way, the lack of necessity and example caused them to remain primitive in their political structures (in comparison with the highly organized empires of Mexico or Peru, or even with the democratic federations of the Iroquois and the Blackfoot) and equally primitive in their day-to-day dress, since in prehistoric times they never developed the tailored garments used by the peoples of the cold mountain and plateau regions of British Columbia, preferring to be clad often in a rough wrap of skins or cedar bark in the manner of an early paleolithic hunter, or even to go naked; there was no taboo among them regarding male nudity.

Thus, it is evident that the Coast Indian culture evolved over several millennia in an isolation unusual in the Americas, with a closed trading, social, and ceremonial system, disturbed only by migrations from beyond the coastal mountains which were absorbed into the areal pattern. This explains why in certain directions — particularly the plastic arts and ceremonial drama — the peoples who lived beside each other in this Pacific enclave developed a wealth of invention and a sophistication of technique and imagery rivalled nowhere else in the New World (for even the imaginations of the Maya and the Chimu were pedestrian in comparison with those of the Kwakiutl and the Tsimshian); and why, in yet other directions, they remained far less developed than their unseen and presumably unknown neighbours south of the California desert and east of the Cordillera.

Yet, though the Coast Indian culture shows obvious signs of having developed for so long in a virtual geographic and ethnic isolation, there are still the haunting echoes which suggest that, at some even more distant epoch, the seed of this whole primitive civilization germinated in Asia. At the same time, we have seen the massive evidence which suggests that there were no migrations from Asia after the arrival of the Eskimos in North America, and no regular links between the Coast Indians and the peoples of Asia at any time since the development of pottery and metalworking in China. As an alternative explanation it is suggested that the stylistic elements, which early and historic Coast Indian arts appear to have in common with Asian arts, may be due to fugitive contacts. There have been theories of Chinese traders coming to the Coast, of Chinese junks being blown across the Pacific and fetching up on some Alaskan or British Columbian shore. But here one faces the difficult fact that no single sherd of pre-nineteenth century Chinese pottery has turned up in British Columbian excavations, whereas in places where the Chinese are known to have traded — like Quilon on the Malabar Coast in India — one can hardly walk along the beach without discovering some scrap of Ming export pottery. And if Chinese junks, with their distinctive and dramatic-looking high poops, were blown upon Canadian or Alaskan shores in prehistoric days, why was not their arrival recorded with appropriate pecked outlines on the petroglyphs, as was the arrival of the first European sailing ships, not to mention the first horse to be seen by the Indians of the village of Clo-ose on Vancouver Island, ridden by a top-hatted Englishman well over a century ago? It is also curious, if Chinese did visit the Pacific Coast of North America, and return (as some of them must have done if such voyages were more of a habit prehistorically than they became in history) that the only reference in the Chinese imperial records should be one whose relevance is highly dubious.

This is the tale of the journey of a Chinese monk named Hoei-Shin, who in the fifth century A.D. travelled with a group of Buddhist priests from their home of Kophen in central Asia, northwest across Siberia until he reached a land called Fusang; he returned in 499 to report his mission. Fusang, inhabited by a people of high culture, has been variously interpreted as Mexico and the Pacific Coast, but there are features which cannot be reconciled with either — like the oxen with horns "so large that they hold ten bushels," the wagons drawn by "horses, oxen and stags," the "hinds" that are milked for the making of butter, and the "red pears of the Fusang-tree," which "keep good throughout the year."

There are indeed only a few features in the whole description of Fusang that might fit the Coast Indian culture: the people use bark to make "a kind of linen"; they have houses "built of wooden beams" and no "fortified or walled places"; they make reed mats; suitors, as among the Salish, wait outside the houses of their prospective brides until their merits are recognized by the girls' parents. But these are the kind of features one might encounter in many places of Asia, not to mention the Americas, and there are other features of Fusang which have no relation to the reality of Coast Indian society at any time, particularly the account of its system of writing and its rule by a king who goes out to the tune of horns and trumpets and wears different coloured clothes every year, as well as the tale of "the religion of Buddha, and with it his holy writings and images" being "extended over the land."

It seems as though the tale of Hoei-Shin is in fact a synthetic account, prepared for promotional purposes by fifth century Buddhist missionaries and including features of a number of lands, the only clearly identifiable one being the northern Siberian region where "hinds" (i.e. reindeer) are indeed used as milch cattle. There is no reference that points specifically to the Pacific Coast and nowhere else, and it is certain that, except in small details, the Kingdom of Fusang bears no real resemblance to any tribal territory in British Columbia or Alaska.

And yet the mention of Buddhist images stirs again the feeling of strange affinities that came to me recently when I looked at a photograph of a stone figure from British Columbia, perhaps two thousand years old, and found its formal and perhaps iconographical analogue in a little bronze Burmese figure of the Buddha, six or seven hundred years old, which had been found in a Vancouver shop about a hundred miles from the place where the stone image was discovered. Both were of seated figures; the posture, the placing of the arms and hands, the disproportionately large head on the small body, all corresponded; and the British Columbian figure had a protuberance on the crown of the head that resembled closely the projection called the *ushnisha* that appeared on the cranium of the Buddhist figure. I am not suggesting that in this case the resemblance I saw was anything but fortuitous, yet the very fact that two objects should present such formal similarities while being obviously so divided from each other by time and place of origin is itself significant; it is typical of the echoes that constantly haunt one when one looks at the art of the Pacific Coast of North America with the art of Asia at the back of one's mind.

The stone figure — which actually came from Lytton in the dry country just above the Fraser Canyon, and thus shows the close links about two millennia ago between the coastal peoples and the ancestors of the Interior Salish — is representative of one of the most interesting types of stone carving being made at the time of the Marpole culture, round about the beginning of the Christian Era. These are seated anthropomorphic images; in each case the figure, which has no overt sexual characteristics, holds a bowl between knees and hands. In almost every case the head bears the topknot that resembles the *ushnisha;* the eyes are usually large and protruding; often the features have an expression of agonized ecstasy; sometimes the figures are represented as emaciated, with thin arms and ribs sharply marked; in a few cases a jutting lower lip, perhaps indicating the presence of a labret, suggests that the figure is feminine.

Sometimes the human image is alone and undecorated; more often it is accompanied by an animal spirit familiar. Most frequent are the serpents, recognizable as rattlesnakes even on figures that have been found in coastal regions where since the Ice Age the only serpents have been harmless garter snakes. Either the figures were all carved in rattlesnake country east of the Fraser Canyon and traded to the coastal settlements, or they represent an example of the ancient serpent cult that spread far over Asia and the Americas in ancient times.

If one takes into account the animistic beliefs of the Coast Indians in historic times and the curiously intimate relationship that in these carvings seems to exist between the human fig-

The cranial protrusion on this prehistoric figure is similar to that of many Buddhist figures.

ure and the serpent, the latter seems the more likely explanation. The serpent cult in South Asia is well known; the Nagas, or supernatural serpents, appear to have been universally worshipped in pre-Aryan India and the Himalayan regions, to the extent that there were castes, like the Nairs in Kerala, and peoples, like the Newars of

A 2,000-year-old Fraser Valley carving. The snake behind the human figure and the bird heads at the base are reminiscent of later Coast Indian art.

in another carving a double serpent raises itself in a free-standing and curiously protective stance behind the human figure. The analogue, of course, is to be found in the widespread Buddhist image that represents Sakyamuni meditating under the protection of the Naga king, the supernatural seven-headed cobra. This resemblance suggests that the human figure in the British Columbian bowl carvings of two thousand years ago is defined by the presence of the serpent; he is the shaman.

In south and east Asia, the seated figure is used to represent not only the Buddha, who was only one teacher-ascetic among many. There are Hindu statues of yogins, and even of the god Siva in his manifestation as the great yogin, which assume the same seated form, as do figures representing the Tirthankaras, or super-human teachers, of the Jains. In other words, there is a universal tendency in South Asia — from which it spread into Tibet, Mongolia, China and Japan — to represent spiritual power in the form of the seated human being, with or without the attendant serpent. The seated posture can represent one of two things: enlightenment achieved through meditative practices, or the power attained through yogic magic. And though the yogin (who seeks through the establishment of total control over himself to control the universe) is different from the shaman (who depends for his power on ecstatic possession by spirits more powerful than himself), their origins clearly meet in the medicine men of the paleolithic hunters — the shamans of Lascaux and Altamira, who performed the necessary magic of the hunter. There is no evidence at all that allows us to relate the Indian seated figures of Buddhas and yogic deities directly to the seated Coast Indian bowl-figures, yet it is evident that they both derive from a more ancient tradition relating to the acquisition by human beings of superhuman powers.

Nepal and the Nagas of Nagaland, who not only worshipped snakes but took their names from them. Perhaps more immediately germane to snake images on the Pacific Coast of North America is the fact that a serpent cult was associated with shamanism even in areas of Siberia where also snakes were rare and usually harmless.

Nevertheless, it is again a hauntingly South Asian echo that reawakens in my mind when I examine Fraser Valley bowl-figures and see that in one carving the serpent crawls up the man's back so that its head forms a kind of diadem, and

The serpent — which has been found carved on paleo-Siberian mammoth teeth antedating the emigrations from Asia over the Bering Strait, and which therefore belongs to the common cultural inheritance of all the American peoples — was regarded by the Coast Indians, as it was by the Siberians, not as a symbol of fecundity but as a being who could confer fearful and potentially destructive power. He was one of the important spirits connected with the guardian spirit quest, which in one form or another was universal on the Coast. If the spirit a novice encountered chanced to be the supernatural snake, he would fall into a coma, bleeding from all orifices, but he would be given the powers of a shaman and his vocation would be determined from the point of this visionary encounter.

As a consequence, the figure of the snake was frequently used as a charm by shamans; snakes were represented in the head-dresses of Siberian shamans; among the Haida the wands of shamans were decorated with serpent motifs; and I have seen carved rattles used by young Salish men in their spirit dances that were tipped with the head of the serpent. The most dreaded form of supernatural serpent was the Sisiutl, a being to whom the Kwakiutl in particular paid a great deal of attention. He was associated with the thunderbird, and indeed one of his manifestations appears to have been the lightning bolt; he was also associated with the sun, who could be represented by a Sisiutl mask. Those who saw him fainted, and only by biting one's tongue and spitting blood before losing consciousness could one avoid being turned into stone by this American equivalent of Medusa with her hair of living serpents. Because of its destructive powers and general fearsomeness, the Sisiutl was regarded among the Kwakiutl as the special patron of warriors, and it was they who wore its emblems in their dances. Because of this concept of the supernatural serpent projecting a malign power

The shamanic snake head-dress is shown on this ancient bowl figure found on Vancouver Island.

that could only be harnessed by shamans or warriors for their own somewhat sinister purposes, all snakes were regarded with fear, even ordinary garter snakes, since although they were not poisonous, they were thought to creep uninvited into the rectal orifice and breed in the bellies of their victims, causing great swelling and discomfort.

This fearsome Coast Indian view of the serpent, and of its peculiar role in the shaman's spirit quest, makes it evident that the prehistoric bowl-figures of two millennia ago are certainly shamans, since no ordinary Indians could endure the company of snakes, and the fearsomeness to historic Indians of some of the other beings associated with the figures confirms this conclusion. Frogs appear on several sculptures, and a toad crawls up the back of one of them, and although in historical times the frog became a clan crest of some importance among the Gitksan, frogs and toads were also associated with sorcery. The owl, which also appears on the prehistoric bowl carvings, is another dread being, linked with death as well as with wisdom; Coast Indians, like the Shropshire peasants among whom I grew up, regarded the owl as the harbinger of death who called out the names of those about to depart from life; and the Bella Coola believed the souls of the dead were transformed into owls. Another being whose head or mask appears between the feet of the seated bowl-figures is the hawk, which in historic times has been associated with the sun in some of the most splendid of the Kwakiutl transformation masks. The association of the hawk or falcon with a sky-being like the sun is natural enough, yet it brings to mind the analogical Old World identification of bird and heavenly body in the myth of Horus, the hawk-headed sun god of the Egyptians.

There has been a great deal of controversy about the uses to which the Fraser Valley bowl-figures were put by the people who made them so long ago. Modern Indians usually claim no knowledge of their origin or their function, though Franz Boas was told before 1890 that Indians in the Yale area were then using a bowl of this kind to sprinkle water on a girl at puberty to ensure that she should breed prolifically, and the anthropologist Charles Hill-Tout picked up a similar story in Kamloops at the same period. But this may well have been a recently devised ceremonial in one of the synthetic mission-influenced cults that arose during the nineteenth century — it sounds very much like an adaptation of Christian baptism — and it seems more reasonable to assume that the bowl-figures of two thousand years ago were in fact used by the shamans in connection with their curing or divining functions. Historic Indian shamans always included a bowl of water among their paraphernalia when they were called out to deal with a case of sickness or possession.

Among the other stone carvings dating from this earliest age of Coast Indian art (or at least the earliest age whose relics have been found) a few are purely decorative or utilitarian. These include the labrets of smoothed stone, which like the pierced septum of one of the carved figures (obviously intended to hold a shaman's nose ornament), suggest that Indian ideas of personal adornment did not change greatly over twenty centuries. There are also the carved stone spindle whorls, decorated with patterns of conventionalized eyes or coiling snakes, which remind us that in prehistoric as in historic times the peoples of the Coast had time to decorate domestic utensils, most of which, being made of wood, have long decayed. Even the undecorated tools and implements of two thousand years ago were often models of simple functional design, like the stone hand hammers shaped like old-fashioned telephone receivers which date from this period.

Among the nonutilitarian but doubtless ritually functional objects were carved heads, some containing a bowl behind the face, presumably used for the same purpose as the bowl-figures. One face without a bowl, carved on a round stone about six inches in diameter and looking like a man-in-the-moon image, bears a striking resemblance in miniature to the great baby-faced heads of unidentified beings that were carved on immense boulders by the Olmecs of ancient Mexico. On another stone a disclike carving of a feline face reminds one of the jaguar masks carved by the people of Chavin in the earliest days of Peruvian civilization about three thousand years ago, and there is a battered sandstone image from a Fraser Delta site which portrays a being with whiskered, catlike face. The large native cat of the Coast, the cougar, played a scanty role in Coast Indian iconography; it was not found north of Vancouver Island and was never used by the northern peoples as a clan crest.

The same Fraser Delta site near Ladner that yielded the sandstone catlike figure also contained a unique representation of human deformity in terms of Coast Indian art — the figure of a hunchback with withered legs and the purse-mouthed face of constant pain. It reflects the wealth and complexity of the Fraser Valley society so long ago that a man so obviously ill-adapted to the basic occupations of hunting and fishing should be able to survive and become an object of artistic representation. But by far the most impressive of all the human figure sculptures produced in these early generations of Coast Indian art is the massive and powerful figure of a mother and child, called the Sechelt Image, carved with monumental power and, at twenty inches high, the second largest figure created during the Marpole period. Given the clearly marked vulva at its base, the image's function as a fertility fetish is obvious; it at least must have played a role in the magic associated with childbirth.

A small number of the Marpole period stone figures are pure zoomorphic images, including the oldest of them, a little large-eyed figure, just over two inches long, with the neck, backbone and four feet clearly defined, which was found in the Milliken site at Yale and has been estimated by its discoverer, C.E. Borden, to be about three thousand years old. It is well worn by handling and seems to have been a talisman intended to bring good luck to its hunter owner. Dr. Borden

Prehistoric stone head from the lower Fraser Valley. There is a bowl behind the face.

has suggested that it represents a seal, but that seems unlikely in a carving found so far from the sea, and I prefer to be guided by its general resemblance — even though it is done in a less naturalistic manner — to the paleolithic bear figures of Scandinavia and Siberia, and to the small bear images dating back two thousand years which have been found near Kamloops and which suggest that early Indians in British Columbia were influenced by the circumpolar bear cult that was strong in Siberia and reached its greatest complexity among the Ainu of Japan.

Other figures clearly linked with hunting magic are the representations of marine animals etched on pieces of caribou horn just large enough to be held in the hand.

Of a different nature, and perhaps with a different function, are the small figures of birds, also about the right size to hold in the palm of one's hand, and probably — as in Siberia — associated with shamanism. Those I have seen seem to be hawks; one which I possess, and which came from the Fountain Valley north of Lytton, is a highly stylized carving, all sharp geometrical planes and masses, with the plumage and wing forms indicated in deep hatching in which the traces of red ochre still lie, yet indisputably a small falcon with all the condensed power of the bird merely accentuated by the abstract treatment.

Somewhere between these animal figures made for free handling and the anthropomorphic bowl-figures, are the little dishes — again hand-sized — in zoomorphic forms. They are occasionally round or even square in shape, but more generally oval, which has led some anthropologists with too heavy a taste for psychoanalytical interpretations to describe them as vulviform, as if every oval in art were the representation of the female sexual organs. In fact, it is obvious that if one's magic requires an animal form for a bowl, the fact that most animals are longer than they are wide will demand an oval as distinct from the round bowl that can be grasped in the arms of a seated figure. Many of the animals in such cases are hard to identify, but I have seen obvious representations of owls, seals, and turtles. One in my possession (which came from the Lillooet region, well north of the Fraser Canyon, but is obviously closely related to the bowls of the lower Fraser Valley) is unusually complex, with different figures above and below. On top is a swimming batrachian — one would call him a frog if he did not have an evident tail — with a head carved boldly in quite high relief, an oval bowl scooped out of his back, and lines to represent his ribs in a stylized way stretching out on each side. Clearly the necromantic power of the frog was intended to strengthen whatever potion or ointment was mixed in the bowl, and the power was enhanced by the surrounding of the bowl on the underside by a snake, equipped with three pairs of minute legs and circling back upon itself like the Ourobouros, the world-embracing serpent of the Greeks.

While the bowl held by the human figure disappeared after the end of the Marpole culture almost two thousand years ago, small zoomorphic bowls of the kind I have just described remained in continuing use and were still being carved from stone up to historic times by the Kwakiutl and the Haida; not only the form but the motifs were persistent, the frog — with its magical associations — remaining an especial favourite and indicating that it was still shamans for whom such bowls were made.

Another item of carving produced almost unchanged into historic times was the carved skull. The small bone skull, that was found at a pre-Marpole site well over two thousand years old, is identical in form with the tiny wooden skulls that are used to this day in the Hamatsa, or cannibal, dances and the ghost dances of the Kwakiutl. Miniature skulls, of course, were also part of the paraphernalia of the shaman, as they were around the whole great arc of shamanic culture that extended through Siberia and as far as Tibet, where they figured regularly in the costumes and in the ceremonials not only of the pagan and shamanic Bonpo priests but also of the tantric magicians adhering to some of the red-hat Buddhist sects, and particularly the Nyingmapa — the Old Ones.

There are other, more stylistic elements in prehistoric Coast art which suggest a clear continuity between the culture contemporaneous with the early Christian Era, and that of the late eighteenth century which Cook and Mackenzie encountered. The heavy accenting of the eyebrows and the bold outlining of the prominent eyes are present in both Marpole-age work and in the masks of recent Coast Indian artists. The outlining of ribs on the bodies of men and sometimes of animals in early sculptures anticipates the X-ray treatment of animals' bodies which one often sees in nineteenth century Coast Indian paintings and carvings; and in at least one case, when a snake, whose head lies between the feet of an early figure, is divided for its body to pass on both sides of his body, we see the beginning of that curious custom of splitting open an animal and laying it out like a kipper to fill a space, which the Coast Indians practised in their art. Also, on at least one Marpole-period figure, there are forms closely resembling the ovoid shape that was used in reliefs and paintings of the historic era both to represent the joints of figures and also to fill fragments of space that offended the Indian artist's *horror vacui*. Looking, as one must, through the narrow opening in the past which is offered by the stone sculptures that are obviously only a tiny fragment of the artistic production of their culture, it seems that the Indian artists of two thousand years ago were more expressionistic and less stylized in their vision than their splendid successors. The absence of any abundance of stone figures attributable to an earlier age suggests that the Marpole period two thousand years ago was indeed one of those cultural eras when a good many things were happening at once, and this may explain why there appears to be so great a variation in quality among the surviving work; some of it is very rough and unco-ordinated, but the best, like the Sechelt Image, combines power of vision with an extraordinary control of form and material, and rivals anything produced by the later

culture at its highest points of inspiration.

If we can learn a great deal from prehistoric stone figures about the development of Coast Indian art and the distant resemblances that suggest a common origin with historic Asian art, it is much more difficult to read the message of the petroglyphs that occur at almost five hundred sites on the Coast, in Alaska, British Columbia, and the State of Washington, usually cut on some seashore or lakeshore cliff or boulder but sometimes found in secluded places, even far from water.

The greatest unsolved problem in connection with the petroglyphs is their age. Their exposed positions mean that they cannot be dated by the carbon 14 method, since usually no organic material that we know to be contemporary lies in intimate contact with them. Nor is there any reliable means by which we can estimate the age of a carving pecked or scored into a rock surface by measuring erosion from weather or water. Nevertheless, there are a few cases in which very rough guesses of period have been possible. When a series of petroglyphs was found in an area of woodland near the Nanaimo River on Vancouver Island, geologists estimated from the depth of the earth cover that it must have been a thousand years since the glyphs were clear to the sky, which means that they were cut and in use more than a millennium ago. In another case a stylistic resemblance between a petroglyph and a datable bone comb found in a nearby site suggested that the glyph must be about a thousand years old.

Some of the glyphs are so worn that they are obviously of great age and may indeed be the earliest stone carvings of any kind on the Coast, made by pecking with pointed stones before the technique of carving soft stone with hard blades was developed. But others are equally obviously recent. The Clo-ose representation of the *Beaver* cannot be more than 140 years old, and the glyphs representing sailing ships are probably between one and two centuries old. Others, especially in the north, seem to belong to the late pre-contact or even the historic period of high potlatching, since they often display the outlines of coppers and are evidently records of the achievements of local chiefs in acquiring the wealth that confers prestige.

In most areas they appear to have been cut long enough ago for the memory of who carved them, or why they did so, to have receded out of oral tradition by the time the first serious inquirers appeared at the end of the nineteenth century. Such a loss to memory would require two or three centuries, depending on whether the genealogical record was meticulously kept — as among the Tsimshian and the Bella Coola (who actually had remembrancers or oral chroniclers to sustain the ancestral family traditions) — or somewhat laxly preserved as among the southern Salish. It is surprising, indeed, how few accounts of the carving of petroglyphs remain even where they were made comparatively recently, particularly at spots like Clo-ose where the villages are no longer populated. Often it happens that, even though the original purpose of the glyphs is forgotten and their history lost, an aura of supernatural power lingers long afterwards, so that petroglyphs are still frequented for purposes that may have nothing to do with their original intent. At Kulleet Bay on Vancouver Island, for example, there is a very interesting frieze of petroglyphs around the rim of a rock pool. In the twenties the glyphs were almost entirely covered with earth, and when the archaeologist C.E. Newcombe uncovered them in 1921 the old people knew nothing about them. Today, now that the Salish spirit dance has been greatly revived, the young novice dancers come in the depth of winter to bathe in the bitterly cold water of the pool. Similarly, in the 1940s, T.F. McIlwraith found at Bella Coola that the place where the Kusiut Society met — a place carefully avoided by the uninitiate — was a ledge jutting out over a waterfall where there were ancient petroglyphs; nobody knew any longer what the carvings signified or when they were made, but the awe remained and the place was still a gathering spot for those who performed the somewhat degenerated rituals of the secret society.

There is only one account of a petroglyph being carved in historic times that is detailed and circumstantial enough to have much meaning. Franz Boas, in 1895, records a tale he was told by his Kwakiutl informant, George Hunt, regarding the last petroglyph made at Fort Rupert:

> In olden times, when the hamatsa was in a state of ecstasy, slaves were killed for him, whom he devoured. The following facts were observed by Mr. Hunt and Mr. Moffat in the early days of Fort Rupert:* When a hamatsa had returned from the woods, a slave, a man of the Nanaimo tribe named Xuntem, was shot. They saw him running down to the beach, where he dropped. Then all the nulmal of the Kuexa tribe went down to the beach carrying knives and lances. The bear dancers and the hamatsas followed them. The nulmal cut the body with their knives and lances and the hamatsas squatted down dancing and crying 'hap, hap,' then the bear dancers took up the flesh and, holding it like bears and growling at the same time, they gave it to the highest hamatsa first and then to the others. In memory of this event a face representing Baxbakualnu Xsiwae was carved in the rock on the beach at the place where the slave had been eaten. The carving is done in sandstone, which was battered down with stone hammers. Near this rock carving there are a number of other and much older ones. The Indians have no recollections of the incidents which they are to commemorate. They say that they were made at the time before animals were transformed into men.

Yet, despite our general ignorance of who

*Fort Rupert was founded in 1849, so that the account probably refers to the 1850s.

carved the petroglyphs and why and when, there is a great deal to be learnt from studying these strange outlines scored or pecked out of the sandstones of the British Columbian coast. The images they present are varied in spirit and — one quickly assumes — in intent and in period. There is a quite perceptible geographical division; in the southern reaches of Kwakiutl territory one begins to encounter more complex forms and images, and it becomes evident that the development of the northern styles of art and also of the northern crest and potlatch system had a considerable effect even on these rock drawings in their usually remote settings.

The two most interesting motifs, in terms of tracing the origins of the Coast Indian culture, are the *oculi* or eye patterns and the humanoid faces around which radiate the strokes of haloes. These are symbols of great antiquity and they proclaim perhaps more emphatically than any other evidence the links between the original Coast Indian peoples and the paleolithic peoples of prehistoric Eurasia.

The *oculus* consists of two emphatic eyebrow curves which unite at a straight nose line; beneath them the eyes are represented by dots; rarely an oval or a line will represent a mouth. This is a sign that is amazingly widespread in Stone Age cultures. I have seen examples from as far away from the British Columbian coast as Denmark, Britain, and Spain, and they appear in pottery-making agrarian cultures as well as in preceramic hunting and fishing cultures, which shows how distant in the common past the origin of the *oculus* symbol must lie. It is generally thought to indicate the face or presence of a spirit, and this suggests that it may have been connected with the guardian spirit quest which in one form or another was common to all the Pacific Coast cultures.

The halo of radiating lines, on the other hand, does not appear in early European art, but it has been identified frequently in Siberia, where it is associated both with sun deities and with shamans, whose reputed power to journey to the sky as well as to the underworld links them to the heavenly bodies. There seems little doubt that among the Coast Indians it was also associated with shamans, and the fact that almost all the humanoid figures on the petroglyphs, with or without haloes, are shown frontally in a dancing posture is a further hint that in such glyphs we are in fact dealing with the products of an ecstatic cult.

A high proportion of the petroglyph images are not human at all, and here a division seems to be necessary, since although almost all of them appear to have some kind of magical and quasi-religious intent, they may not all be shamanistic in context. The bird images, indeed, may often be associated with shamanism, since birds were among the familiar spirits of shamans and at the same time were symbols of the soul and of transcendence. In the case, however, of whales portrayed in whale-hunting areas, or salmon at the mouths of streams where the fish run, it seems that a simple pictorially sympathetic magic is involved and that the representation of the marine animal or fish is intended — as representations of game seem to have been at Lascaux and Altamira — to tempt the whale or salmon people ashore for the benefit of their human friends and dependents.

But there are other beasts which are clearly mythological: the strange sea wolf figures of Nanaimo and Sproat Lake, and the sea serpents portrayed at other sites. The sea wolf, which appears on the petroglyphs of the Nanaimo River, is very close indeed to the similar figures in Coast Indian paintings or sculptures made during the historic period; the representations of the same type at Sproat Lake and at the famous Petroglyph Park near Nanaimo are more distant in style and therefore doubtless older, but distinctly in the tradition, which provides us at least one sign of the antiquity of the motifs and manners that we encounter in classic Coast Indian art.

While links between eye figures and spirit quests seem relatively comprehensible, as do links between haloed figures and shamanism, and between whale or salmon figures and the sympathetic magic by which the clan or village chiefs sought to provide for the needs of their people, nevertheless the monsters raise some crucial questions. In later periods they enter into lineage myths and are used as the crests of clans, but in contexts like the Nanaimo River site and the Petroglyph Park they appear in connection with shamanic haloed humanoids and with birds, which suggests they were meant to represent supernatural beings encountered on the vision quest. It has been suggested that sites like the two I have just mentioned, which were well removed from known villages, may have been the places where shamans gathered in secret in the same way as European witches held their covens in remote spots.

Another type of image appears rather rarely on the petroglyphs and always in the southern part of the area permeated by the Coast Indian culture complex. These are female figures with prominently drawn sexual organs; present also are the divided ovals which in prehistoric and primitive art frequently represent the vulva. There is even, at Clo-ose, a unique representation of a couple engaged in copulation. Overt sexual imagery is in fact surprisingly rare in Coast Indian art, and like the peoples of Siberia, the peoples of this region had no earth mother figure resembling that which is so prominent in European paleolithic art. When erotic practices occur in Coast Indian myths and stories, as they often do, they are dealt with in a remarkably matter-of-fact way and are rarely elevated to a high symbolic level, while there is no evidence that sexual activity played any part in Coast Indian shamanism, as it undoubtedly did among some types of Siberian shaman and among the tantric magicians of Tibet. Certainly there is nothing at any period in Coast Indian art that resembles the extraordinary vigour and variety of sexual imagery in the arts of India and Nepal, and attempts to find in it some kind of yoni-lingam polarity have notably failed. This makes the occasional representation of sexual organs and sexual acts on the petroglyphs more difficult to explain. Do they represent a local phallic cult? Or were they merely the obscene graffiti of their day?

Finally, in the later period, and particularly — though not exclusively — in the northern areas, there seems to have been a tendency for the petroglyph to be used for the recording of mundane events. However, it is unwise to make too close a distinction. Any unusual event tended in the Indian mind to take on supernatural connotations. The first sight of a ship with sails or a steamship was so out of the ordinary that it appeared as much a visitation from the spirit world as a thunderbird or a sea serpent. Similarly, crests were not merely signs of a man's social standing; they were also records of the supernatural encounters he or his ancestors may have experienced. And when we remember instances like the Tsimshian man, who was so intrigued by his first sight of a white man's dog that he adopted the creature as a crest, duly validated by potlatch ceremonial, we get some idea of the Indian's reaction to the unfamiliar; to him the appearance of this strange barking creature was a supernatural encounter. Similarly, when a chief commemorated his coppers on a petroglyph, he was not merely boasting of his triumph in acquiring or destroying objects that represented so much wealth; the copper itself was symbolic wealth, and as a symbol it entered into the whole quasi-religious ceremonial complex of Coast Indian life. We should therefore be cautious about making any interpretation that dismisses the petroglyphs as being intended merely as historical records or as journalistic notations. Everything the Coast Indian considered significant in his life was, almost by that very token, raised above the level of the mundanely material, as it is in all animist societies, which endue every object and every event with at least latent spirituality.

Although their age is so difficult to estimate, it is obvious that the Coast petroglyphs cover a long period — possibly several millennia — and that some at least of the simpler figures represent the earliest use of stone for artistic, or perhaps rather for ritualistic purposes, since one of the particular characteristics of the glyphs as compared with other Coast Indian artifacts is their unprofessional look. In almost every case they appear to have been made with the roughest of tools — sharp pebbles or (as in the case described by Boas) stone hammers — and without the consummate artisanship evident in the work of professional carvers in historic and late prehistoric times and also in the best of the Marpole period stone carvings. It is evident that their unprofessionalism is part of the meaning of the petroglyphs; they were made by men whose special skills did not run in an artistic direction but who made their images in response to highly personal experiences, or, in the case of the magical salmon and whale figures, of pressing social needs.

It is notable that almost all the petroglyphic designs were figurative; the main exceptions are the fairly frequent circles and concentric circles, but even these may be solar or lunar images. Certainly there is no attempt to reproduce the geometrical designs that appeared on textiles and blankets made by women, and which were never used by male artists, and this suggests that petroglyph making, like image making in general, was a male activity. But the figurative designs do differ greatly, and one can say that they are freer and more expressionist in the southern part of the region, the area where the individual spirit quest was most important, and more stylized (and doubtless later in their first appearance) in the northern area where, in the secret societies, the spirit quest took on a collective form.

At the same time, the refinements of later northern art — as it flourished among the Haida, the Tsimshian, and the Tlingit — are not present in the petroglyphs, and this is perhaps a further indication that few of them were done during recent centuries when the peoples of this area turned towards an elaborate ceremonial art. Yet at least one of the peculiar attributes of classic Coast Indian art appears, and in a more developed way than in the stone figures of the Marpole era. This is the X-ray vision. There are figures of pregnant whales and women with their young shown inside them, and there are animals and supernatural beings with their skeletal framework clearly defined. Such a device seems to be related to the shamanistic preoccupation with the novice's dismemberment and his reconstitution as an initiate during some forms of the spirit quest, and it suggests once again how important the shamanistic tradition is in helping to explain both the origins of the Coast Indian peoples and the development of their culture.

CHAPTER FOUR

Shamanism: The Link with Asia

There is a special poignancy about the final remark which ends Franz Boas's description of the Hamatsa ceremony and the making with stone hammers of the late petroglyph at Fort Rupert. He refers to the older glyphs at the same time and remarks that living Indians have no memory of the incidents they commemorate. "They say that they were made at the time before animals were transformed into men."

Transformation, of course, is one of the ruling concepts of Coast Indian culture. In the great transformation masks of the winter dances, in which invisible strings literally changed faces, all the duality of existence was displayed, and especially the ambivalence of man's own position in his universe, conscious of his affinities with the animal world but also of the aspirations that drew him towards the mythical world of supernatural beings with its extensions into the heavens and the underworld. But the remark quoted by Boas suggests something different: the progression by which man developed out of animal innocence, the pagan version of the Fall, and also a suggestion that just as the Indian condition under the rule of the white man was perhaps degenerated from what it had been up to that fatal hour when Cook's tall ships sailed into Nootka Inlet, so the most complex stage of Coast Indian culture, just before Cook's arrival, was in some way a degeneration from the simplicities of an earlier past. The myth of Eden, the legend of

the Golden Age, is by no means an exclusive possession of European traditions, as the Tsimshian myth of the lost paradise of old Temlaham reveals.

The idea of animals being transformed into men might of course be interpreted as a bizarre parallel of evolutionary teachings, but this would assume a progressive kind of philosophy and even a historical view which the Indians themselves almost certainly did not extract from the picture that we, as alien outsiders from another civilization, have of their culture: the picture of a culture that had advanced materially and had acquired not merely cultural complexity but also a certain artistic sophistication. For though they had emerged from the precarious insecurity of a paleolithic hunter's life into the state of material well-being usually associated with settled agrarian communities, they still depended on the death of wild creatures for their survival; and so they never lost that symbiotic sense of identity which has always bound the hunter with his quarry and in so many pre-agrarian cultures has produced elaborate rituals for placating the spirits of slain animals or the deities — to be encountered even in classical mythology in such personifications as Diana and Cybele — who serve as the masters or mistresses of animals.

Such basic assumptions — more deeply rooted in a man's sense of being than mere theories or beliefs — arise out of a consciousness of the unity of the world that men experience, a world in which the visible and the invisible, the phenomenal and the spiritual, form one continuum whose differing aspects one sees through various ways of perception, so that the visions of the shaman at times of ecstasy are as real — and even as tangible — as what the ordinary man going about his daily occupations perceives with his physical eyes.

To the Coast Indian there was no qualitative difference between the animal and the human spheres. The Judeo-Christian idea that animals had no souls would have seemed absurd to him in his animist assumption that all things were imbued with spirit; the Hindu-Buddhist conception of a wheel of life, on whose hierarchical rungs the animals were placed irrevocably lower than men, would have seemed equally incomprehensible to him with his sense of the wisdom and power of animals. The Bella Coola believed that their ancestors were sent down from the heavens clad in animal cloaks, and although the descendants no longer possessed such overt signs of identity with other kinds of creature, they still commemorated the relationship in their crests. In another way the feeling of interconnection between the human and the animal world was expressed in the belief, common to all the Coast peoples, that in their essential forms the all-providing salmon were really no different from men and lived their lives in human form below the sea until the time when their king decided to lead them to the assistance of their human brethren. They then put on their salmon bodies and allowed themselves to be caught, or died after spawning. But their essential being resided in their bones, and if these were carefully collected and returned to the rivers up which they had ascended, then they would be reconstituted in human form beneath the ocean and in due course return once more in their salmon

Tsimshian marionette representing a woman shaman.

71

form, in an everlasting round of regeneration and death.

This was the world of the shamans, who have traditionally applied to themselves the same myth of death and rebirth, and the related myths of an essential continuity between human and animal existence and between the natural and the supernatural, so that they themselves passed into the underworld and the heavens, sometimes under the guidance of spirits who were also animals, and sometimes themselves transformed into animals — just as the great supernatural animal spirits, and even the heavenly bodies, had their human manifestations that were revealed when the transformation masks opened out in the firelight of the winter ceremonials to display the men within the beasts and the elemental forces that were also deities. In such a world the possible was not governed by the probable; every natural happening had its supernatural aspect and meaning.

Such a world view was more than a matter of hunting magic, to which many writers have tried to reduce the significance of the art and ceremony of pre-agrarian peoples — even of the great paleolithic frescoes of Lascaux, Altamira, and many other early monuments of human art. Before European arrival, the world of the Coast Indian — like that of the Siberian shamanists — was shaped according to an elaborate cosmology. There was, as writers like Norman Newton have pointed out, a great deal of intricate thought about planetary relations involved in the stories in which the Haida and the Tsimshian gave symbolic form to their astronomical beliefs; and in general one is aware of a serious attempt by visionary and inquiring minds, whose logic may not have been systematically the same as ours, to establish the relationships that seemed to exist not only within the natural world but also between earthly beings and those remoter entities that filled the skies, the ocean depths, and the heart of the earth, and governed the destiny of all men except those who could defeat or evade them by the proper use of spiritual force.

We have already seen how prehistoric artifacts display the centrality of the shaman in the early millennia of Indian settlement on the Pacific Coast. There is hardly a stone sculpture among the many pieces recovered from the Marpole culture that does not relate to the shaman or his activities, and it seems likely that a considerable majority of the petroglyphs were also connected with shamanism or with the related guardian spirit quest. On such carvings we see many of the attributes of Coast Indian shamans in historic times already present: the topknot of hair on the cranium, the nose bored to receive a bone ornament, the bowl which shamans habitually used in their curing ceremonies, and in the case of some of the petroglyphs what appear to be crowns of grizzly bear claws. Also, as we have seen, the familiar spirits of the shamans are incorporated into the Marpole sculptures, and they seem to be acting in a direct relationship with the shamans displayed on such large and complex petroglyphs as those near Nanaimo. At the same time, it is significant of basic changes in Coast Indian society over the past two millennia that there is nothing in the early sculpture to suggest the highly stratified and crest-obsessed world of the Kwakiutl and the more northerly tribes in historic times, with its secret societies and potlatches, in which both ceremony and art became diverted towards ends of social aggrandizement. In this situation the role of the grandiloquent, name-obsessed chiefs grew at the expense of the shamans, whose standing appears to have diminished greatly in recent centuries, a tendency in all societies that moved from precarious nomadism to a degree of settled security and even prosperity.

Yet, if any strain in Coast Indian society is central to establishing the ancestry of the culture, it is undoubtedly shamanism. Archaeology is beginning to tell us much about the material life of the people who lived in British Columbia between two and three millennia ago, but not much about their antecedents. Legends and languages enable us to sketch out with a fair plausibility the movements after migration to the Americas of the peoples who eventually came together to form the Coast Indian cultures as we have know them. The prehistoric art tells us a little about the material and a good deal more about the spiritual life of the early inhabitants; and it provides some stimulating hints about the origins of the Coast Indian styles of sculpture and painting, and suggests at least indirect relations with Eurasia even after the Bering Strait land bridge was submerged and the migrations came to an end. But it is only shamanism that provides clear and copious evidence of a common origin between the Coast Indian cultures and civilizations, and those of prehistoric Eurasia.

In its classic form shamanism exists in Siberia; the very word *shaman* is a Russian adaptation of an original used among the Tungus. In his basic work on the subject, *Shamanism, Archaic Techniques of Ecstasy*, Mircea Eliade presents the basic definition, "shamanism = *technique of ecstasy*," but he immediately qualifies it by remarking that "any ecstatic cannot be considered a shaman; the shaman specializes in a trance during which his soul is believed to leave his body and ascend to the sky or descend to the underworld." One can add that though a shaman is also a magician and a healer, all magicians and healers are not shamans; the shaman has his own techniques which are related to the totality of his experience and his vocation.

The origins of shamanism lie far in the human past. It is possible that the painters of the Lascaux caves were recording shamanistic concepts of the linked destinies of men and animals as well as carrying out mere hunting magic, for which much less naturalistically elaborated figures of animals would have been sufficient; it is possible even that a primitive form of shamanism was emerging in the quasi-religious rituals which we now believe Neanderthal men to have practised in their caves fifty thousand years ago.

Forms of shamanic practice in fact occur in most parts of the world and survive to colour our own customs and religious beliefs (so that even in putting up a Christmas tree every year one is replanting the shamanic Tree of Life). It is likely that beliefs of this kind developed in all hunting societies in response to primitive man's direct and often highly stressful relationship with the forces and beings of the natural world; the first shamans were probably hunters who discovered the ecstatic condition accidentally through a hallucinatory state brought on by solitude, cold, and starvation, and then repeated the experience deliberately. But the particular current of shamanistic beliefs and practices that produced the cult among the Coast Indians of British Columbia originated in Siberia and was brought over the land bridge with the first waves of migrants. It is significant that the last migrants, the Eskimos, retain a type of shamanism almost identical with the cults surviving in present-day Siberia, whereas both practice and doctrine have undergone some modification in Pacific North America, but not enough to leave any doubt as to the common origin of the Siberian and Coast Indian variants.

In a later chapter I shall discuss the role that the shaman played in the life of the Coast Indians in historic times; here, I will note the basic beliefs and practices that relate Siberian and Coast Indian shamans to each other and serve to establish the roots of the Pacific Coast culture in Asia.

The Siberian shaman may reach his vocation by a number of ways; he may set out deliberately

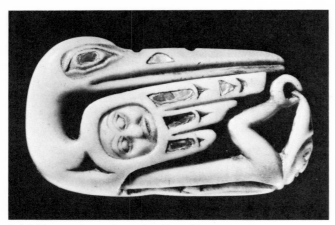
Inlaid bone charm from the Nass River.

to seek a qualifying spiritual experience, particularly if he is the son of a shaman, but such experience may equally well come to him without seeking, and then he is virtually being conscripted by the spirits, and particularly by the spirits of dead shamans.

While the theory that shamans are usually psychotics, epileptics, or physically sick people seems to be unfounded, there is no doubt that a sickness often precedes a shaman's first experience and that becoming a shaman provides a cure. Through meeting a supernatural being or through some other extraordinary experience, the novice falls into a deep trance. In this trance he encounters the spirit who will be his guardian. As part of the experience he descends or is taken into the underworld, and there, at the hands of spirits who are really dead shamans, he undergoes the dismemberment of his body, the reassembling of his bones, which are its essential structure (as in the case of the salmon whose bones are returned to the sea), and the renewal of his organs. He undergoes, as Mircea Eliade says, "ritual death followed by resurrection." He is symbolically, spiritually, and — since he believes the trance experience to be as real as any other experience — "physically" reborn. He believes himself an entirely transformed being, and from this basic original transformation he has gained the power of further transformation at will.

From this point onwards the shaman acquires knowledge in two ways: by repeated entrancement, and through the esoteric oral teachings of the older shamans who have accepted his initiation. He can change himself into an animal form, acquiring the power of interchangeability which all beings possessed in a happier past, and he can detach his soul from his body for journeys into the underworld or into the heavens. The universe, through which he moves with such facility, is centred on a great World Tree or Tree of Life, up which he can climb to the heavens which its branches touch, and down which he can descend into the underworld. A great supernatural bird perches on the topmost branch of the tree and a serpent coils around its base, like the serpent that lived in the roots of Yggdrasil, the great ash tree that in Nordic mythology united all the levels of the cosmos. As Tree of Life, the World Tree was created for the happiness of all earthly beings, and its branches served as roosts for innumerable birds which were the transformed souls of dead people.

The very vocation of the shaman involves, as Eliade remarks, a "separation," and this lies not merely in the spiritual crisis that divides him from his unregenerate past self, but also in the way his experience has placed him apart from other men. Yet his ecstasies have not detached him from the world. Far from it; they have allowed him to experience that world more vividly. And though the shaman constantly retreats into solitude to renew the ecstatic experiences that give him his powers, it is in the world that those powers are made manifest.

The influence that a shaman can wield as a wise man in the community varies greatly in accordance with the social structure; there are

The shaman used a bone soul-catcher to retrieve the wandering spirit that had caused a person to fall ill.

situations in which he acquires temporal power, but among the Coast Indians, at least in historic times, his role tended to be restricted to that of spiritual technician, with much of the socially necessary aspects of contact with the spirit world having passed into the hands of ritualists of other kinds, like the chiefs who performed the welcoming rituals for running fish. The particular role the shaman always played in the community was that of the healer, but even here his functions were related strictly to his ecstatic role, to the insights and powers he had acquired on entry into the freemasonry of the world of spirits. There were other kinds of healer in most societies where shamans flourished; herbalists, usually women, had a wide knowledge of the medicinal properties of local plants, and primitive chiropractors were also often present. Like all specialists in such societies, they regarded their skills as the gifts of spirit helpers, but this did not mean that they shared the ecstatic experience which was the hallmark of the shaman.

Specifically, the two areas of healing in which the shaman specialized involved illnesses attri-

buted to soul loss, and illnesses attributed to the intrusion of evil forces or actual foreign substances into the body, either by sorcery or through the anger of supernatural beings. When a man's soul was lost, it could have been kidnapped by a hostile shaman or an evil spirit, or it could have strayed away during sleep or as the result of an accident; dead men's souls were particularly prone to lure away the souls of living men so that they should have company on their journey into the land of death. In this case the shaman must leave his body and journey in spirit until he discovered the errant soul; the journey would often be represented by energetic miming on the part of the presumably entranced celebrant.

In the case of the intrusion of an alien spirit or object, the shaman would chant and beat his drum or shake his rattle, but the climax of the treatment was always reached when he energetically sucked at the subject's body and produced some object which he claimed must have caused the sickness. At the same time he would divine who had willed the illness, which would mean accusing someone of sorcery, or informing the sick person how he had offended by breaking a taboo or neglecting a ritual.

In almost every respect the initiation, education and function of the Coast Indian shaman, even in historic times, corresponded with that of his Siberian counterpart. There was, to begin, the encounter with a supernatural being resulting in a prostrating trance, which was described with great vividness by a Gitksan shaman named Isaac Tens in an account recorded by Marius Barbeau in his *Medicine Men of the North Pacific Coast*. Tens tells how, when he was thirty, he went one day into the forest to gather firewood as it was growing dark:

> Before I had finished my last stack of wood, a loud noise broke over me, and a large owl appeared to me. The owl took hold of me, caught my face, and tried to lift me up. I lost consciousness. As soon as I came back to my senses I realized that I had fallen into the snow. My head was coated with ice, and some blood was running out of my mouth.
>
> I stood up and went down the trail, walking very fast, with some wood packed on my back. On my way, the trees seemed to shake and lean over me; tall trees were crawling after me, as if they had been snakes. I could see them. Before I arrived at my father's home, I told my folk what had happened to me, as soon as I walked in. I was very cold and warmed myself before going to bed. There I fell into a sort of trance. It seems that two *halaaits* (medicine-men) were working over me to bring me back to health. But it is now all vague in my memory. When I woke up and opened my eyes, I thought that flies covered my face completely. I looked down, and instead of being on firm ground, I felt that I was drifting in a huge whirlpool. My heart was thumping fast.

When Tens recovered from this trance he found the two shamans attending him; they told him that it was time he himself became a shaman, but he refused to heed their advice. A second and decisive spiritual encounter followed. Tens had gone to his hunting grounds in the region of the old paradise of Temlaham and he was looking for a bear's lair among the trees:

> As I glanced upwards, I saw an owl, at the top of a high cedar. I shot it, and it fell down in the bushes close to me. When I went to pick it up, it had disappeared. Not a feather was left; this seemed very strange. I walked down to the river, crossed over the ice, and returned to the village of Gitenmaks. Upon arriving at my fishing station at the point, I heard the noise of a crowd of people around the smoke-house, as if I were being chased away, pursued. I dared not look behind to find out what all this was about, but I hastened straight ahead. The voices followed me in my tracks and came very close behind me. Then I wheeled round and looked back. There was no one in sight, only trees. A trance came over me once more, and I fell down, unconscious. When I came to, my head was buried in a snowbank. I got up and walked on the ice up the river to the village. There I met my father who had just come out to look for me, for he had missed me. We went back together to my house. Then my heart started to beat fast, and I began to tremble, just as had happened a little while before, when the *halaaits* (medicine-men) were trying to fix me up. My flesh seemed to be boiling, and I could hear Su_____. My body was quivering. While I remained in this state, I began to sing. A chant was coming out of me without my being able to do anything to stop it. Many things appeared to me presently: huge birds and other animals. They were calling me. I saw a *meskyawawderh* (a kind of bird), and a *mesqagweeuk* (bullhead fish). These were visible only to me, not to others in my house. Such visions happen when a man is about to become a *halaait*; they occur of their own accord. The songs force themselves out complete without any attempt to compose them.

Tens does not mention the underground abduction by spirits as part of his experiences, perhaps because by the time he spoke he had been converted to Christianity, but it occurs in many other accounts of shamanic initiation among the Coast Indians, such as the story of the Tsimshian shaman Qamkawl or Only-One, recorded by William Beynon as recently as 1954 and also reproduced by Barbeau. Strange noises and singing had been heard coming from a pit near one of the Tsimshian villages, and finally a young chief with two companions set out to investigate. The companions descended in turn on the end of a cedar rope, but were attacked by swarms of stinging insects. Then the young chief went down:

> When he landed at the bottom of the pit he found it very dark, and felt his way round. A great sound as of thunder almost deafened him. Then a door opened from which a very bright man stepped and came straight to the Gyilodzau man, and asked, 'Where are you from, and what do you want?' 'Oh! supernatural one, I have come to get halaait power, to cure my people.' The bright man said, 'Come with me, I will take you to my father. He may help you.' The Gyilodzau followed this shining man, who led him into a large house. A number of people sat about, and at the rear was a great chief, with many rattles which looked as if they were alive. Along the side of the great fire there were a number of people, and across from them, on the opposite side of the fire, was an empty space. The Gyilodzau man was seated near the big chief, at the rear of the house. The chief wore a crown of grizzly-bear claws, and in each hand he held a rattle which appeared to be alive. They rattled of their own accord. While he sat there, another door opened through which a young man entered and came to where the Gyilodzau sat. He also had a rattle in each hand and wore an apron which was fringed with deer hoofs. These hoofs gave a rattling sound with every movement that he made. While he stood there, one more door opened, and boards came out as if alive and spread out in front of the fire. Then live clubs appeared. They went to the boards and began to beat time on the boards. The people in the house began to sing, following the tune

A Tsimshian shaman's crown made of carved and inlaid mountain goat horns.

> sung by the young man with the rattles in his hands. A live drum then ran out and began to beat itself with one of the beaters. Everything seemed to be alive. The Gyilodzau heard the singing and the dancing. The great chief arose and rubbed the Gyilodzau-man's eyes. Then all became quiet in the great house. He no longer could see. Everything was in darkness. He felt that the rope was still fastened to him. So he called out, and his companions pulled him out.

Later, Only-One went through the experience of death and rebirth common to the shamanic experience. He vanished for many days. One night a crash was heard behind his house, and he was found lying face down in the mud, apparently dead. His two companions took him into the house, covered him with a mat, and left him. Then they heard singing, and when they went back they found him alive; he told how he had gone again among the underground spirits and had learned the secret of restoring the dead to life, an ability Coast Indian shamans were generally held to have possessed in past ages but to have lost in the degenerate present.

A shaman's charm box

The myth of dismembering at the time of the shamanic initiatory vision was not so frequently mentioned among the Coast peoples as in Siberia, but its universality in prehistoric times can be inferred from the fact that symbolic death and dismemberment play their part in the rituals of the Kwakiutl dancing societies; dismemberment was re-enacted theatrically during the winter ceremonies, especially in the performances of the ghost dancers, when burial alive and decapitation were regularly mimed.

The theme of dismemberment and recreation occurs also in the high art of the Kwakiutl and the northern peoples, represented in a concept of design which involved what Audrey Hawthorn, in her *Art of the Kwakiutl Indians*, has called "the use of X-ray painting to establish the design form of a whole animal, disposed over the area to be covered." The literal forms of nature were cavalierly butchered as the spirits symbolically butchered the shamanic initiate. An animal might be shown kippered down the backbone, his body spread out on each side to fill the space involved; his bones and organs might be clearly delineated within his body; he might be rep-

resented in a composite design merely by a recognizable beak, tail, or claws; his joints and genitals might be metamorphosed into eyes or faces; his organs and features might be moved into quite unnatural compositions to satisfy the needs of design and the symbolic expression of clan or secret society myth. Such examples demonstrate how strongly the shamanic myth of death, dismemberment and renewal influenced the mental life even of Coast Indians who were not themselves shamans (and predisposed them long afterwards to be attracted towards the pentecostal aspects of Christianity).

Once initiated, the Coast Indian shaman, like his Siberian counterpart, was free to leave his body and journey to the higher regions through the "Hole in the Sky," represented on the famous pole of that name which still stands in the Gitksan village of Kitwancool. He might climb there up a chain of arrows, as in many legends, or up a magic pole or even a Tree of Life, for the Bella Coola had their legend of the magic tree belonging to Alkuntam, the supreme deity who resided in the heavens; in that tree the souls of men roosted, transformed into a vast company of owls. This tree was in the upper world, but the Bella Coola also conceived of a great pillar somewhere in the west, which kept the sun from falling down on the earth and which also served as the ladder by which the ancestors first made their way to earth from the upper world. The title, "Post of the World," was also applied to a pole erected in the dancing house during the Kwakiutl Hamatsa ceremonials; it was also called the "Cannibal Pole," because it represented a similar and much larger post of cosmic significance in the supernatural dwelling of Baksbakualanu Xsiwae, the "Cannibal from the North End of the World."

Such analogues of the World Tree or the Tree of Life have led some anthropologists to conclude that the totem poles, the heraldic and mortuary poles so central to the ceremonial lives of the Kwakiutl and the northern peoples, were originally in fact shamanic representations of the Tree of Life. A great deal of colour is given to this theory by the fact that many poles were topped by images of birds, like the poles which Siberian shamans climbed to mime the journey to the heavens. In fact, it is likely that the plain, bird-topped pole may have been the original form of the Coast Indian pole, which later became elaborated by the need to record the crests of the name-proud chiefs. It seems significant that on the peripheries of the culture, far up the Skeena in the villages of the Gitksan and of the neighbouring Carriers of Hagwilget, simple poles bearing perhaps a single crest and a bird on top, or even only the finial bird, were still being erected in the early years of the present century.

The curing activities of the Coast Indian shaman were entirely similar to those of his Siberian counterpart. He underwent journeys in search of lost souls, of which the most spectacular were undoubtedly the mimed voyages by spirit canoe in which whole groups of Salish shamans would take part. Nootka shamans, who had to contend with maritime spirits who stole souls, would dive in ecstasy to the sea bottom and return with the lost spirits wrapped in a pinch of eagle's down. The Coast Indian shaman also practised with dramatic ritual the extraction of foreign influences and substances by a process in which sucking was the culminant and the most important element.

Apart from these general similarities, there were other very specific similarities between the beliefs of the ancient Siberians and the Coast Indians, which reinforce the idea of a common shamanic inheritance. Among both peoples great store was set on rock crystals, which conferred supernatural powers and which were held to embody the spirits of dead shamans; every Siberian and Coast Indian shaman included such

A Tsimshian shaman performing his cure.

crystals in his magic equipment. Among Siberian shamans, and universally in Coast Indian society, the eagle appeared supernaturally in the form of Thunderbird, lord of the elements, and among the Siberian Chuckchi, as on the Pacific Coast, Raven appeared as an animal trickster who was also, in every essential point, a shaman pitting his knowledge, his skills, and his insolence against the impersonal forces of the universe and so becoming the favourite culture hero of peoples on both sides of the northern Pacific.

So much evidence leaves one in no doubt about the common ancestry of the shamanism which until long after the communist assumption of power in Russia remained the moving heart of life among many northern and eastern Siberian peoples, and which among the Coast Indians had already retreated before the social and ceremonial pretensions of the secular chiefs, by the time the first Europeans arrived. Among the shamans themselves the tradition had been continued almost unchanged, as rigidly controlled oral traditions often do. (The extraordinary lack of change over many centuries in Tibetan religio-magical practices before the Chinese communist invasion is a strikingly similar example.)

79

The most evident difference between the Siberian and the Coast Indian cultures, indeed, does not rest in differences of shamanic vision or practice, but rather in the wide diffusion among the Coast Indians, as among other North American groups, of spiritual quests and aspirations which elsewhere tend to be regarded as the concern and privilege of the elect few. Mircea Eliade, who dealt mainly with Siberian shamanism, nevertheless recognized this crucial difference between the spiritual tempers of East Asian and Pacific Coast societies. He remarked on what one must describe as the almost pantheistic attitude of the Indian to a world where spiritual power was latent everywhere, where "any spiritual, animal or physical entity can become a source of power or guardian spirit, whether for the shaman or for an ordinary individual."

The guardian spirit quest extends in all Coast Indian peoples far beyond the reach of shamanism. Every man with a special skill, whether he was a carver, a canoe maker, a hunter, or a warrior, felt that he had gained this ability from a spirit helper. Every nobleman traced his crests to encounters with the supernatural which he or his ancestors had experienced. Membership of the prestigious secret societies of the Kwakiutl and the northern tribes depended on real or simulated spirit encounters. Among the Salish, where the social order was less stratified and society more naturally democratic, probably a majority of individuals of both sexes underwent guardian spirit quests which might bring them special skills, might even turn them into shamans, but usually merely provided them with a personal song and a dance that established both their position in mundane society and their links with the supernatural. As Eliade puts it in trying to define the relations between shamans and the secret brotherhoods which exist not only among Coast Indians but almost universally in aboriginal North America:

> In North America the differences between "consecrated" men and the "profane" multitude are not so much qualitative as quantitative; they lie in the *amount* of the sacred that the former have assimilated. We have shown that every Indian seeks religious power, that every Indian commands a guardian spirit acquired by the same techniques that the shaman uses to obtain his own spirits. The difference between layman and shaman is quantitative; the shaman commands a greater number of tutelary or guardian spirits and a stronger magico-religious "power." In this respect we could almost say that every Indian "shamanizes," even if he does not consciously wish to become a shaman.

Just when this generalization of spiritual searching among the Coast Indians began, and how much can be attributed to such factors as the greater leisure enjoyed during the winter months, or the spectacular and alarming features of the setting of coast and rain forest and mountain, it is virtually impossible at this stage to determine. But the ultimate fact is that, though we cannot doubt the common origin of Siberian and Coast Indian cultures, and especially of shamanism in the two regions, by the end of the eighteenth century there was a striking difference between the hard and frugal existence of the Siberians, rich only in the ecstatic fantasy of their shamanic cults, and the materially wealthy and ceremonially complex life of the Coast Indians with their surplus economy, their conspicuous spending, their love of overtly displayed honours, and their remarkable artistic and inventive talents. It was the latter society, at the height of its prehistoric flowering, that the first European voyagers encountered in the 1770s.

This beaver mask of the Haida has eyes of abalone shell and shows in its
fluted surface the fine marks of the finishing tools.

This original frame of a Kwakiutl house, which now stands in the Totem Pole Park at the University of British Columbia, shows the carved house posts and central frontal post with door opening.

No original Haida houses survive, but during the 1960s the carver Bill Reid
supervised the construction of this replica, with a typical housefront post,
at the Totem Pole Park.

Original Haida posts (left) from the Queen Charlotte Islands show in their weathered greyness the models from which contemporary.Indian artists have carved modern posts (right), which now stand in Canadian and foreign outdoor museums.

These house posts, now standing in the great Museum of Anthropology which Arthur Erickson designed for the University of British Columbia, were brought from the Kwakiutl village of Koskimo.

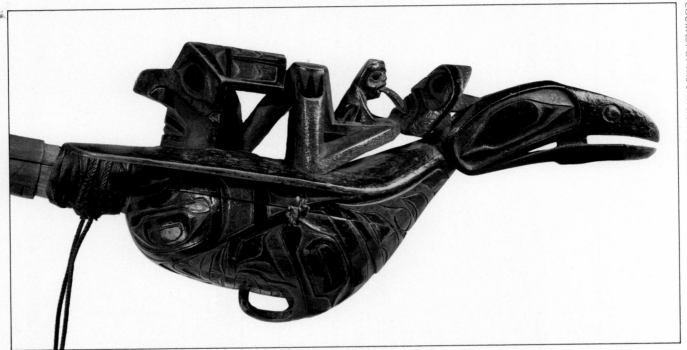

This Kwakiutl raven rattle is made of alder wood and was part of the ceremonial regalia of the chiefs at potlatches and on other public occasions.

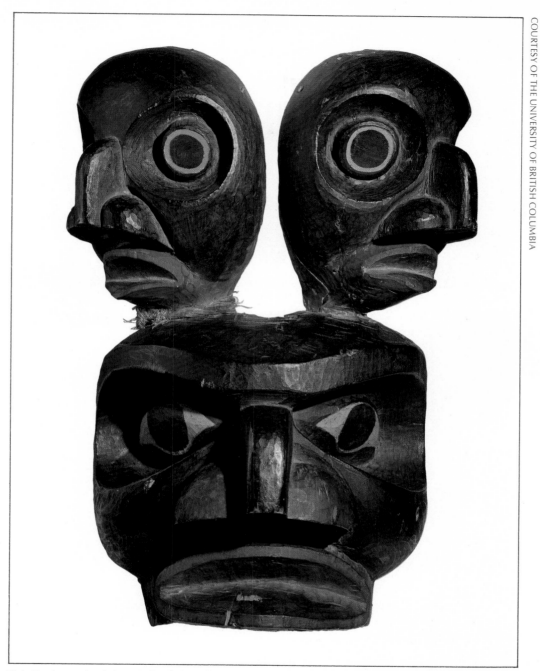

This Tanis mask of the Heiltsuk (northern Kwakiutl) was collected in 1893 at Kitlope, where it had been found in a cave, but it is much older than the date of discovery and is thought to have been used in early forms of the Hamatsa ceremonials.

A celebrated example of Bella Coola artistry, this mask with movable jaw shows a frog's head superimposed on the head of a bear.

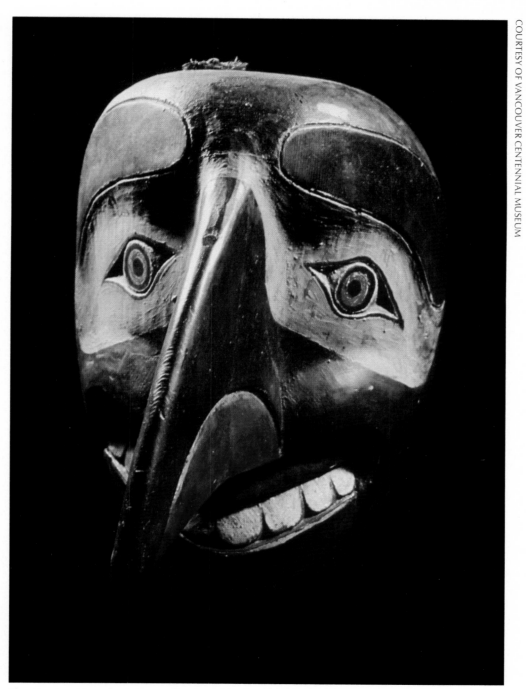

The Noolmahl, or fool dancer, took part in the Kwakiutl winter ceremonials as representative of one of the cannibal spirits attending the initiation of the Hamatsa dancer

This relatively early Kwakiutl bear mask may well have been used by one of the masked wedding dancers photographed by E. S. Curtis.

This eloquent and unusual bear mask is a fine example of Tlingit craftsmanship.

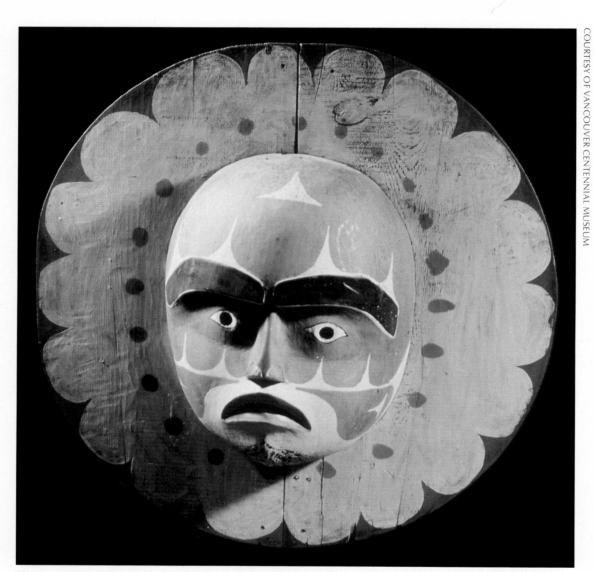

The sun mask, highly lyrical in its presentation, shows the originality of Bella Coola workmanship and particularly of the colour combinations favoured by that relatively isolated people.

Boxes of cedar wood were made to store food, and the best made were used for storing oolichan oil. Secured with cedar bark ropes, they were often carried on men's backs over the grease trails as part of the coastal trading complex.

This moon mask of the Bella Bella (a Kwakiutl group) was used in the dances of the winter ceremonials.

The chiefs of the northern peoples wore diadems with carved frontlets of alder wood, usually decorated with abalone shell, and with ermine skins attached which fell like manes over the wearers' shoulders.

Part II

Interior of a Nootka house, as seen by John Webber.

CHAPTER FIVE

History Begins: The Fatal Encounter

The Coast Indian culture was a tough and tenacious growth that in its essential elements resisted the pressures of alien impact for several generations. It was not until the missionaries mounted their frontal assault in the later nineteenth century, and were supported by the Canadian federal government in such infamous measures as the legislation of 1884, forbidding both the potlatch and the Salish spirit dances, that the culture disintegrated, and even then the disintegration was incomplete, as the recent revival of the basic ceremonial structure and of the artistic traditions has revealed.

During the whole century following the arrival of Juan Perez in 1774 and of James Cook in 1778, the Coast Indians showed a remarkable ability to assimilate alien technologies into their ceremonial lives without the central structure of their societies being destroyed. Yet the appearance of strength and impermeability was deceptive, and even if it took several generations for the old native order of the Coast to disintegrate under the impact of a greyer but stronger alien power, the change began from the very moment when foreign explorers and traders appeared, not only as the purveyors of such desired substances as copper and iron, but also as models to imitate. And because of the perishability of Coast Indian dwellings and of most of their contents, which two generations of rain forest weather are enough to dissolve back into the woodland soil, the accounts of these early explorers who saw the society in its pristine condition are especially precious, particularly as up to now only one archaeological discovery has been made that gives us a really broad view of the Coast Indian culture immediately prior to the first European contacts.

This is the discovery of a buried village at Cape Alava on the ocean shore just south of Cape Flattery, a region inhabited by the Makah, a branch of the Nootka who were once famous whale hunters. The Makah had the reputation in early European times of being a particularly hostile and intractable people; traders were repeatedly attacked by them and as late as 1808, when the Russian ship *Saint Nicholas* was wrecked off this shore, most of the crew were captured and either killed or enslaved by the Makah.

Sir Francis Drake appears to have sailed through these waters in 1579, claiming all the land he sighted for Queen Elizabeth I under the name of New Albion, though if he did sight the land he does not appear to have sighted any of the people. But the Cape Alava discovery at least in part makes up for the omission, since about the time when Drake sailed here (the carbon 14 datings give us a century or so each side of his date), an avalanche of mud slid down on the village which the Makah called Ozette and which they had been inhabiting for at least fifteen centuries. It engulfed eight great houses; and the slurry, which has kept perpetually damp over the centuries, preserved the dwellings and their contents as the dust of Vesuvius preserved Pompeii. The slide appears to have happened at night, for at least twenty people, as well as dogs, were found in sleeping postures in the first four houses to be excavated; and it happened also in the spring, for there were fresh cedar bark and fresh evergreen leaves which withered once the air struck them.

The find at Cape Alava, made in 1971, reveals at least two important facts. The first is that the material abundance and artistic fertility of the Coast Indian culture, as it was seen by early anthropologists in the later nineteenth century, had not resulted merely from the influx of goods and of metal tools through the establishment of the fur trade. In the first four houses, no less than forty-five thousand items of local manufacture or of intertribal trading were discovered, including examples of every art with which we are familiar from later Coast Indian production. There were cedar bark blankets and rugs of goats' and dogs' wool with the looms and spindle whorls used in making them and even the skeletons of the extinct wool-bearing dogs. There were carved wooden bowls, sewn boxes of cedarwood elaborately painted with the owners' crests, and a multitude of woven baskets. There were wooden sculptures, and ceremonial clubs carved out of stone, and the elaborate woven hats that appear in all the early prints of the Nootka peoples. One house contained all the whale-hunting equipment proper to a chiefly harpoonist, including not only the great harpoons and lances with their blades of sharpened giant mussel shell, but also a complete whale skeleton with a harpoon tip lodged in the skull, a fourteen-foot long carved and painted wooden screen bearing the image of a whale, and a wooden sculpture of a killer whale's fin inlaid with seven hundred sea otter

teeth in the form of a thunderbird, either a symbol to indicate that the chief belonged to the killer whale clan, or part of the ceremonial paraphernalia used when a whale was killed and the flesh and blubber were distributed according to strict precedence to the noblemen and the common people.

The second extraordinary fact about the Cape Alava find, which confirms what the early explorers repeatedly asserted when they talked of the Coast Indians' knowledge of metals, is that iron knives and chisels had reached the village in small quantities at least two hundred and possibly four hundred years before the arrival of the first European traders. The iron discovered there bore no resemblance to that being made at that period in the only three possible European countries — Britain, Spain, and Russia. It was nearer to early mediaeval Japanese iron, and this accords with the observation of more than one of the early Spanish and British explorers, that the "rough knives with coarse wooden hafts" — as Cook's marine sergeant, John Ledyard, called them — were of unfamiliar manufacture. A few diarists thought they might have been traded through successive Indian intermediaries from the English post at Hudson's Bay, but that would not explain the dating from before the foundation of the Hudson's Bay Company of the finds at Cape Alava, or the unfamiliarity of the kind of iron; it seems that the knives must have been traded from some Asian source, carried over the Bering Strait by the Eskimos who inhabited both its shores, and found their way through the Aleuts to the northern Tlingit; once at Yakutat Bay, they would enter the North Pacific coastal trading area and would find their way down the Coast in the chain that circulated products as far apart in their origin as the copper of Alaska, the abalone shell of northern California and the obsidian blades found in the interior plateaus of British Columbia and Oregon.

The finds at Capa Alava confirm the descriptions which the early explorers give of the physical accoutrements of the Coast Indian life at the point of first contact, though they also suggest an abundance and an intricacy which the first Europeans do not make evident in their accounts, perhaps because until John Jewitt was captured by the Nootka in 1803 and lived for more than two years as the chief Maquinna's slave, none of them saw that life with the intimacy of which the Cape Alava finds give us a flavour. But only a flavour, since if it were not for the increasingly close observation of actual Coast Indian behaviour — and particularly of the ceremonial life — that has gone on for the past two centuries, we would not reach more than a very rudimentary interpretation of the later prehistoric artifacts so miraculously and liberally preserved at this site.

The early explorers were not the best of observers, though they are the only ones we have relating to that period. They went to the Coast with the preconceptions of eighteenth century men. Many of the Spaniards were devout Catholics — some were even priests — and were so intent on conversion that they would buy child slaves for this purpose with sheets of copper. The best of the British tended — like Cook, Vancouver, and their officers — to be rather rationally-minded Anglican latitudinarians with an inbred sense of the superiority of their people and of their stage of civilization. The English and American traders, some of whom were extremely ruthless and insensitive men, were interested mainly in making quick money out of the sea otter skins which (as Cook's expedition had revealed) sold for high prices in China, and only a few of them had any sympathetic or even detached interest in the people among whom they moved.

Even the best of these early visitors arrived with the view that the Indians were uncouth

Maquinna, the celebrated chief of Nootka Sound, as seen by an eighteenth century Spanish artist.

savages, and when they were forced to acknowledge the high craftsmanship and unique design of Coast Indian artifacts or the solidity of Coast Indian houses, they still reacted merely with astonishment that so crude a people could execute such exquisite work, and did not pause to consider that perhaps the artistic tradition concealed a way of life far more complex, and in its own way far more civilized, than it might appear at a first cursory glance.

They were, of course, hindered from any profundity of observation by many circumstances. They rarely understood more than a few words of the local languages and usually communicated in

Maquinna's potlatch to celebrate his daughter's puberty. By an eighteenth century Spanish artist.

what was called Chinook, not the actual language of that tribe, but a debased pidgin which had absorbed English and French expressions as well as words from almost all the peoples up and down the Coast. They usually traded or voyaged in the summer months, when the Indians were living in their temporary fishing camps and were occupied with fishing and other economic activities. For reasons of safety they rarely penetrated into the secluded coves and inlets where the winter villages were situated, and only rarely did they see — and then usually misinterpret — some fragment of the potlatch ceremonials. None of the early explorers appears to have seen any of the dramatic winter dances or to have had much insight into the views of existence that underlay such performances. And it was not long before

the brutalities of impatient sea traders (like the American Captain Gray's burning of a whole village of great houses with carved and painted fronts in 1792, over some small affront) created an atmosphere of mutual distrust that made even the kind of ceremonial visits exchanged between Indian chiefs and visiting captains in the early days a practical impossibility by the end of the eighteenth century, when the Coast became infested with Yankee speculators interested only in profits and willing to resort to such measures as kidnapping the local chiefs in order to extort furs from their peoples.

As early as 1793, when Alexander Mackenzie descended the Bella Coola valley and reached salt water, he was to experience difficulties owing to the insults the Bella Bella believed they had received from Vancouver's men — and Vancouver was more considerate of native feelings of dignity than most other visitors to the Coast. The incident of the *Boston* in 1802, during which John Jewitt and his shipmate, Thompson, were captured by the people of Nootka Sound, illustrated the way in which mutual distrust could build up into deadly hostilities. Maquinna — the successor and name-inheritor of the Maquinna who had welcomed Cook in 1778 — had endured a series of insults from American traders, and some of his people had been killed by them. When Captain Salter of the *Boston* called him a liar over an incident of a broken musket, and in various other ways showed his contempt, Maquinna — who knew enough English to understand the insults — took his revenge by surprising the boat and killing all but two of the twenty-seven men on board. The news of the cutting out of the *Boston* spread up the Coast, and when visiting captains heard it they avoided not only Nootka Sound but also the neighbouring villages, and this in turn aroused the hostility of other Nootkas against Maquinna and his people, whose actions had deprived them of trade.

It is possible that such hostile behaviour on the part of both American traders and Indian communities had a double effect, not only delaying European acquisition of knowledge about the Indian peoples but also slowing down the pace of acculturation among the Indians. Perhaps the most interesting conclusion one reaches from reading such an account as *The Adventures and Sufferings of John R. Jewitt, Captive Among the Nootka, 1803-1805* is that despite more than a quarter of a century during which Nootka Sound was the centre of European attention on the Pacific Northwest — during which a Spanish settlement existed there and many European and American ships arrived for trade, or for political manoeuvres in the Spanish-British conflict over jurisdiction in the north

Pacific — the actual lives of the Nootka had changed remarkably little. They had acquired considerable quantities of European goods, including many muskets and much cloth and metals, but a great deal of this material they appear to have used merely as gifts in the round of potlatches, and except for an increasing use of iron in tools and weapons, their daily life remained surprisingly unchanged. They do not seem to have used their firearms to any great extent in hunting, and when Jewitt accompanied Maquinna and the local warriors on a murderous night attack on a neighbouring village, only he and Thompson took pistols; the rest of the attacking band was armed entirely with traditional weapons. As for social and ceremonial patterns within the community, these appear to have been entirely unaffected.

One can in fact draw quite a sharp line between the period when the traders operated from ships which appeared off the coast with no regularity, and the later period, beginning with the establishment of the Hudson's Bay Company post at Fort Langley in 1827, when they became an established part of coastal life. Once the fur trade was anchored in the posts, the changes in Indian life accelerated. Almost as soon as Fort Simpson was established in 1834 near the present site of Prince Rupert, the people from all the nine Tsimshian villages of the lower Skeena migrated there to set up a great compound settlement on the beaches near the fort, and the same thing happened among the Kwakiutl of northern Vancouver Island and the neighbouring small islands after Fort Rupert was established in 1849. This gathering in close proximity of groups who had come together in the past merely for trading, or for occasional potlatches, or in war, resulted in the development of extraordinary rivalries among the chiefs, and there is no doubt that the extravagantly competitive potlatching of the middle and later nineteenth century first developed in places like Fort Rupert and Fort Simpson.

The establishment of Fort Victoria on Vancouver Island in 1843 affected Indian life on the Coast in a different but equally potent way, for it soon became the headquarters of the Hudson's Bay Company's activities on the Coast, and, after the establishment of the crown colony of Vancouver Island in 1849, the local centre of British power on the Pacific. This meant that warships as well as trading and survey vessels began to appear, with a consequent and growing imposition of an alien political power and alien concepts of law and justice. Less than a decade later, the Fraser Valley gold rush of 1858 turned Victoria into a frontier town that became an irresistible magnet for the northern tribes, and especially the Haida, who would set up their camps and remain for months — to the great perturbation of the local authorities and the white inhabitants — until the fear of smallpox rather than of Governor James Douglas finally drove them away.

But perhaps the establishment of the Hudson's Bay Company posts had its greatest effect by attracting missionaries to the sizeable flocks of potential converts who gathered around the forts. The famous William Duncan, the Anglican lay missionary who founded the mission colony of Metlakatla, forced himself on the reluctant fur traders at Fort Simpson in 1857; and the effects of that event on the whole nature and structure of the Indian societies in the northern part of the coastal area was profound and to a great extent irreversible, as we shall see later in more detail. The traders had wanted as little material change as possible in the Indian way of life, so that a hunting economy could continue to produce a steady flow of furs; the missionaries believed that they could change the spiritual condition of the Indians, which was their first objective, only by approximating the Indians'

way of life to the Victorian norm, and so they aimed from the beginning at a total transformation of the Coast societies and at a destruction of their rich ceremonial life and its artistic manifestations, so aggressively pagan to the evangelical mind.

The great agglomerations of peoples around the trading posts also attracted the first and in many ways the best of the anthropologists, for it was at Fort Rupert that Franz Boas found his most reliable informants and carried out most of his crucial studies of Kwakiutl society. In their own way, anthropologists change the societies they observe, and where the cultures are simple and fragile, as so often in the South Pacific, the mere presence of such intruders can markedly hasten the process of acculturation. It is doubtful, however, if the anthropologists working on the coast of British Columbia and Alaska, during the crucial phase of late blossoming and quick decay among the Indian cultures, had much to do with the changes that took place at that period — though their successors have played a definite (and on the whole positive) role during recent decades in encouraging that pride in the past which has helped to bring traditional concepts back as a directing force in the lives of Indian peoples, who for generations had felt disoriented as they became absorbed irrevocably into the general material culture of the modern Western world.

One traces backwards in a diminishing ratio the knowledge that these various alien groups acquired of Indian society. To the early anthropologists in particular, like Franz Boas and John Swanton and Thomas McIlwraith, who operated before academic vested interests became a distorting factor, we owe the kind of knowledge, recorded almost at the last possible time in the decades of rapid change and disintegration between 1880 and the First World War, without which books like this would be much more difficult to write. The missionaries, for their part, learnt and recorded the languages, and in this way they furthered our knowledge of the cultures, but the rest of their information they acquired very selectively and principally with a view to discovering what, from their point of view, was bad in Indian life (which included all the rich native ceremonial) and should be eliminated in the process of turning the Indians into model and industrious Victorian Christians. Only in very recent years have the representatives of any of the churches shown much real sympathy for Indian cultures or understanding of their genuinely religous aspects.

As for the fur traders who staffed the Hudson's Bay Company posts, we owe to them surprisingly little of our knowledge of the Coast Indian cultures; even the freelance sea traders were more informative. There were certainly no Samuel Hearnes among the company's officers on the Pacific Coast, willing to share the life of the native people in the interests of knowledge; and even the lesser degree of intimacy which North West Company explorers like Mackenzie, Fraser, and Thompson achieved through land travel in the interior regions was rarely reproduced on the Coast. Mackenzie's few days among the Bella Coola at the end of his overland expedition to the Pacific and Fraser's equally short time among the Fraser Valley Salish are perhaps the most notable of the infrequent exceptions. Otherwise, the Hudson's Bay Company men tended to stay on their ships or in their forts, seldom even learning the languages of the people with whom they traded, and showing so little interest in their cultures that there is not a single book of recollections by a Hudson's Bay Company man operating on the Coast which we can now regard as a major source of information on local Indian life — though many of them have a great deal to tell us in their memoirs which an Indian anthropologist might find useful if he

were studying small societies of white people living on the edge of an unsympathetic wilderness.

The fur traders developed, indeed, what Northrop Frye has defined as a garrison mentality, turning inward in mental self-defence and self-congratulation, and the same phenomenon showed itself equally strongly among the people who came to the region for other purposes, such as gold mining, settlement, or government administration. The Indians lived as alien presences on the periphery of their vision, to be feared, to be pitied, to be converted, to be exploited when it seemed profitable, but rarely to be seen as a people interesting in their own rights and worth the trouble of studying. It is this collective racial blindness of the average early Victorian transplanted to the Pacific Coast that makes so exceptional the achievement of Gilbert Malcolm Sproat who, when appointed government agent on the west coast of Vancouver Island, became deeply interested in the lives of his Indian neighbours and in 1868 published *Scenes and Studies of Savage Life*, which despite its slightly condescending title is a pleasantly written book, reflecting an observant and fair mind and much acquired knowledge, and is altogether a notable predecessor of the more overtly scientific studies of the ethnographers.

But the more one reads, the more it is evident that Sproat's account is almost unique in the period between the era of the early visitors, ending by about 1810, and the era of the anthropologists and ethnographers, beginning not before 1885. The first men to reach any country are necessarily concerned with encountering and understanding its inhabitants, since whether they come for trade or to explore, their success and their survival alike will depend on such understanding, particularly as traders and explorers travel usually in small groups, unsupported by the force of invading armies or navies. But

The first European village in Coast Indian territory was built at Nootka Sound in 1789 by Esteban Martinez.

before the scientific investigators of the indigenous culture get to work, there is usually an intervening generation of the settlers, who have quite different problems from either explorers or scientists; since their aim is to take over the land they occupy, they concentrate, once they have taken measures to defend themselves, on the business of exploring the riches of their new country, and it is now with vigilance rather than interest that they observe the older inhabitants, whose lands and resources they in any case intend to appropriate. Most of the nineteenth century on the Pacific Coast of North America was dominated by people of this kind.

Even apart from this nineteenth century shift of emphasis in western Canada and Alaska, there is the purely literary fact that the eighteenth century was not merely a time of high exploration but also a time when exploration literature was widely read, and when men held

nominally to the myth of the noble savage — at least until experience destroyed it. The great explorations of the South Pacific stimulated the appetites of European readers for more accounts of strange places and peoples, and so there were ghost writers and publishers in London and Edinburgh, in Boston and Paris, willing to cooperate with any sailor who had a good tale to tell of travels in a remote land. Thus, a surprisingly high proportion of the men who went to the Pacific Northwest in the last quarter of the eighteenth century found their way into print. Many of them, like the notorious Captain Meares, were consummate rascals, and their tales of their own exploits were often either boastful or evasive; but even the most vain or rapacious among them tends to be objective when he is describing concrete details about Coast Indian ways of life, and it is possible by putting together the details culled here and there from their ghosted narratives to produce a very interesting panoramic view of the Coast Indian world as seen from the outside two hundred years ago.

It is essentially the visible world that we see, with a few sounds and smells added, presented by people whose linguistic inadequacies gave them hardly the slightest peephole glimpse into the Indian mind. Whole vast areas of Indian life, of which we now know, are absent from such accounts by men who had not the time or the wish to settle down among the people they encountered, and so we miss entirely such phenomena as the guardian spirit quest, the winter ceremonials, the whole complex of shamanism; while, since the explorers and traders met the Indians in the restricted circumstances of trading encounters and gift-exchanging ceremonies, even what they saw of intimate and domestic life was gathered by observing eyes unaccompanied by explaining voices. Tomas de Suria, the artist who accompanied Malaspina's expedition in 1791, wandered along the beach at Yakutat Bay, and with his painter's eye watched the gamblers playing with their finely etched sticks of bone and the children with their dolls that had heads of carved marble. None of the other observers saw the Tlingit marble-headed dolls, yet they have turned up in collections. But even Tomas de Suria, observant as he was, had nothing to say about such a phenomenon as the guardian spirit quest, though he seems the kind of man who would have been intensely interested if he had known about it. He watched from behind the barriers of language.

The Indians as well saw the white men through their own perceptions limited by experience and tradition, and if many of the visitors had noble savage expectations to shed, the native people too were caught within their own myths, so that the Tlingit when they first saw the white-sailed ships of their visitors imagined that the great transformer Raven was returning in supernatural form; and when Simon Fraser travelled down to the Coast by the canyon that now bears his name, the Salish thought that the spirits of Sun and Moon with their attendants were now appearing at the command of the other great transformer, Coyote.

It did not take long for the concept of noble savagery to wear away on the side of the whites, or for the Indians to recognize that it was not Raven or Coyote who had appeared among them but mortal and not entirely estimable beings like themselves. Yet out of the mutual disillusionment of those first encounters an astonishing amount of vitally important information did in various ways become perpetuated.

Partly this was because European men by the eighteenth century had become inveterate collectors of specimens, which were accumulated and preserved to find their way into the crowded cases of ethnographic galleries in nineteenth century museums and eventually to be recognized as something far more than mere savage curiosities; as works, in fact, of highly original art. Thus, almost four hundred artifacts were brought back by Cook to be lodged in the British Museum, or by Cook's and Vancouver's associates to be preserved in various British and continental European collections, not to mention the considerable number of still incompletely classified or even counted objects that reached Spain as a result of the various expeditions from Mexico northward during the late eighteenth century.

These objects from the very first years of Indian-European contact, together with the recent finds from earlier centuries at Cape Alava, carry more emphatically than words could ever do two most important messages. First, the Indians of the Pacific Coast of North America had reached as high a point of material achievement as was possible for a nonagrarian society, which despite possessing a few iron blades and some copper used mainly for prestigious adornment, was still technically in the New Stone Age. Secondly, everything these Coast peoples created during the nineteenth century to fulfil a tradition that we now accept as one of high, rather than primitive art, was already in the process of full development when the Europeans arrived. It did not — as some historians have suggested — develop out of the strange conjunction of a natural abundance, a yet unfulfilled native sense of form, and a kit of tools and techniques introduced by European strangers. Anyone who reads the accounts of the eighteenth century travellers and sees the artifacts they brought back must agree with Erna Gunther's remarks:

> That metal became much more common in the late eighteenth century cannot be denied, but the art style was already well established, as can be seen in many of the objects of the period. The more extensive use of the metal increased the rate and scope of production and made larger pieces possible, but it did not change the fine smaller carvings.

The full implications of what the eighteenth century men saw did not occur to most of them, but there was one man of the time who perceived the true achievement of the Coast Indians more clearly than his contemporaries and expressed himself eloquently on the subject. He was Claret Fleurieu, who accompanied the French navigator Etienne Marchand on his circumnavigation of the world between 1791 and 1793. In their *A Voyage Round the World* (published in London in 1801) Fleurieu wrote enthusiastically of the solidly built and elaborately carved houses of the Coast peoples, and particularly of the Haida, and it is to him that we owe descriptions of the tall, house front poles, which confirm, as emphatically as the finds at Cape Alava, that the characteristic Coast Indian iconography and style were both well established by the time the white explorers arrived. This is how Fleurieu describes one such pole:

> This door, the threshold of which is raised about a foot and a half above the ground, is of an elliptical figure; the great diameter, which is given by the height of the opening, is no more than three feet, and the small diameter, or the breadth, is not more than two; it may be conceived that it is not very convenient to enter the house by this oval. This opening is made in the thickness of a large trunk of a tree which rises perpendicularly in the middle of one of the fronts of the habitation, and occupies the whole of its height: it imitates the form of a gaping human mouth, or rather that of a beast, and it is surrounded by a hooked nose, about two feet in length, proportioned, in point of size, to the monstrous face to which it belongs. It might, therefore, be imagined that, in the language of the inhabitants of North island, of Queen Charlotte's Isles, the door of the house is called *the mouth*.
>
> Over the door is seen the figure of a man carved, in the attitude of a child in the womb, and remarkable for the extreme smallness of the parts which characterize his sex; and above this figure rises a gigantic statue of a man erect, which terminates the sculpture and the decoration of the portal; the head of this statue is dressed with a cap in the form of a sugar loaf, the height of which is almost equal to that of the figure itself. On the parts of the surface which are not occupied with the capital subjects, are interspersed carved figures of frogs or toads, lizards and other animals, and arms, legs, thighs, and other parts of the human body.

Anyone familiar with late Coast Indian art will recognize not only the characteristic *horror vacui* which led the carvers to fill every part of a surface, and also the inclination to dismember bodies and reassemble them as part of that process. The tall figure crowning the pole is clearly that of the chief who erected it, topped by a ceremonial hat whose height was increased by a number of rings recording the potlatches which the chief had given. The foetuslike figure below him, with the diminutive sexual organs, doubtless represented a family myth linked with a supernatural encounter. The beaked face surrounding the entrance oval would be that of the eagle, representing the clan to which the lineage owning the house belonged, while the frogs, toads, and other beasts were almost certainly lesser clan crests. Many of the posts shown in nineteenth century photographs and even preserved in modern museums show essentially the same characteristics.

Accounts like Fleurieu's and those of other mariners of this early period seem also to answer the theory advanced by Marius Barbeau, and for a period widely accepted, that the development of pole carving, as it appeared in the later nineteenth century, was recent and could be traced to the presence of larger quantities of iron tools. There is no doubt that more poles of an elaborate kind were indeed carved during this later period, but Fleurieu is not alone in noting large and intricate wooden sculptures during the last decade of the eighteenth century. In 1791 Captain Ingraham saw two elaborately carved house front poles forty feet high in one of the Haida villages. Nor were the free-standing heraldic poles entirely absent even at this period. The unpublished diary of Bernard Magee, first officer of the *Jefferson*, commanded by Captain Roberts, records that in 1794 Roberts and his men assisted in the planing, painting, and erection of what appears to have been a free-standing pole in the Queen Charlottes. It seems unlikely that this was the only or the first pole of its kind to be raised, and since a potlatch was given immediately afterwards, it seems clear that Roberts and his crew took part in a ceremonial occasion — the carving and raising of the heraldic pole — already established in Coast Indian custom. Magee described the principal figures in the ceremonial arriving to the sound of their personal songs, the display of the presents (consist-

ing of armour, garments, weapons, and ornaments), and the ceremony, combined with the celebration of the pole-raising, of boring the lips and noses of four girls to receive nose ornaments and labrets. Afterwards the presents were distributed, and in acknowledgment of the work he and his men had done, Captain Roberts received five prime sea otter skins.

The close resemblance between the potlatch which Magee describes and those seen by anthropologists a century later suggests a continuity in the Coast culture which allows us to believe that such ceremonial patterns are indeed ancient. In fact, since they rarely visited the winter villages, few explorers or traders actually took part in occasions of this kind, which formed the very core of the native culture. They met the Indians, in fact, in a curious twilight zone between everyday life and festival life. They saw everyday life in a very superficial way, when they happened to go ashore at summer camps or villages and watched the people engaged in fishing or preserving fish or cooking, but they rarely saw such essential activities as carving, weaving, basket-making, or the fabrication of stone tools, all of which were winter occupations carried on in the villages hidden at the heads of inlets, so that in their accounts one is often glad and astonished to find some revealing notation like Whidbey's remark of having seen among the Salish "40 dogs in a drove shorn down to the skin like sheep." In such a moment the dogs' wool blankets move in one's mind's eye out of the museum into actual life.

Since trading was in the hands of the chiefs (with women playing an important role as advisers among the northern peoples), the explorers and traders were mainly in contact with a rather limited section of Coast Indian society (though some of the English and Americans had sexual encounters — disapproved of by the Spaniards — with the slave women whom their owners were happy to prostitute for suitable payment in copper or iron). They usually saw the Indians in festival clothing, since the welcoming of a stranger was always regarded as a good excuse for ceremony, and it was in this way that in 1774 Juan Perez encountered the first Coast Indians to enter history, when on 20 July, at 53°58' north latitude, in the Queen Charlotte Islands, a great canoe almost as long as the ship put out from the shore and paddled towards them, with a man in the prow dancing and scattering eagle's down upon the water. Other canoes followed, filled with singing people clad in cloaks of sea otter with hats of reed.

At Nootka, Perez received a similar welcome, and when Cook arrived four years later and sailed into Nootka Sound with the intention of staying long enough to repair his ships, he was greeted by masked performances and by orations. David Samwell, surgeon of the *Discovery*, gives a description of one of the dances, which shows that the wolf cult so prominent in historic times was already well established among the Nootka:

> The principal or indeed the only performer appeared in a mask which was made of wood, not badly painted in the manner they generally do their faces; of these he had two expressing different countenances which he changed every now and then. Over his body was thrown a fine, large wolfe Skin with Hair outwards and a neat border worked around its edges; thus accoutred he jumped up and down in his canoe with his arms extended, he moved his head different ways and shaked his fingers briskly, while he was acting in this manner all the other Indians sat down in their canoes and sung in concert and struck the sides of their canoes with the but end of their Paddles keeping exact time.

For all the cordiality of the welcomes and the effectiveness of trading carried on by sign language, the degree of communication at this early point between the Indians and their visitors was so slight that, after a month among the Nootka, Cook was still speculating rather wildly about the functions of the masks he had seen:

> Whether these masks are worn as an Ornament in their public entertainments or as some thought to guard the face against the arrows of the enemy, or as decoys in hunting, I shall not pretend to say; probably on all these occasions. The only times however we saw them used was by some of the Chiefs when they made us a ceremonious and in some of their Songs.

With his usual shrewdness, Cook had guessed at the general purpose of the masks, but beyond that his speculation could not go, and throughout the period of the early explorers and traders, who moved around without benefit of local language, one seldom finds an account that even approaches any understanding of how the Coast Indian society operated.

Rare indeed are the shrewd observers like Captain Dixon, who managed by watching the patterns of trading to gain a sound approximate idea of the corresponding patterns of social organization. Dixon discovered that there were various ranks among the Haida chiefs, some ruling over whole villages, some over clans or houses. It was the chiefs who traded, but there seemed, Dixon observed, to be some degree of democratic control, and if the people in general were discontented with a chief's achievements, they could appoint one of the lesser chiefs to trade in his place. And though Dixon did not fully understand the matrilineal system among the northern peoples on the Coast, he did realize that in some way the women were powerful in the clans and households, and that their opinions had a great deal of bearing on the success or otherwise of trading; he even heard stories of chiefs who were beaten by their wives when they did not bargain in the clan's best interests.

Such insights into the actual structure of the society are rare before the end of the eighteenth century, among traders and even among explorers, though in justification of the latter one must add that they were sent out by their respective governments to explore and lay claim to the land and, in Vancouver's case, specifically to survey a coastline and its islands; they had scientific assistants, mainly botanists who doubled as zoologists, but anthropology was still an uninvented science, waiting for Darwin in *The Descent of Man* to release humanity from the grip of theology; and so the view which travellers took of strange peoples tended to be one of ignorance compounded by moralism and irradiated by curiosity.

It is for this reason that one treasures the objective evidence, scanty though it may be, that emerges from the early expeditions: evidence like the artifacts that were brought back and still survive, like the meticulous drawings of the Nootka and their houses done by John Webber, the artist to Cook's expedition, like the extraordinary description given by the Spanish mariner, Jacinto Caamano, of the feast to which he was invited by a Tsimshian chief in 1792, presenting in uniquely vivid detail not only the dancing customs and costumes of the time but also the ingenious theatrical effects for which the Kwakiutl and the northern peoples were in later decades to be celebrated. The chief, Jammisit, arrived at Caamano's ship with a singing company of relatives:

He, together with his nearest relatives, arrived in one of two canoes lashed alongside each other. Jammisit's head appeared from behind a screen formed of brilliantly white deerskin; on it, accordingly as the action demanded or his own particular fancy dictated, he would place various masks or heads of the different animals that he proposed to imitate; the deerskin serving as a curtain by which he was entirely hidden when he wished,

unseen to put on or change one of these masks or faces. They remained alongside thus for some time, singing and continuing their antics, until Jammisit with great eagerness explained that he had come to conduct me to his village.

Caamano agrees, and immediately he gets into his cutter the canoes race to the village to make preparations:

By the time we in the cutter reached the strand, there were already six lusty natives carrying a very clean deerskin awaiting me on the beach. These at once dashed into the water up to the waist alongside our boat, making signs to me to sit on the skin to be carried ashore on their shoulders. At first I declined, but they were so vehemently insistent, that I gave in and let them do it; not, however, without considerable apprehension lest I should be dropped upon the ground on my back.

The moment that I placed myself on the deerskin these six fellows hoisted my 150 lb. carcass on to their shoulders and carried me at a run across the shingle and up the pretty steep slope leading from it to the village, whither they brought me at a surprising speed. To pass through the narrow doorway of the chief's house, over which was painted a huge mask, it was necessary to make a litter or hammock of the deerskin. Two of the strongest of the Indians did this, with the other four assisting as best they could, while I was shrinking myself into as small a compass as possible (though my bearers were careful enough) to avoid being bumped against the door posts. Once inside, I tried to get on my feet, but this they would not allow before bringing me to the place prepared for my seat, which was to the right of the entrance. The seat was formed of a case or chest, raised higher than those for the others, fitted for only one person, and covered with a new mat; while a similar one was spread before it. The seats for my officers, ranged on either hand of mine, were made in similar manner; those for my men, were formed of mats spread on the floor. . . . By this time, the whole native company, amounting to about eighty people of both sexes, was arranged on the floor. Jammisit, his three wives, and grown family, were in front. Myself, with all my officers and men, were on the right; and only women were allowed behind us. On the left were the remainder from Jammisit's village, and those from that of Gitejon. In this situation, then, Jammisit began to emit piercing howls in a pitiful key; after which, throwing back his head as if about to faint, he sat down, clutching at the collar laces of his cloak, as if wishing to throw it off. Several of his family nearby, who were watching to give him any help that might be necessary, when they noticed this, gathered around him forming a screen so that he might not be seen changing his garments in which some of the others were assisting him.

So soon as he had put on the ones in which he was to show himself, they would break up and sit down out of his way, leaving only a couple of his nearest relations standing by ready to help him as he might require. When he was ready, these also left him, and the actor arose.

On his head was a large well-imitated representation of a seagull's head, made of wood and coloured blue and pink, with eyes fashioned out of polished tin; while from behind his back stuck out a wooden frame covered in blue cloth, and decked out with quantities of eagles' feathers and bits of whale bone, to complete the representation of the bird. His cloak was now of white calico, bearing a blue flowered pattern, trimmed with a brown edging. Round his waist hung a deer skin apron falling to below the knee, whose fringe or flounce was made from narrow strips of the same leather, every one being split into two tails, each of which carried half the hoof of a deer. Over this apron or kilt he wore another, shorter one, of bluejean ornamented with numerous metal buttons arranged symmetrically, and two rows of antelope hide pendants or tassels, each finished off with an eagle's claw. On his legs were deer skin leggings, tied behind with four laces, ornamented with painted masks and trimmed with strips of hide bearing claws. Clad in this weird rattling rig, he then began to leap and cut capers, reminding one of a rope dancer trying his rope. He also waved his arms, keeping them low down. . . . After two or three preliminary attempts, he started a song. This was at once taken up by every one inside the house, man or woman, and produced a terrific volume of sound, to whose measure he then began to dance, while a specially chosen Indian beat the time on a large drum.

Having danced till he appeared to be exhausted, Jammisit retired behind a hide screen, and during the interval boiled salmon was served to the guests, after which the curtain was withdrawn and he appeared "with a half-length wooden doll on his head."

Two Indians at some distance behind him, who endeavoured to conceal their actions, then proceeded — by means of long fishing rods — to open and close the eyes of the doll, and raise its hands, in time to another tune that was struck up, while the dancer himself imitated the movements of the doll's face, which was sufficiently frightful in appearance, being coloured black and red, and furnished with an owl's beak and nostrils. For this scene, he wore a bear skin cloak, with the remainder of his costume as before. So soon as the music ceased, his attendants again hid him from sight. Before long, however, he again appeared, this time wearing a heavy wooden mask on his head, of which the snout, or upper jaw, was moveable. (Translated by Harold Grenfell, *British Columbia Historical Quarterly*, July 1938.)

In his third costume Jammisit danced himself into a frenzy and then appeared about to collapse, when his attendants squirted water on him from a distance, and one of them, applying his mouth to his side, shouted loudly. Although Caamano did not suspect it, this may well have been a piece of deliberate clowning, for it ended the dance, after which Jammisit gave Caamano a nutria skin and the Spaniards were allowed to depart. In virtually every detail the scene might have taken place during a Tsimshian feast a century later, and there are places where very similar dances might be enacted even today, so constant is the tradition.

It is obvious that very few European travellers at this time had any more understanding than Caamaño of the significance of the dances they saw, and consequently very few of them perceived the Coast Indian culture as a unity. Even those who admired parts of it failed to understand how its aspects fitted together, and here again Claret Fleurieu was typical of the best of them, with his intense admiration for the artistic achievements of the Haida and his wonder that a people so apparently primitive in other respects could achieve so much. After detailing the merits of Coast Indian art and architecture in tones a modern enthusiast could hardly excel, Fleurieu goes on to conclude that the tradition cannot possibly be indigenous:

> It may, therefore, be concluded that the people, at this day given up to hunting, among whom the taste of these arts is prevailing and their general employment, have not created them in the solitude of the woods; that they brought them thither from some other place; that they have borrowed them; and that it descends not originally from a people who have been nothing but hunters.

Perhaps the most complete view at this time of the Coast Indian way of life was that of John Jewitt, who after all lived on intimate terms with the Indians for more than two years, and in the next chapter I shall make use of Jewitt's excellent account of the material aspects of the Nootka society. But even Jewitt suffered from the limitations of his education and his prejudices. He was too conventionally Anglican to understand the peculiar kind of spirituality that permeated Indian life, and he wholly failed to comprehend even what he saw of shamanism and of the winter ceremonials, though he did grasp the significance of the rituals connected with the whale

A woman of Nootka Sound, drawn by Webber.

hunt which followed a rather easily understood pattern of prescriptive magic. Finally, he had little aesthetic sense, and the beauty of much that the Nootka created merely passed him by.

It was Alexander Mackenzie who in the end attained the most balanced and understanding view of the Coast Indian culture at the point when it emerged into history. He had a number of advantages. He was accustomed to the Indian cultures of the prairies and of the northern forests, and so he could make appropriate comparisons and grasp immediately the greater sophistication of the culture he came upon when he walked down from the Coast mountains into

Bella Coola. He saw that culture in its pristine state, for though the Bella Coola had heard of the presence of European ships off the coast, they had not yet, in 1793, encountered any of the explorers or the sea traders. Also, since he travelled through and stayed in the riverside villages of the Bella Coola, Mackenzie was able to see at least their material life as a totality.

He watched their ingenious methods of fishing; he saw women weaving and spinning and preparing preserved foods; he saw the kind of trade between the coast and the interior for which the Bella Coola valley was one of the funnels; he saw shamans and carpenters at work; he ate the native foods and did his best to fit in with the taboos imposed during the salmon running season, giving up his iron kettle to use a wooden one and refraining from eating the venison he had brought with him; he examined houses and canoes, tools and weapons, and found out about burial customs and slavery, though he admitted his failure to understand the religious beliefs of the Bella Coola, except that he correctly guessed that they acknowledged a heaven and a deity to rule it.

Still, considering that he was in the valley only for a few days, arriving at Friendly Village on 17 July and leaving it on his way back into the mountains on 26 July, and that the people did not entirely welcome his presence for fear the salmon might be offended, he saw a surprising amount, and saw it with a fair eye, commenting on the exactness of the carpentry in the houses of the Bella Coola, on the "unexpected correctness" of their painted images, and yet adding justly, "But the sculpture of these people is superior to their painting." Finally, he understood, as none of his contemporaries had done, how narrow a margin lay among these people between culture and civilization. "Of the many tribes of savage people I have seen," he concluded, "these appear to be the most susceptible of civilization." But even Mackenzie thought in terms of transformation; he did not see the culture in its own light or as capable of development within its own traditions.

Part III

John Webber's drawings of artifacts collected by Captain Cook show that they bear a striking similarity to later Coast Indian work.

CHAPTER SIX

The Hunters of Leviathan

The Nootka have attracted less attention from anthropologists and connoisseurs of primitive art than most of the Coast Indian peoples, and it is true that they did not produce such remarkable artifacts as the Tsimshian and the Haida or evolve such elaborate dramatic ceremonials as the Kwakiutl. They also inhabit a part of British Columbia, the stormy western coast of Vancouver Island, which has been off the ordinary traveller's trail for more than a century and a half, though in the early days of European presence on the Pacific Coast it was a noted calling place for sailing ships — to such an extent that the high chief of Yuquot became, under the name of Maquinna, the most celebrated of all Coast Indian chiefs, rivalled only by his fellow Nootka potentate to the north, Wickanninish of Clayoquot Sound.

There is only one good anthropological study of the Nootka, Philip Drucker's *The Northern and Central Nootka Tribes*, and even that has never been available to the general public, so that this rather remote Indian group tends to be known — when it is known at all — through early accounts: the records of fleeting encounters preserved by the explorers and the sea traders; Jewitt's narrative of his captivity; and Sproat's *Scenes and Studies of Savage Life*, the last of which dates from the 1860s. By the time of the last great frenzy of potlatching and pole building among the Kwakiutl and the northern tribes, the Nootka,

less affected by such fevers than their neighbours, had largely become forgotten, and when the anthropologists arrived in the 1880s they were attracted, like the more ambitious missionaries, to the northerly groups that seemed most flamboyant and aggressive in their cultural manifestations, and therefore most in need of study as well as of salvation. It is no accident that both Franz Boas and William Duncan headed northward rather than westward from Victoria.

Yet there are excellent reasons for beginning a survey of the historic cultures of the Coast with a visit to the Nootka. Apart from the Salish, who remained somewhat peripheral to developments on the Coast after the decline of the ancient Marpole culture, the Nootka probably display the basic elements of the Coast civilization in their simplest and most easily comprehensible forms. Moreover, because of the extremities of their environment, they show at its best the combination of audacity and specialized adaptability, which enabled the Coast Indians to devise a technology that would take full advantage of the natural abundance of their setting and provide not merely for survival but also for leisure, and hence for ceremonial and for art. Nowhere does the Coast Indian mastery of the environment seem more dramatically portrayed than in those contests with Leviathan, in which the Nootka chiefs vindicated their names and at the same time fed their people by hunting and killing the great whales of the Pacific from their sea-going canoes. Finally, one must acknowledge the Nootka's pride of historic place, which manifests itself in two ways: they were the first Coast Indians to be brought to the attention of the European and American educated public in the late eighteenth century through the various narratives that emerged out of Cook's third voyage; and they are also, again apart from the Salish, the Coast people in whose culture one seems to detect the greatest proportion of archaic elements, which appear to confirm that like the Salish, the Bella Coola, and the Kwakiutl, they belong to an earlier wave of migration than the peoples of the north.

At the time of the first contact with the Europeans, the Nootka were one of the most numerous of the Coast peoples. About ten thousand of them, in twenty-five villages of varying sizes, lived on a two-hundred-mile stretch of the western shore of Vancouver Island, bounded roughly by Cape Cook on the north and to the south by Port Renfrew at the entrance to the Strait of Juan de Fuca. An outlying group, the Makah, occupied a small piece of coastline around Cape Flattery on the south side of the Strait of Juan de Fuca, in what is now the State of Washington. The outer beaches of this coast were exposed to the open ocean and swept by Pacific storms, and here the Nootka established only temporary camps for fishing and for hunting sea mammals. It was on the sheltered shores of the deeply penetrating sounds and inlets that they built their real villages. Some groups, like the Moachat — of whom a line of Maquinnas were the head chiefs — had summer and winter settlements even within the inlets. It was at his summer seat of Yuquot that Maquinna received his famous European visitors, but as we know from John Jewitt, as soon as the winter storms began, the planks would be taken off the Yuquot houses and the whole company would load their canoes —

Nootka seafood gatherers.

joined together like catamarans — and make their way up to the head of the inlet, where in the shadow of the mountains their other village of Tahsis was an appropriate setting for winter ceremonials.

On this coast the Nootka were more isolated, except from ocean-faring sailing ships, than other Coast peoples. The mountain spine of Vancouver Island, rising at some points to more than seven thousand feet and heavily forested, presented a frightening barrier to people used to the openness of water and beaches, and only a couple of trading trails penetrated this barrier eastward to provide a tenuous link with the Kwakiutl and Salish, who lived on the eastern side of Vancouver Island. With the Nimkish Kwakiutl, who occupied a few villages on the northwestern corner of Vancouver Island, there were closer links through which not only trade goods were exchanged but also less tangible possessions like dances, songs and ceremonies by which Nootka rituals were slowly modified.

Jewitt tells us that in his day the Nimkish brought vermilion for face painting and a "black shining mineral called *pelpelth*," by which he may have meant obsidian, and he also mentions various commodities coming over the trails from the east, including "train-oil," or oolichan grease, and

> an excellent root called *Quawmoose*. This is the size of a small onion, but rather longer, being of a tapering form like a pear, and of a brownish colour. It is cooked by steam, is always brought in baskets ready prepared for eating, and is in truth a very fine vegetable, being sweet, mealy, and of a most agreeable flavour. It was highly esteemed by the natives, who used to eat it, as they did everything else, with train-oil.

Quawmoose was in fact the camas (*Camassia Quamash*), a member of the lily family with a blue flower so clear in colour that Meriwether Lewis likened the great beds of it in the meadows of the Pacific slopes to "lakes of fine clear water." The tubers of the camas were eaten by many western Indian peoples as a source of starch, but there were few open meadows in Nootka territory where the plant grew freely, and it was imported as something of a delicacy from the oak-studded savannah country around the present site of Victoria, where the Salish gathered it in abundance.

Yet the environment in which the Nootka lived was so generous in most of the things necessary for existence that the goods imported over the trading trails and by canoe along the shores were mainly luxury items. The rugged coast provided the basic subsistence of a surprisingly numerous population, but only because of the riches of the sea. For it is a region which would have been the despair of a primitive agriculturist; to this day only a few farms have existed — and for the most part disappeared — in isolated pockets of this land of rock and conifers.

The Nootka territory could also have supported only a small population of land hunters, even though Vancouver Island in pre-European days harboured in its somewhat impenetrable rain forest large numbers of blacktail deer and Roosevelt elk, as well as black bear and smaller game like beaver and raccoon, and there were large communal deer drives at the beginning of winter. Vancouver Island is also on the great Pacific flyway for birds migrating to and from the western Arctic, and this ensured at spring and autumn a supply of wild geese and ducks, which, as Jewitt recorded, were taken with nets woven out of cedar bark:

> Those who take them make choice for that purpose of a dark and rainy night, and with their canoes stuck with lighted torches, proceed with as little noise as possible to the place where the geese are collected, who, dazzled by the light, suffer themselves to be approached very near, when the net is thrown over them, and in this manner from fifty to sixty, or even more, will sometimes be taken at one cast.

Game of this kind was almost always eaten fresh by the Coast Indians; there was not enough to preserve it in great quantities and so it provided merely a seasonal variation in the diet. Some game, indeed, was so spiritually potent that its consumption was hedged around with elaborate taboos, and this applied especially to the bear, towards whom the Nootka behaved with a reverence reminiscent of that accorded to this creature by the Ainu of Japan.

Jewitt once saw a bear brought into the village of Tahsis. It was cleaned of dirt and blood and then seated in an upright position in front of Maquinna. A chief's ceremonial head-dress was placed on its head, and it was honoured with a dusting of eagle's down, after which food was placed before it in a dish, which it was invited to eat. Only after this ceremony was it skinned and its flesh cooked into a stew. A feast was then given, at which Maquinna's son danced. Yet very few people ate of the bear stew, since nobody who partook of this meat would be allowed to eat fresh fish for two months lest the salmon be offended. A few — about ten according to Jewitt — did take part in this strange eucharist, and it seems likely that these bear-eaters were members of a secret society or perhaps even shamans, though Jewitt evidently did not realize it. Certainly this evidence of the circumpolar bear cult in full operation on Vancouver Island is another very tangible proof of the ancient links between the people of East Asia and the Coast Indians.

The west coast of Vancouver Island provided almost the whole range of marine life on which Coast Indians depended for their main subsistence. The most reliable and abundant of all the creatures who came from the sea were the various species of Pacific salmon which, each at its proper season, ran up the inlets and the rivers to end its life cycle by spawning and dying. There are five species of salmon which visit Nootka territory; the most important in the Indian economy were the spring, the coho, and at the very end of the season just before the autumn storms began, the dog or chum salmon which was preserved to provide food for the winter.

Salmon was caught in many ways. Before the fish reached the rivers, they were swept up in nets of nettle fibre trawled between paired canoes, were caught with lines using hooks formed of a piece of straight wood with a bone barb, were speared with ingenious harpoons with detachable heads. On the streams the Indians built fish weirs, leading into funnel-shaped basketwork traps as much as twenty feet long and five feet in diameter; the fish would be driven through an outer funnel into an inner cage where they were caught; they were also caught in dip-nets wielded from the weirs.

The Indians would never have been able to utilize this abundance of salmon as well as they did if they had not developed efficient techniques of preservation. Large quantities of fish were of course eaten fresh in season, boiled or roasted in barbecue fashion, but enough was filleted and air-dried by the autumn to provide for a winter not merely of eating, but also of feasting. The very seasonal nature of the salmon runs contributed to the special character of Coast Indian life. If the people had been forced to fish or hunt every day of the year for their subsistence, they would never have had the long winter months in the great houses when the carvers could work and the chiefs give and the dancers dance, and when the quality of life was changed.

Every other kind of available seafood was utilized, with the exception of dogfish and sharks, which appear to have been taboo. The Nootka had ingenious special ways of catching each species of fish. The largest catches of halibut were made in the early summer from off the ocean beaches, though there was a certain amount of all-year fishing for them in the inlets; they were caught with springy U-shaped hooks of fir devised to lodge the bone barb firmly. The various species of fish, which on the Coast in European times have been inaccurately described as cod, were attracted to the surface with shuttlecocklike lures of light wood, and then speared.

The herring runs were times of particular activity, for then the Nootka both caught the fish to eat fresh or to dry, and also collected the spawn. The instrument used for catching herring was a kind of rake, whose use Jewitt describes:

A stick of about seven feet long, two inches broad, and half an inch thick, is formed from some hard wood, one side of which is set with sharp teeth, made from whalebone, at about half an inch apart. Provided with this instrument, the fisherman seats himself in the prow of a canoe, which is paddled by another, and whenever he comes to a shoal of herrings, which cover the water in great quantities, he strikes it with both hands upon them, and at the same moment, turning it up, brings it over the side of the canoe, into which he lets those that are taken drop. It is astonishing to see how many are caught by those who are dexterous at this kind of fishing, as they seldom fail, when the shoals are numerous, of taking as many as ten or twelve at a stroke, and in a very short time will fill a canoe with them.

Jewitt, a close and accurate observer of the material processes of Nootka life nearly two hundred years ago, also describes the way in which herring roe was collected and preserved:

> At the seasons of spawning, which are early in spring and the last of August, they collect a great quantity of pine branches, which they place in different parts of the Cove at the depth of about ten feet, and secure them by means of heavy stones. On these the herring deposit their spawn in immense quantities; the bushes are then taken up, the spawn stripped from the branches, and, after being washed and freed from the pine leaves by the women, is dried and put up in baskets for use. It is considered as their greatest delicacy, and eaten both cooked and raw; in the former case, being boiled and eaten with train-oil, and in the latter, mixed up with cold water alone.

Salmon roe was similarly dried into flat hard cakes and appreciated during the winter as a delicacy.

Octopus, sea slugs, sea urchins, crabs, and all kinds of shellfish were eaten freely by the Nootka. Clams were dried, and in times of scarcity when the salmon run had been small or when food had been wasted over the winter because of excessive feasting, the people might turn to the beaches to supplement their remaining dried fish with fresh clams and mussels. Evidence of the importance of shellfish in the Coast Indian diet ever since early prehistoric days is provided on a grand scale by the immense shell banks and middens which are found everywhere in the region, and which have assisted notably in the archaeological reconstruction of the past.

Some of the shells were used for other purposes than food. The giant mussel, found all the way down the west coast of Vancouver Island, was not only used to make the fish knives with which the women cut the salmon for drying (it was long before the taboo on iron was allowed to lapse), but also provided the sharp tips for the whale hunters' great harpoons. And the peculiar cream-coloured and tusklike *Dentalium pretiosum*, found only in offshore beds facing onto Nootka beaches, though it had no utilitarian function, played a considerable role in the aboriginal Nootka economy as an item of trade, since it was not merely prized among Indian peoples as an ornament even as far off as the Blackfoot of the prairies, whom it reached by a long chain of trading contacts which extended over the Rockies, but it was even used by some of the California Indians as a kind of currency. Certainly it was recognized everywhere in the Coast Indian area as one of the most prestigious signs of wealth.

The dentalium fishery was the inherited property of certain clans who guarded carefully their knowledge of the landmarks defining the beds which they visited. The device they used for taking the dentalium shells was a remarkable example of the functional efficiency of the Coast Indian peoples. It consisted, according to Philip Drucker,

> of a bunch of hardwood spikes, elongated oviates in shape, tightly lashed at one end around the tip of a long slim pole so that their points diverged, thus suggesting in form our traditional Halloween witches' broom. Over the 'broom' was fitted a board with a hole at the centre of such a size that it passed freely over the bundle of splints at the point of attachment but was too small to be forced over the diverging points. Heavy stone sinkers were lashed one to each end of the board.

This contrivance was lowered, on a series of rods, until it was close to the sea bottom, when the fisherman jabbed downward.

> The resistance of the water retarded the descent of the flat board so that the bunch of splints, uncompressed and therefore flared apart, reached bottom first. The board with its stone sinkers slowly slid over the splints, compressing them strongly. The fisherman hauled the apparatus surfacewards, unlashing the joints as he went. Were he lucky, he would find a shell or two, or even several, pinched between the tips of the splints. Then he put the contraption back into the water to make another try.

Together with the highly-regarded canoes which the Nootka made, dentalia were probably the most important commodities which the Nootka contributed to the trading complex of the Pacific Coast region.

Nootka canoes were built in several forms. The large voyaging canoes, some of them more than forty feet long and only less massive than the great Haida war canoes, were the most popular in terms of trade, being sold to almost all the peoples in the southern part of the culture complex; but the most highly functional and perhaps the most typical of the Nootka craft were those made for the sea mammal hunts which were the most prestigious of all lordly activities.

These hunts also had a considerable economic importance, since the oil-rich oolichan, or candlefish, never ran in the Vancouver Island streams or in those of the Queen Charlottes, so that both the Nootka and the Haida could only obtain the prized grease of these fish in relatively small quantities through trade. Animal oils played a peculiarly important role in the diets of all Coast Indian peoples, especially in the winter when dried fish was dipped in some kind of fish or sea mammal oil to make it palatable, and some observers have suggested that this abundance of fat in fact compensated for the very low starch

The Nootka whaler went on his quest clad in a bearskin. His harpoon had floats attached to it.

content of the Coast Indian diet, particularly in regions where such foods as camas root did not grow in plenty. Certainly the Nootka made great use of the oil rendered down from seal, sea lion, porpoise, and especially whales. (The killer whale was generally exempt from hunting because of his peculiar role in the mythology of Coast Indian peoples). The seal were harpooned from special narrow canoes carefully smoothed so that they would move silently through the water, but they were also clubbed on the rocks where they congregated along the ocean coast; and there too the formidable sea lions were hunted, but only after great ritual preparation, since this was regarded as an occupation that required a spiritual power second only to that needed for the great whale hunt.

Whales were not merely hunted; they also drifted dead onto the wide beaches of Nootka territory, and it was held that they could actually be induced to do so by a magic which utilized the power the dead were regarded as wielding over whales. The chief who undertook such a powerful ritual had — for his own protection as well as to ensure success — to go through the cleansing procedures that were thought necessary for any kind of hunting venture, on sea or on land: to fast, to bathe in cold water and scarify the body with rough barks, to refrain from sexual intercourse. The potent core of the whale-calling ceremony consisted of vigils and chants at a secret forest shrine, where the chief and his closest kinsmen gathered around the image of a whale, before which an assemblage of corpses stolen from graveyards, or of wooden puppets surmounted by actual human skulls, were arranged in such a way that they appeared to be dragging the whale on a rope. When, after such a ritual, a whale did float ashore, he was welcomed with all the ceremonial proper to an honoured guest. Even if the flesh of such a notable piece of flotsam happened to be putrid, this did not matter greatly, since the blubber could still usually be rendered down to oil that was edible, though somewhat rank smelling.

The more spectacular of the whale adventures, at least to an outsider, was the actual hunt for a live whale, though to the Nootka themselves the fearful perils of an encounter with the dead, which ensured the arrival of a drifting whale, might seem just as alarming and might confer an almost equal repute for heroism on the chief who undertook it.

For the whale hunt a very strict ritual was followed. Two special whaling canoes went out, and the duties of the crews were carefully apportioned by custom. The harpoonists were always the men of highest rank in the village — the head chief and his nearest brother — and it was only men of such high rank who had the right to kill the whale. The head chief thrust the first harpoon, the brother had the privilege of thrusting the second, and it was usually the head chief who made the final cut into the heart with a stone-headed lance.

The whaling season lasted through May and June, and for some time before the first trip the crews of the vessels went through a process of ritual cleansing; it was important that this should be observed meticulously, since any lapse in continence on the part of a single member, any eating of a taboo food, might mean that the whale would be reluctant to appear or would break away from the harpoon once it had been struck. It was on the chief and his wife that the greatest burden of ritual preparation lay. He would go for days to the solitude of his hereditary whaling shrine, and he and his wife would bathe together in a cold secluded pool. While he sang songs addressed to the whale and scrubbed his body with hemlock twigs, his wife would imitate the whale spouting and diving, and would call out, "This is the way the whale will act." Jewitt describes Maquinna's mood at such time as "thoughtful and gloomy, scarcely speaking to anyone."

The chief set out clad in a bearskin robe, with a cedar bark fillet around his head into which hemlock twigs had been thrust. His wife accompanied him to the beach, saw the canoe depart, and then returned to her house where she was expected to lay motionless, without food or drink, until the return of the hunters. Her immobility, it was held, would ensure the docility of the whale.

The canoe was not a large one. It held merely eight men and their equipment. At the front, where the raised prow would on occasion give him some protection, sat the harpoonist. There followed three pairs of paddlers and a helmsman, who was usually old and experienced in the hunt so that he could act as the adviser to the chief. The canoe carried minimal supplies of food and water — enough for frugal subsistence — and its most important cargo consisted of the great yew-staffed harpoon (which might be fourteen feet long), a spare harpoon staff, a lance, a kind of spadelike instrument on a long pole that could be used to immobilize the whale's flukes towards the end of the fight, and four sealskin floats which were strung together, the first of them being attached to the detachable head of the harpoon, which itself consisted of a blade of sharp mussel shell and two elkhorn barbs.

The canoe, of course, was much smaller than any whale its occupants were likely to encounter, and — apart from the magic spells and songs that had been chanted before the silent approach to the whale — everything depended on accurate timing, both in attack and in evasion. A good whaler could anticipate the position in which the whale would sound, and then, provided the canoe was in the right position, the harpoonist had to calculate the right time for his powerful first thrust when the whale had sunk just far enough for his tail to be harmless. The pitch head of the harpoon would explode on impact, freeing the staff, and the mussel cutting edge would probably break inside the whale's blubber; but if the thrust had been a good one, the barbs would hold, and the lanyard attached to them would drag out the floats as the whale sounded. When it surfaced again, the second harpoon would be thrust, with more floats attached, all of which would hamper the whale's progress and help to exhaust it. When it seemed near the end of its strength, the canoes would close in, the whale's flukes would be cut, and the killing lance would be driven between the appropriate pair of ribs into the heart. Then one of the paddlers would dive to cut holes in the whale's lips so that its mouth could be held closed to prevent it shipping water and sinking. The hunt ended in the slow tow towards the home village, until its people became aware of the catch and paddled out to help in the tow, while the chief's wife danced on the beach, sang a welcoming song to the whale, and scattered honouring eagle's down upon its snout. As Jewitt adds, "All who were on the shore, men, women and children, mounted the roofs of their houses to congratulate the king on his success, drumming most curiously on the planks, and exclaiming *Wocash — wocash, Tyee!*"

The successful beaching of the whale was followed by a great feast at which all the people of the locality, together with any visiting chiefs, gathered together and were seated according to their rank, as at a potlatch. The chief's kin were responsible for dividing the blubber, which was shared among the guests according to rank; speeches were made reciting the whaling exploits of the chief's family; and finally the commoners were allowed to scramble for the remaining flesh and blubber left on the whale's carcass. How often whales were in fact caught it is hard to tell with any accuracy, since the legends tell of heroes who killed ten whales in a single season, but no chief in historical times seems to have averaged more than one killing a season in his active whaling life, and many others could boast of only two or three in a career. Yet the prestige attached to success, and even to the right to make the effort, was so great that to the end of the nineteenth century the Nootka chiefs still went out in their fragile canoes to hunt Leviathan.

The whole character of the whale hunt suggests the extent to which the Nootka chiefs had taken on what were essentially magical and even sacerdotal functions, since the chief was not merely performing magic rituals intended to compel the whale to be caught, but by catching the whale or even embarking on the unsuccessful quest for it, he was also symbolically — like the chief-ritualist welcoming and placating the first salmon — assuring the prosperity of his people at the same time as he enhanced the prestige of his lineage (which of course were two aspects of the same thing). To that extent he seems to have encroached on the province of the shaman, as Coast Indian chiefs regularly did in their ritual functions, and in this context it is interesting to note how small a role the shaman seemed to play in the view Jewitt evolved of Nootka society after more than two years as the enforced guest of Maquinna, for there is only a single slighting sentence devoted to the subject:

> Neither have they any priests, unless a kind of conjuror may be so considered who sings and prays over the sick to drive away the evil spirit.

Jewitt, it will have been noted, referred to Maquinna as a "king," and certainly most of the early explorers appear to have considered him and other powerful chiefs, like Wickanninish at Clayoquot, as something in the nature of absolute monarchs of the kind to whom they were accustomed in Europe. Jewitt's misconception is understandable, since Maquinna's personal relationship with him was an absolute one — the only absolute one in Coast Indian society — that of the captor to the slave who is his chattel and over whom he has all the power of life and death. The misconception of the explorers is equally understandable, since they encountered Maquinna in a trading-diplomatic relation, in which, as was the custom among ranking chiefs in all Coast communities, he talked of everything his group owned as his property. But this was not literally the case, and there was no form of absolute rule among the Nootka, largely because there was neither the political nor the social structure to support it.

The basic structure of social as of political life among the Nootka was the extended family, which inhabited a single large house divided between a number of nuclear family groups belonging to the same lineage, and was presided over by a hereditary chief. A large Nootka house might in fact contain as many people as a small village; Captain Meares, as we have seen, described one he saw in the 1780s as being large enough for eight hundred people to assemble there, while Maquinna's house in 1803 had a ridgepole a hundred feet long, and as late as the 1860s Gilbert Sproat saw Nootka winter houses which suggested to him "what the wooden halls of the old northern nations may have been like." In these great houses the nobles, consisting of the chief and his close kin, lived together with the commoners whose relationship with the mythical ancestor-founder of the lineage was too tenuous to carry any of the titular rights that were so important to the nobles. On each side of the central aisle, series of low partitions gave at least a nominal privacy to small family apartments, with the chief, his wives and children occupying the end of the great house farthest from the entrance.

Unlike the northern tribes, the Nootka counted inheritance patrilineally, and a chief's heir would begin to assume titles — and the masks and dances appropriate to them — at a quite early age, though the real authority would still rest with the father, or even, if he were alive, with the grandfather who had nominally given all his titles and privileges to his heirs. The Nootka also differed from the northern peoples in belonging to neither phratries nor clans; nor did they have the elaborate system of crest privileges that went with such organizations, or insist on exogamous marriages of any kind, though they would not allow the marriage of close blood relatives.

Thus, the Nootka extended family unit was even more autonomous than among the Tsimshian or the Haida. Externally and internally it was in the fullest sense a community, since all the rights that were essential to its existence were in its collective control. The family group, not the chief, owned the vital fishing, berry picking, and hunting rights, and when the chief traded he did so on behalf of the group. Even songs, dances, and the very titles the chief held were possessions of the lineage and could only be alienated with its consent. Personal property existed only in such things as clothes and domestic articles, tools, and hunting and fishing equipment. Even a chief's name was not, in the strict sense, his own; it was part of the collective property of the lineage.

How far political organization went beyond this extended family structure at the time of the first contact with Europeans is by no means certain for the whole of the Nootka-speaking area. It seems likely that some of the southern settlements were in fact no more than unaffiliated extended families. In most of the area, however, the custom had already arisen of wintering together in places where several houses, occupied by large family groups, shared the village site and automatically became each other's most convenient guests for feasts and potlatches; here, incipient tribal structures began to arise, with the various house chiefs settling into their places in what was the beginning of a social grading system, and one of them becoming virtually the village chief, a primacy which he would owe to a combination of ancestral prestige and the wealth of his particular kin group. On large protected stretches of water, like Nootka Sound and Clayoquot Sound, these wintering tribes even combined further to form confederacies (the nearest things on the West Coast to the great leagues of the prairie Indians and the Iroquois), which would live together for a period in the summer season, share in rituals, act together in war, and present a common front to strangers

when their highest ranking chiefs would speak for the confederacy.

Far from being in any true sense a king, Maquinna was in fact the highest ranking chief — by virtue of ancestral titles frequently validated by wealth — in the Moachat confederacy, of which the extended family he ruled as house chief was a constituent unit. It was therefore as representative of the confederacy rather than as absolute king that he welcomed Cook and the Spanish captains. Even Jewitt (who had seen the chiefs of the confederacy seated in their ranked positions below the man who in 1803 bore the name of Maquinna) observed that the high chief had no power over the property of members of other houses; Jewitt's report of the debates that took place in 1805 over his own release, when the *Lydia* put into Nootka Sound in search of him, suggest that so far as anything affecting the welfare of the confederacy was concerned, Maquinna had at least to listen to the general opinion of the confederation. On this occasion he actually called a general council of the people, attended apparently by all but the slaves, at which commoners as well as chiefs had their say, by no means always agreeing — though, to Jewitt's relief and benefit, the views of the chiefs prevailed in the end and he was able to secure his freedom. All this suggests that the loosely structured nature of Nootka society allowed a fair degree of that democratic freedom of expression which distinguished the councils of the prairie Indians.

Of course, there were the slaves who had no rights at all, and whose condition, as Jewitt's experience showed, could vary from extreme comfort to extreme misery according to the caprices of their owners. But the very shame that was associated with the idea of having lost one's freedom through capture or — in rare cases — through the local equivalent of bankruptcy, suggests how greatly the liberty practised within the context of the kinship community was valued. We have perhaps not considered sufficiently deeply how far, in an analogical situation, the presence of slavery among the Athenians led them, even while they exploited the slaves, to establish the material and theoretical foundations of democracy as the Western world has known it.

The structures of property and authority among the Nootka were mingled inextricably, as they were among all other Coast peoples, with the ceremonial patterns of the community. The principal ceremonies were feasts, potlatches, and the celebrations connected with the winter festival of secret confraternities. Feasts were distinguished from potlatches in that the first were convivial social gatherings in which food would be distributed and either eaten on the spot (daintily by the nobility and voraciously by the commoners) or carried home by the guests. On such occasions there would be speechmaking, without which no social occasion could take place, and there would be the display by the host of his privileges in the form of masked dances with appropriate songs, in which the assembly would join. As in the case of the whale-catching celebration which I have just described, the feast always had an occasion — if only the welcome of a visiting English or Spanish captain.

The potlatch was a much more elaborate and expensive affair, which might last for days and which involved the generous giving of accumulated wealth to guests who were not part of one's own kinship group; the kin, who shared collectively in the honour accruing from a potlatch, were expected not only to assist at the ceremony as orators, ushers, or tallymen with their little bundles of sticks that kept a record of the gifts, but also to contribute materially to what very often amounted to a distribution of the extended family's whole surplus wealth, except of course for its ceremonial regalia. (Such a distribution of

property was, incidentally, never regarded as an impoverishment, since the value of the intangible privileges belonging to the lineage had been enhanced, and the material property would always in the long run return in some form or another when the guest chiefs held their own potlatches).

In later historic times, particularly after 1850, potlatches appear to have been held, nominally to validate the assumption of a name or some other inherited privilege, but in fact for individual self-aggrandisement whenever enough goods had been accumulated by trading to justify the occasion; and out of this situation arose the competitiveness that Ruth Benedict described so sensationally in her account of Kwakiutl potlatches in *Patterns of Culture*. But even in this later period, the Nootka seem to have been less extravagant in their potlatching than either the Kwakiutl or the northern peoples. And certainly, at the time of early contact with the Europeans, potlatches were held comparatively rarely among the Nootka, as on other parts of the Coast, and usually at the time of some life crisis: for example, on the death of a chief and his successor's assumption of the title; on the assumption by a boy of a name — with its dance and song — of ancestral potency; on the puberty of a girl, again with the assumption of a valued name.

Where the potlatch originated is by no means certain; all we know is that it is shared by all the peoples of the area, from Yakutat Bay down to Oregon, and has spread to many tribes on the periphery, such as the Athapaskan-speaking Carriers of the interior of British Columbia and the Yurok of northern California. But it was among the Nootka that Europeans first encountered it, and the author and artist George Clutesi, himself a member of this people, has suggested in *Potlatch* (his moving evocation of the tribal past he knew in early childhood) that the very word *potlatch* may be derived from the Nootka verb *pachitle* "to give," which was constantly in use on such occasions. The Nootka themselves called it *tlooqwahnah*, meaning a feast to which guests from other villages were invited, as distinct from *tleedstoo*, a feast within the village. Certainly occasions recognizable as potlatches were witnessed by early Spanish visitors, and in 1792 Dionisio Galiano and Cayetano Valdez visited one at Nootka which Maquinna gave to celebrate his daughter's attainment of puberty. It was held at Copti, one of the tribe's wintering villages. A platform had been set up outside the house "supported by four thick pillars, painted white, yellow, scarlet, blue and black, with various badly drawn figures on them and two busts at the corners with open arms and hand stretched out as if to signify the munificence of the monarch." The "two busts" were clearly the welcoming figures which were a standard feature of Nootka potlatches. Meanwhile, Maquinna's daughter, in a dress of the finest "cypress" (actually red cedar) fibres, had been lying on a bed of rushes within the house. At the appropriate time Maquinna took her out on the platform and, accompanied by his brother who acted as orator, he gave her the formal name — a high female title in the lineage — by which henceforward she would be known. The assembly applauded, and then valuable gifts were distributed to everyone present, dances were performed with the appropriate singing, and there were wrestling matches, to which the Nootka at that time were especially addicted. Some of the Spanish sailors took part in the wrestling matches, and they also were given presents of sea otter skins, since by their participation in one phase of the ceremony they had played their parts as witnesses to the validation of the name giving.

The winter ceremonials of the Nootka were not so complex as those of the Kwakiutl, though they may have been influenced by them. Essen-

tially, they centred around the activities of a single dancing society, who are generally referred to in English as Wolf Dancers, but who among the Nootka are called "the Shamans," an illuminating instance of the way in which the shamanic function was diffused among the Coast peoples, since initiation was by no means restricted to those who were shamans by vocation, but tended to be regulated by the social position of the sponsor and the initiate.

The wolf, who is widely recognized among Coast peoples as a guardian spirit of warriors, was accepted by the Nootka as their special patron, to be celebrated in rituals deriving from the myth that in ancient times an ancestor had found his way to the house of the wolf spirits, who in four days and nights — which on his return to the village turned out to have been four mortal years — taught him the necessary songs and dances to assure their assistance. Each year, during the winter season, the legend was re-enacted by the Nootka with the initiation of the young men.

At the onset of the festival, wooden horns sounded eerily in the woods and bullroarers hummed, signalling the approach of the spirit wolves. Then men disguised as wolves, in masks and skins, entered the village on all fours and mimed the kidnapping of the novices. The boys were secluded for several days, either in the woods or in a secret compartment of a ceremonial house, while they were taught the dances appropriate to their initiation. During this period the village was given over to a kind of saturnalia, with comic dances and a great deal of horseplay. Then, on the appropriate day, the horns sounded eerily again, and the wolf pack, with their captives, appeared on the far bank of the river or bay nearest the village. The people set out in canoes tied together into catamarans to rescue their children. There followed feigned attacks by the people on the wolves and vice versa, until the

This Nootka spirit mask shows interesting affinities with masks of Alaskan Eskimos.

have been somewhat neglected as artists, so that exhibitions of Coast Indian work, as well as books on the subject, contain hardly any references or illustrations devoted to their work. It is always the Haida or the Tlingit, the Kwakiutl or the Tsimshian to whose baroque power or expressionist fantasy our attention is likely to be drawn when the achievements of Coast Indian artists are discussed. The Nootka are rarely mentioned; the Salish almost never.

Yet Nootka art does have an austere strength which needs to be recognized. There is, to be sure, not the colour nor the fantasy nor the complexity that so often attracts us in Kwakiutl or Tsimshian art, nor is there that peculiar compulsion that one encounters among the Haida to cover every surface of every object with a complex pattern in relief sculpture or paint.

The Nootka chief's rattle, for instance, is most often carved in the shape of a bird. But it is not the kind of meticulously detailed carving, a bird burdened with mythical appendages, that one encounters among the Tsimshian; the Nootka tends to carve merely a bird, and with extreme restraint of detail, so that the natural form is subtly suggested without marring the stylized simplicity of the conception.

The great carved support posts of a house at Yuquot, drawn by John Webber, were the first examples of Nootka figure sculpture to become known to the outside world, and again the quality is one of grand simplicity. Cook and his men wondered about these great figures, which they saw at the entrance to or inside many of the Nootka houses, and decided correctly that their purpose was not religious, since nobody seemed to worship them. At the same time, Webber had a curious experience when he was sketching them, which was more illustrative of Indian attitudes towards such matters than the artist perhaps understood. A Nootka man approached somewhat menacingly with a knife in one hand

wolves finally retreated, leaving the boys on the beach, dressed in hemlock-bough kilts, with their faces painted, and carrying cedar bark emblems as tokens of their initiation. Like most initiates, they behaved with simulated fury as they were being taken home, knocking people down and breaking things until they were subdued; on the final day of the festival they sang the spirit songs and danced the dances they had been taught during their seclusion, and announced the special names they had received.

The masks used in the ceremonies connected with the wolf cult, and the splendid onion-domed conical hats made for the chiefs with representations of the whaling hunt woven into them, are probably the best-known products of Nootka artistry. Generally speaking, the Nootka

and in the other a mat with which he covered the image Webber was sketching.

> Being certain of no further opportunity to finish my Drawing & the object too interesting for leaving unfinished I considered a little bribery might have some effect, and accordingly made an offer of a button from my coat, which when of metal they are much pleased with. This instantly produced the desired effect, for the mat was removed and I left at liberty to proceed as before. Scarcely had I seated myself and made a beginning but he returned to renew his former practice, till I had disposed of my buttons after which time I found no opposition to my further employment.

It seems clear that the man regarded the image which the carving represented as the property of his household, so according to custom it could not be reproduced unless appropriate payment were made, which the artist did in his brass buttons.

It is evident from the very scanty descriptions provided by the early explorers that most of the large Nootka carvings of this period were like those which Webber drew, simple and highly stylized figures with their salient details picked out in paint. Unfortunately few among the visitors to Nootka responded with as much appreciation as Mackenzie did to the carvings he saw at Bella Coola. Cook merely remarked that they "bore some resemblance to the human figure, but monsterous large"; a member of Vancouver's expedition dismissed them as "strikingly preposterous"; and Jewitt committed himself no further than to call them "curiously wrought." However, Cook did grant that Nootka masks were "most of them well designed and executed."

Many of the early travellers noticed the fine carving of the wooden bowls and trays, which were used by the Nootka on special occasions, and the neat carpentry of their lidded boxes, but the very fact that they mention the local inclination to simple inlaid decorations of small white opercula shells or sea otter's teeth (which some travellers mistook for human teeth) suggests that then, as in more recent times, the Nootka did not indulge greatly in the carving and painting which other Coast peoples applied to their bowls and boxes. Yet if one is looking for true proportion and meticulous craftsmanship, the Nootka work in this area is remarkably fine. Carving with few tools and none of the squares or other instruments of precision used by Western workers in wood, these people produced square boxes true to perfect right angles, bowls whose sides were of uniform thickness and whose shapes were completely balanced, and surfaces that were carefully finished and meticulously smoothed. The very beams of the houses, made of massive cedar logs eighty or a hundred feet long and often two feet in diameter, were fluted with the adze to give a finish to the look of the house, and the same carefulness persisted down to the smallest object.

During the nineteenth century a tinge of Kwakiutl expressionism permeated the austerity of traditional Nootka art. The Kwakiutl were less dedicated than the Haida and the Tsimshian to the idea of a large carving as an emanation from the tubular shape of the tree trunk, within which — except for the occasional jutting beak or killer whale fin — everything must be contained and at the same time liberated by the use of expressive high relief. Following the example of the Kwakiutl, the Nootka became more concerned with the form of the mental image rather than with the natural bounds of the material, and so among their characteristic later carvings would appear figures with dowelled appendages, like the thunderbirds with spread wings that often appeared on memorial posts. Yet the free-standing heraldic, or "totem," pole never replaced the single-figure caryatid house post as the most frequent Nootka form of large carving,

The Nootka canoe, which was used extensively in the southern regions, did not have a high stern as well as a high prow like the northern canoes.

mainly because the Nootka never caught the obsession with clan crests that justified the totem pole.

Wolf and bird masks for a few ancient rituals, frugally inlaid but superbly finished wooden utensils, grandly simple but massive house posts, beautifully made hats illustrating the epic whale hunt, a few massive chiefly maces of engraved whalebone: there is a homeric simplicity, a noble functionality about the art of the Nootka that has passed most of the aestheticians by in their bedazzlement with the more vivid and inventive art of other Coast peoples. Such qualities deserve to be acknowledged, yet they cannot be fully celebrated without some reference to the fine craft of canoe making, at which the Nootka excelled.

Canoe making was one of the sacred arts among all the peoples of the Coast. The canoe maker was believed to be inspired by special guardians (the pileated woodpecker in spirit form was often his helper); never of noble rank, he nevertheless acquired, like shamans, mask makers, and pole carvers, a special consideration within the community, received good payment for his work and lavish gifts at feasts and potlatches, and was even somewhat feared in his role as craftsman, which had a touch of the supernatural about it, so that he was allowed to work in private for fear of disturbing his familiar spirits, and any interruption by all but immediate kin was regarded as a personal injury.

Like the houses and most other things of wood that the Nootka used, canoes were made from the red cedar. The other great trees that filled the rain forests were remarkably neglected by Coast Indians; the Douglas fir was virtually ignored; merely the roots of the spruce were used, for weaving baskets and hats; and of the hemlock only the twigs (for ceremonials) and the inner bark were taken, the latter dried into a kind of dull biscuit to be eaten in winter soaked in fish oil. Maple and alder were used for solid utensils and for masks, but for everything else the easily-splittable and universally useful red cedar, whose bark provided fibre for clothes and blankets, was utilized.

Often, instead of felling a whole tree, a canoe maker, with his jade or elkhorn chisel hit by a big stone maul, would cut halfway through a straight and knot-free tree at the bottom and again as far up the tree as the length of the canoe he intended to make. Then, by wedging open a crack at the top, he would thrust a pole into it and go away, certain that the working of wind and frost would enlarge the crack in the straight-grained cedar and bring the half-trunk down to the ground without his being involved in felling a whole tree that would become entangled in others during its descent, presenting an insoluble problem to a man with primitive tools.

With his chisel and hammer, supplemented by a hand-adze and a gimlet, the canoe maker would then set to work on his boat, as Gilbert Sproat, who saw it more than a century ago, describes the process:

> The hand-adze is a large mussel-shell strapped firmly to a wooden handle. The natural shape of the shell quite fits it for use as a tool. In working with the hand-adze, the back of the workman's hand is turned downwards and the blow struck lightly towards the holder, whose thumb is pressed into a space cut to receive it. The surface of the canoe, marked by the regular chipping of the hand-adze, is prettier than if it were smooth. The gimlet, made of bird's bone, and having a wooden handle, is not used like ours: the shaft is placed between the workman's open hands brought close together, and moved briskly backwards and forwards as on hearing good news; in which manner, by the revolution of the gimlet, a hole is quickly bored. . . . Fire is not used here for

the hollowing of canoes, but the outside is always scorched to prevent sun-rents and damage from insects. After the sides are the required thinness, the rough trunk is filled with fresh water, which is heated by hot stones being thrown into it, and the canoe, thus softened by the heat, is, by means of cross-pieces of wood, made into a shape which, on cooling, it retains. The fashioning is done entirely by the eye, and is surprisingly exact. In nine cases out of ten, a line drawn from the middle to the extremities will leave, as nearly as possible, the same width all along on each side of the line. To keep the canoe in shape, light cross-pieces fastened to the inside of the gunwales are placed about four feet apart, and there remain. The gunwale is turned outwards a little to throw off the water. The bow and stern pieces are made separately, and are always of one form, though the body of the canoe varies a little in shape according to the capabilities of the tree and the fancy or skill of the maker. Red is the favourite colour for the inside of a canoe, and is made by a mixture of resin, oil, and urine; the outside is as black as oil and burnt wood will make it; the bow and stern generally bear some device in red.

What Sproat does not add is that the singeing of the outside of the canoe was also devised to burn off any splinters, and that for a whaling or sealing canoe a final "sanding" with shark or dogfish skin was given so that it could move through the water completely silently.

It was indeed the needs of the whale hunt, when the chiefly harpoonist required perfect equipment for challenging the largest of earth's creatures, that turned the Nootka canoe into a work of functional precision whose beauty lay in its meticulously gauged equilibrium — an example, like so much the Coast Indians did, of art produced by the intelligent response to necessity.

A Salish *swaihwe* dancer with his characteristic mask and his garment of feathers. The *swaihwe* dancers are unique to the Salish culture.

CHAPTER SEVEN

The Spirit Questers

In population, the Coast Salish were the most numerous group among the native peoples of the Pacific Coast of North America, and they occupied more territory than any other of the local Indians. As late as 1835, after considerable depopulation through smallpox and other epidemics, they still numbered twelve thousand in British Columbia alone. It is fair to assume that in the late prehistoric period, just before the arrival of the Europeans, the Salish in what later became Canadian and American territory must have numbered between twenty and twenty-five thousand, and this despite the fact that they were liable to considerable slave raiding by their Kwakiutl neighbours in the Strait of Georgia, by the Nootka on Vancouver Island, and even by the Haida who raided in historic times as far south as Puget Sound and in doing so were probably perpetuating an already established custom.

Coast Salish territory when the Europeans arrived included the eastern shore of Vancouver Island from Comox southward and the southern shore of the island facing over the Strait of Juan de Fuca; the mainland sounds and their hinterlands from Bute Inlet south to Burrard Inlet; the delta of the Fraser and the broad river valley up to the lower end of the Fraser Canyon east of Yale; and, in the State of Washington, from the mountains westward to the ocean in an area surrounding Puget Sound and to the south bordering the territory of the non-Salish Chinook who inhabit the valley of the lower Columbia. Today, in the Fraser Valley and western Washington, this area includes some of the most productive farmland of North America west of the Rockies, and in prehistoric days — with its rivers and still undrained lakes and sloughs, its great sheltered sounds, marshes, and tidal flats, its forests and marginal mountains — the territory was already, in terms of fish and shellfish, game and wild plant food, the most productive part of the rich Pacific Coast.

Many early travellers applied to all Salish the name of "Flathead Indians," which more recently has been used only to identify one specific group of them, a tribe of Interior Salish living in the mountains of Montana. This was because of the custom, which all Salish (including those of the Coast) shared with some other western Indian groups, of changing their physical appearance by reshaping the skulls of their infants while the bones of the skull were still soft. Their concepts of human beauty led them to believe that a high forehead gave an ugly, narrow look to the face, and they went about improving on nature by a process which the Canadian painter, Paul Kane, still saw in operation when he visited the region in 1847:

> The Indian mothers all carry their infants strapped to a piece of board covered with moss or loose fibres of cedar bark, and in order to flatten the head they place a pad on the infant's forehead, on

the top of which is laid a piece of smooth bark, bound on by a leathern band passing through holes in the board on either side, and kept tightly pressed across the front of the head, — a sort of pillow of grass or cedar fibres being placed under the back of the neck to support it. This process commences with the birth of the infant, and is continued for a period of from eight to twelve months, by which time the head has lost its natural shape, and acquired that of a wedge: the front of the skull flat and higher at the crown, giving it a most unnatural appearance.

Apart from the artificially induced shape of the head, the Coast Salish differed from other people of the area, and even from their own Interior Salish relatives, in being rather short and stocky people, with an average height of five foot three. Although the cultural continuity between them and the ancient Marpole people who inhabited the Fraser Delta two millennia ago seems quite evident, the arguments for racial continuity are less clear, since in at least some of the earlier archaeological sites in British Columbia the remains of a small, long-headed people have been found, whereas the Coast Salish tend to be round headed. Yet the fact that they are markedly shorter than the Interior Salish suggests that in coming to the Coast they may have mingled with the earlier long-headed strain and genetically dominated them, and that the pattern in the region centring on the Fraser Delta was one of a continuing culture kept in a state of growth by changing mixes of peoples, until, just after the high flowering of the Marpole culture, the last wave of immigrants arrived and life in the Salish region settled down to the relatively unchanging form which it has retained for a thousand years and more. One circumstance suggesting a long presence on the Coast is that the Salish are divided into at least a dozen dialect groups, which over time have become so differentiated that now a man from southern Van-

couver Island and a man from the Puget Sound area will find it virtually impossible to converse in their own languages and will fall back either on English or on the old trading lingo of Chinook, as I have heard them doing at winter dance festivals.

The sharp linguistic divisions among the Salish are only one sign of their extreme lack of cohesion as a people. Admittedly, none of the Coast Indian peoples in aboriginal times ever had that sense of nationality which emerged among the Iroquois and among some of the prairie Indian peoples, such as the Sioux and the Blackfoot Confederacy, but the Salish excel them all in their lack of any sense of a political or even a racial unity that extends beyond the village (and even there it is likely to be somewhat tenuous). As Homer G. Barnett so aptly expressed the situation in his classic study, *The Coast Salish of British Columbia* (Eugene, 1955):

> Among the Salish, the highest unit of common allegiance was the extended family. There was no tribe or state; hence, there were no offenses against or loyalty to either. There were no tribal officers; no council; no bodies for the enactment, adjustment, or enforcement of regulations. Action involving the rights of others was governed by a set of traditional and theoretically unchangeable rules. These, like other rules of behaviour, were inculcated from early youth by precept and by example. Ignorance of the rules excused no one; every well-bred person was familiar with them and took pride in his knowledge of them. It was a part of good breeding, almost of etiquette, to respect and observe them, and it was beneath the dignity of an aristocrat to commit a breach. It was certainly to his material advantage not to do so, for his social, and therefore political position rested, in large part, upon his support of the commonly recognized group good.

It all sounds rather like Kropotkin's model of the ideal primitive society where every man

Swaihwe dancers performing at a Coast Salish potlatch at the Songhees Reserve in Victoria in 1895.

knows the natural laws of social behaviour and therefore no authority is needed. But any system of taboos is a system of depersonalized authority, and in practice a great deal of influence, if not of overt power, was wielded among the Salish not only by the class of hereditary *siems* (since it seems better to use their own word than the inappropriate title *chiefs*) who were called "real men," but also by the individual headmen of houses or villages. Also, although there is a great deal of evidence to suggest that life went on very harmoniously in Salish extended families and children were brought up with an excellent combination of toughness and understanding (boys were routed out every winter morning to bathe in the ice-cold rivers and scarify their bodies with branches, but at the same time were prepared for the spirit quest that would determine their lives), nevertheless these little anarchic communities existed in a precarious world where people who spoke a slightly different dialect might turn hostile and start a night attack at the slightest pretext. Slavery, after all, was the other side to the apparently exemplary combination of freedom and responsibility; every Salish house, like every Nootka house, had its slaves, and since the Salish were no match in warfare for the Kwakiutl or the Haida, their slave raids tended to be directed against people of their own language group; as one writer put it succinctly, "Salish preyed upon Salish."

If the Salish were less politically oriented than other peoples in this region, they were also less organized in the ceremonial patterns that underlay the elaborate social structures of the Kwakiutl and the northern tribes. Until the coming of the white men and their authority encouraged better communication between Coast peoples by virtually banning that unheroic combination of ambush, surprise attack, and general treachery which passed for warfare in this region, the Salish lacked both the secret dancing fraternities that developed among the Kwakiutl and the elaborate systems of crested clans that shaped the matriarchal societies of the northern peoples. In historic times, dancing societies and the carving and erection with due ceremony of crested poles began to spread southward among northern groups of Salish, particularly the Comox on Vancouver Island, but the southern villages of the Fraser Valley and around Puget Sound remained virtually untouched to the end by such hieratic manifestations. Inherited family privileges, which played as great a part in their own way as the clan privileges of the northern peoples, tended to be embodied among the Salish in individual dances and songs, in names, and to some extent in inherited rituals, but they were not objectified in such artifacts as poles or paintings.

Related to these differences from the more dynamic peoples, who in recent centuries lived to the north of them, was the relative modesty of the various arts among the Salish. It was in fact — as we shall see — in the geometric designs of the women's crafts of weaving and basketry that they seemed to excel; their imagination did not express itself in so figurative and visually intriguing a way as that of the Tsimshian and Kwakiutl master carvers. But it was, for all that, a strikingly fertile imagination; no group was more mystically active, more universally involved in the guardian spirit quest in all its forms. At first sight, when one compares it with the histrionic flamboyance of the Kwakiutl sequence of extravagant potlatches and dramatic winter ceremonials, or with the artistic richness of the Tlingit, the Haida, or the Tsimshian life styles, the Salish pattern of existence seems remarkably low keyed and even banal, and there are some enthusiasts for Coast Indian culture who never get beyond this first impression. But there remains a special inner intensity to the Salish vision that becomes immediately evident to any person who — even now in the late twentieth century — attends one of their spirit dance gatherings with his senses widely opened.

If one had to pick a single material feature of Salish life as a symbol of the whole culture, it would surely be the great rambling house that was so characteristic of this people. Styles of building say a great deal about the collective characters of peoples, and nowhere more emphatically than on the Pacific Coast. Essentially, there were two forms of house in this region, if one ignores the interior type of conical-roofed underground house that appears only occasionally on the verges of the Coast area. The northern peoples, including the Kwakiutl, built massive and splendidly carpentered gabled houses, rela-

A Salish long house early in this century. Although modifications had been made in the form of building by adding windows and a gabled roof, the carvings were similar to those seen by Simon Fraser a century before.

tively small in regional terms (usually between fifty and sixty feet long, a little less wide, and between twelve and fourteen feet to the ridge pole); but they made up for this compactness in the splendour of their decoration, which among the Haida, who added massive carved portal and corner posts and wall paintings, became the Coast Indian equivalents of Gothic or baroque church facades, except that they were dedicated not to the glory of God (the Coast peoples had no temples as such or the kind of worship for which they might be necessary) but rather to the glory of the resident chiefs and their ancestors and through them to the glory of the clan they headed.

The southern type of house, which existed in a modified form among the more southerly groups of the Nootka and which appears to have been the older pattern, used frameworks of dressed timber but differed from the northern form in a number of basic features. Instead of the gabled roof, it had a simple shed roof (supported on poles) that sloped almost imperceptibly downward — because the frame at the front of the house was a foot or so higher than that at the back. The walls of the northern houses consisted of upright planks which fitted into slotted sills; those of the Salish houses consisted of overlapping horizontal planks lashed to upright poles, which actually formed a kind of outer shell separate from the framework that supported the roof, which also was made of overlapping cedar planks.

But the great difference lay in the dimensions and the divisions of the house. The Salish houses were far larger than anything built in the northern villages; in fact they were very often villages in themselves. With good interior supports, they might reach a maximum width of sixty feet, but the length could be indefinitely extended, and houses have been reported from the Puget Sound region as much as fifteen hundred feet long. Simon Fraser saw from the outside houses eight hundred feet long and went into one near Hope that was hardly less large:

> The whole range, which is 640 feet long by 60 broad, is under one roof; the front is 18 feet high, and the covering is slanting: all the apartments, which are separated by partitions, are square, except the chief's, which is 90 feet long.

The most reliable reports agree that the long houses of the Salish did indeed consist of independent apartments; and it appears, moreover, that though the frame was a common structure, the planks of the walls and roof belonged to the individual households, so that when the time came to move on to a summer fishing camp each family would take down its own planks and carry them off to be incorporated into a summer shelter.

The very plan of these two different types of houses emphasizes the different social patterns governing northern and southern peoples. The northern house was arranged hierarchically, with its triple aisles leading up to the platform at the end that was allocated to the house chief. The remaining living area in the side aisles was allocated in descending orders of rank to the lesser nobles in the house and to the commoners with their wives and children. Real privacy did not exist. Everything was clearly structured within the framework of a pyramidical matrilineal group, itself the microcosm of the clan of which the house was a part. In the Salish house the structure of authority was not nearly so evident. The chief had the largest apartment, and this fact acknowledged both his greater wealth and his hereditary importance as the person in the most direct line of descent, considered patrilineally, from the mythical ancestor of the whole extended family. But the ranking patterns were less definite, less emphasized by ceremonials relating to privilege.

Sometimes a village would consist merely of one large house inhabited by a series of fairly closely related families, like the very large examples which Fraser describes. More often there would be a group of houses, usually between a hundred and two hundred feet long, each of which would contain a joint family head, with his younger brothers and their children, his sons and their children, his unmarried daughters, his parents if they were alive, and usually a few more distant relatives — widowed aunts, orphaned nephews, disabled cousins — who were unable to survive on their own and who were taken in under the vaguely understood mutual aid system that expected kin to assist kin.

Such extended family units were held together far more by a tradition of common ancestry and a sense of mutual interest than by any formal pattern of authority. The headman or *siem* did not really hold any office. He was respected because of his direct descent from the mythical ancestor and because of the names and privileges (dances, songs, rituals) he had inherited. But the other householders, even though they were his younger brothers or his sons, were in no real sense under his authority; rather, he acted as steward of the extended family's general interests, as trustee of its collective property, as its delegate in relations with the outer world, and above all as its ceremonial head, its hierophant. Common household concerns were discussed between the heads of the nuclear families, and the headman's opinion carried weight. But he had neither authority to exert nor the means to assert it, and there was no formal mechanism to check dissent. Nevertheless, dissent rarely occurred, partly because the world outside the big house was a perilous one for unattached individuals and partly because in a primitive society, where formal authority is slight, the forces of public opinion are usually strongly developed.

If a village consisted of several houses, they usually belonged to extended family groups at least related enough to acknowledge a common though distant ancestor who had dropped down, as the legend usually went, from the sky. The pattern of the northern village, comprising several clans claiming different origins, did not exist among the Salish; in fact, the Salish had not developed their concepts of common ancestry into anything so formal as a clan. Within such a village, as within the house, there would be no formal structure of authority. But the headmen of the various houses would meet to discuss in a very informal way any matters that were of common concern to the village — such as the building of fish weirs across a local river — carefully avoiding any appearance of interference in the internal affairs of houses to which they did not belong; and in these councils, if such they could be called, the headman of the largest house, with the most ceremonial privileges, would take the lead without assuming the formal role of a village chief.

Relations with other villages were even less defined and tended to be tempered by distrust, since the lack of any sense of racial solidarity among the Salish made it always possible that, over some slight excuse, the warriors in a house would incite a surprise attack on a house in another village; if such an attack were successful, the men would all be killed, while the children and sometimes the women would be taken away as slaves. But it seems likely that the incidence of such deadly raids has been exaggerated in the accounts anthropologists have gathered from their Indian informants, since if they had been frequent, the Salish population would not have been as large as it was at first contact with the Europeans, and the early travellers would not have been able to remark — as they sometimes did — on the extraordinary longevity that seemed to prevail among these people. Moreover, frequent attacks would have meant a state of armed vigilance and an attempt to fortify the villages, which only occurred when the Salish lived in close proximity to some hostile other people, as in the case of the group Paul Kane found on the Olympic Peninsula, who, out of fear of the ferocious Makah (whom Kane called "Macaws"), had built themselves a considerable stronghold:

> It was composed of a double row of strong pickets, the outer ones about twenty feet high, and the inner row about five feet, enclosing a space of 150 feet square. The whole of this inner space is roofed in, and divided into small compartments, or pens, for the use of each separate family. There were about 200 of the tribe in the fort at the time of my arrival.

It seems obvious that peaceful intervillage relations exceeded by far the hostile occasions. There were, after all, very complicated minglings along the Fraser during the periods of the salmon runs, when the Salish peoples from Vancouver Island would come to fish from summer camps to which they held ancient rights dating from before their migration across the Gulf of Georgia, and there were the spring gatherings known as *klanak*, the Salish equivalent of the potlatch, when the "real men" of a village would invite the "real men" of the other villages to gatherings at which privileges would be displayed and life crisis ceremonies like namings and puberty rites would be carried on to the accompaniment of feasting, dancing, singing, and above all a good deal of bombastic speechmaking; for although a modest and judicious demeanour was regarded as appropriate to the daily behaviour of a house headman, he was expected to be bold and boastful in his assertion of the privileges through exercising which he objectified the pretensions of the lineage. Except in the more northerly villages, where Kwakiutl influences had percolated, the *klanaks* were much less formal ceremonies than the potlatches of other Coast peoples, and a great deal of unprogrammed horseplay was usually permitted.

Salish society, as I have said, was basically patrilineal in its structure. Names, privileges, and the trusteeship of the common family property descended from father to son, usually according to the pattern of primogeniture. As far as personal property was concerned, there was a double pattern; the father's hunting and fishing equipment and his personal adornments descended to his male heirs, but the mother's household implements, personal ornaments, and craft equipment (such as looms and spinning whorls) would be inherited by the daughters. At times, also, valuable privileges might pass from one family to another as part of the rather complicated exchanges of material and nonmaterial property that accompanied marriages.

Marriage, of course, was another situation in which intervillage links were often established. Since the Salish had no clans, they had no strict system of exogamy, nevertheless, the marriage of close blood relatives was not accepted, and this meant that a bride must be found outside the house, and preferably outside the village, since that would create an alliance in a world where friends were always useful.

Marriage customs among the Salish were surprisingly formal for a people so informal in the ordinary political structuring of their lives. Marriages were usually arranged beforehand on the basis of tacit understandings between the parties concerned, since in a society where loss of face could be a reason for suicide, or at the very least for expensive giving to wipe out the

humiliation, no prospective bridegroom's family would take the risk of public rejection. Nevertheless, it was the convention for the prospective bride's family to pretend that the whole matter was a complete surprise when the groom's party sailed up to the beach before their house, with the father and uncles singing their family songs from a platform laid across canoes that were loaded with gifts. The door would be barred, and the orators from the groom's party would stand before it making their elaborate speeches extolling in repetitious phrases the virtues of both families and the advantages of a union between them. The door still remained barred, and then any relatives or connections the visiting party might have in the village were recruited (and paid) to add their personal solicitations. On occasion, the comedy was carried on so far that these intermediaries would threaten to chop down the door before it was eventually opened.

But the opening of the door did not mean the end of the groom's ordeal. He was allowed to enter and sit just inside the door, but the family of the bride (who in the meantime was being kept out of sight) ignored him, and he would have to sit there, silent and fasting, for several days, while his relatives came back each morning to resume their exhortations. At last, the girl's father would go out silently and return with his own team of speakers, who would discuss with the visiting orators the merits of the marriage, and at last the boy would be led to the centre of the room and fed, while his father gave blankets to the girl's speakers.

Next day all the fellow villagers of the bride's family would be invited for the public betrothal. The boy would be seated on a pile of blankets (cedar bark before the traders came, and Hudson's Bay Company blankets afterwards), and the bride would be seated on another, provided by the groom's family. Speakers from both sides would indulge in flowery mutual praise and in exhortations to the young people on the qualities of a good marriage. Then the groom's father presented the marriage gift of food, blankets, and other items, part of which was distributed among the guests. The bride's father always gave the young couple a going-away present, customarily of useful household goods, but his main obligation was the return gift, which he usually presented on his first visit to his daughter during the following winter; it was the convention that if possible the return gift should exceed the marriage gift, and often it included privileges such as the right to perform the prestigious *swaihwe* dance with its characteristic mask.

The basis of the Salish economy was not in any essential way different from that of the other Coast Indian peoples. Salmon and cedar once again were the main staples. The whale was not hunted, though the arrival of dead whales on local beaches was always welcomed, and there were few halibut in nearby waters; on the other hand the Fraser was inhabited by immense sturgeon, some of which as late as Paul Kane's day weighed up to six hundred pounds and were caught in a very ingenious way:

> This is done by means of a long pointed spear handle seventy to eighty feet long, fitted into, but not actually fastened to, a barbed spear-head, to which is attached a line, with which they feel along the bottom of the river where the sturgeon are found lying at the spawning season. Upon feeling the fish the barbed spear is driven in and the handle withdrawn. The fish is then gradually drawn in by the line, which being very long, allows the sturgeon to waste his great strength, so that he can with safety be taken into the canoe or towed ashore. Most of their fishing lines are formed of a long seaweed (kelp), which is often found 150 feet long, of equal thickness throughout the whole length, and about as thick as a black-lead pencil; while wet it is very strong.

This operation was carried out from a keelless and therefore highly unstable dugout canoe, and required a great deal of skill even if it was not perilous in the same way as the whale hunt.

Since the Salish inhabited some of the flattest areas of the coastal region, with large stretches of level forest — and even parkland in some places — as well as a great deal of marshland, they hunted more frequently than most Coast Indians, with the exception of the people of the Nass and Skeena rivers. They were expert at netting wild fowl, and they even hunted for its precious wool the mountain goat which in those days still inhabited the mountains bordering on the Fraser Valley; the goat pastures were the property of families regarded as noble — as "real men" — and only these could hunt them. The bear was killed with respect, being addressed as "grandfather," and when he was killed the hunter sang to his head; only the black bear was generally eaten, since the grizzly, which also then inhabited the local mountains, was believed to be one of the agents of the Transformer. Apart from the small dogs they bred for wool, the Salish bred hunting dogs — said to have resembled coyotes in appearance — which were trained by men who knew the appropriate magic. They were used for driving mountain goats into nets and for chasing deer and elk into lakes, where they were killed from canoes which overtook them as they swam.

The prevalence of hunting, on the mainland at least, led to a certain variation of the Coast pattern of clothing among the Salish. They made blankets and other garments of cedar bark fibre, as the other Coast peoples did, and during bad weather they wore the tightly woven cedar bark capes, which if not completely waterproof, were water-repellent like the Austrian cloaks of *loden* cloth. But they also made many garments, not only of furs but also of tanned buckskin, using methods which they had probably acquired from

A Salish fish weir on the Cowichan River, Vancouver Island.

the Thompson River Indians, an Interior Salish group whose fishing territories in the Fraser Canyon bordered on those of the Coast Salish. Yet in summer, like all the Coast peoples, the Salish preferred to wear as few garments as possible, though, particularly in the Fraser Delta and up the river valley where the insect population was enormous and intrusive, they would apply to themselves a very thick coating of bear grease or some similar cosmetic.

The Salish enjoyed a greater abundance of vegetable foods than most Coast peoples, since the best camas-growing meadows were situated in their region. They made a "sap bread" from the inner barks of maple and alder, and from the Chinook they had learnt to make acorns palatable by pounding them into a paste and then pouring water on them to leach away the tannin.

But such a plethora of material wealth — and the Salish were blessed even more than other Coast peoples with the natural abundance of the region — could produce a leisure filled with artistic creativity, or an extraordinary development of mystical introspection and understanding, or a society imprisoned by its own material desires. The third of these alternatives is the one

that our own modern Western culture has fatally chosen to accept. The first — that of artistic creativity, the objectification of the imaginative vision — was the direction followed by the northern Coast peoples and the Kwakiutl, among whom the histrionic and aesthetic elements eventually overbalanced the spiritual ones in the typical manifestations of their cultures through ceremonial and artifact. The second alternative — an extraordinary development of mystical introspection and understanding — was that followed by the Coast Salish.

One of the consequences of such a choice was that — rather like the Tibetans who followed a similar course — the Salish developed little in the way of an original artistic tradition. Indeed, when one looks at the extraordinary works in stone which were being created in their territory in the Marpole era, the modesty of Salish art in recent centuries is astonishing. There were only two areas in which they might be said to equal and even to excel their neighbours, and these were weaving and basketry, the women's geometric arts.

The Salish were not in fact lacking in good craftsmen. Their canoes were adequate for the rivers and the sheltered sea waters they had to traverse. Their wooden utensils were well carved but unornamented, except for the large spinning whorls, sometimes six inches in diameter, which the men still carved as intricately as their forerunners two thousand years ago had done. Their fish weirs were often masterpieces of simple engineering, as were the platforms for dipnetting and spearing salmon in the narrow passes of the Fraser Canyon, which were still in position when I first went through the region as late as 1950. But except among the Comox, who borrowed it from the Kwakiutl, the Salish did not share in the special tradition of symbolic-figurative art which we commonly associate with the Coast Indian peoples.

140

Salish graves beside the Fraser River, about 1862.

Yet although the museums contain relatively few examples of their work, the Salish were not men completely without art. They belonged, in fact, to a tradition that seems far more ancient than that which the northern Coast peoples developed. Their native style of sculpture may well, indeed, have been a degenerated survival of the lost wood carvings of the far prehistoric days of the Marpole culture. It was an art particularly associated with the celebration of ancestors, sometimes applied to houses but more often to be found in cemeteries. Simon Fraser, who remains in so many ways our great authority on aboriginal Salish life (since the establishment of Fort Langley nineteen years after his arrival changed completely the whole cultural situation in the Fraser Valley) was very definite about the existence of such sculpture. In describing one of the very large houses he saw, he remarks: "Above, on the outside, are carved a human figure as large as life, with other figures in imitation of animals and birds." Later, discussing the

141

Coast Salish grave figures of mourners, from the lower Fraser Valley.

often shown as wearing European hats and sometimes even decked out in actual European garments, but still showing a style of carving that is common to many cultures — in Africa, in the Hindu Kush, among the Nagas, in Southeast Asia and Melanesia — which, even if they have not built megaliths, have retained the styles of the megalithic era, including the boldly carved mortuary images which are so often characterized by flattish heart-shaped faces. These are, essentially, spirit figures. They are not intended to fit the pattern of social hierarchy which produced the formulaic and esoterically allusive art of the northern peoples. They project that sense of a direct relationship with a world of spirits, which was especially characteristic of the Salish view of existence.

It is significant that the Salish have only one mask of their own, and that a very strange one, the *swaihwe*. The *swaihwe* was a mask unlike any other on the Coast, a blind mask whose eyes were large peglike projections through which the dancer could not look, so that he had to perform his curious whistling prance by guesswork; animal heads — like those on the rattles of spirit dancers — were attached to the crown and front of the mask, and plumes surmounted it; it was worn with a kind of feather cloak that covered the dancer's body. All accounts of the origin of the *swaihwe* mask are legendary. A man is said to have caught it while trolling in Burrard Inlet; another man is said to have seen a being who wore it rising out of Beaver Lake in Stanley Park; the first man to descend from the sky and found the village of Musqueam is said to have worn it. What evidence there is points to its having originated in Musqueam which, as we have seen, is an ancient Fraser Delta centre. And this, together with the whole *swaihwe* costume, which is strikingly similar to those worn by certain West African dancers and clearly belongs to an equally ancient tradition, suggests that this very

curious grave houses of the region in which the boxes containing the remains of the dead were arranged in tiered shelves, he described a cemetery which he saw at Spuzzum:

> [The tombs] are about fifteen feet long and of the form of a chest of drawers. Upon the boards and posts are beasts and birds carved in a curious but crude manner yet pretty well proportioned.

Photographs taken later in the nineteenth century reveal similar grave houses, with animal figures in rough relief and with upright and life-sized anthropomorphic figures in the round,

Salish monuments beside the Fraser River.

curious mask may take us back to an era before the artistic traditions we associate with the Kwakiutl and the northern tribes came into being.

The rights over the *swaihwe* mask and its accompanying dance were held only by certain privileged families among the Salish, either descended from the original receivers of the mask from supernatural sources, or co-opted by marriage, or through a gift of the right. The dance, furthermore, could only be performed at the instance of families who held such rights, and although there was no actual dancing society associated with the *swaihwe*, the owners of the right were well known, and the rule was ob-

served, even though the uninitiated were allowed to watch. The dancers' function seems to have been one of purification, since the *swaihwe* maskers were called on such occasions as the termination of the period of seclusion after a girl's first menses, the emergence of parents from seclusion after the birth of a child, and funerals — occasions potent with spiritual peril. In all such instances, individuals through some form of ritual impurity had been made vulnerable to evil supernatural forces, and the *swaihwe* dance, whose effect was sometimes referred to as a "washing," appears to have neutralized such perilous conditions or at least to have validated emergence from them.

143

The *swaihwe* dance was unusual among the Salish since its performance was dependent on no spirit quest; it was merely handed down as an inheritance or transferred as a gift, and the man who received it learnt in a straightforward way from those who were already performers. Such lessons may have been expensive, as *swaihwe* performances certainly were.

The spirit quest was quite another matter. It was not a question of inheriting a socially recognized ritual or performance, for many sons of inspired fathers went uninspired and many men of high social standing with hereditary ceremonial privileges never received the spirit vision.

Essentially, the idea of the spirit quest was based on a completely animistic view of the universe. The Salish had only the vaguest notions of a supreme deity (and what they displayed may well have been implanted after the arrival of the first missionaries). Instead, they believed fervently that everything in nature was permeated by spirit, even inanimate material objects, so that one had to be in tune even with one's tools or one's fishing tackle if they were to operate in the right way. This was not a vague and sentimental otherworldliness of the kind that bewilders so many people in the West. It was an attempt to give a form and an explanation to the universe in which men found themselves living, and once one understands it as the basis of a view of existence and of behaviour in response to existence, everything that the Salish did in response to it followed with that innate and nonrational but extraordinarily precise logicality which Claude Lévi-Strauss has taught us to perceive in the systems invented by primitive peoples.

The basis of this particular system lies in the belief that not only is everything in the universe permeated with spirituality (which is thus a worldly quality like electricity and not in any real way otherworldly), but that everything has its own individual spirit reflecting its special nature which can reveal itself in human form, not necessarily because man is superior (he is often inferior in particular ways to other beings and needs their assistance) but because the human form was the original universal form which only man has retained but to which in exceptional circumstances other beings can return. It is evident, from the way we see them behaving in their ordinary lives, that animals have certain kinds of knowledge which are normally unavailable to human beings; so, presumably, do inanimate objects and forces. It is also accepted as a convenient theory that animals and natural forces are inclined to be benevolent to men, and that just as a man's parents teach him certain forms of knowledge and give him certain gifts (some material and others — like names — immaterial), so the spirits could make him gifts according to their natures which would assist him in his life.

It was mainly the young who went on the spirit quest, while their own spirits were still responsive and unclouded by such experiences as marriage. The young man — for it was usually the men who engaged on the more arduous searches — would go out into the wilderness, on his own, without any previous instruction by his elders in what he might expect; he had to remain continent, to fast, to go without sleep, to mortify the flesh in every possible way. Then, if he were fortunate, he might have a waking vision (which we might regard as a hallucination) of an animal or a "supernatural" being. But this in itself was not sufficient. There also had to be a dream or a trance in which the spirit came to the novice — often in shining human form — and actually spoke to him and instructed him. For the benefit of the experience to be secure, moreover, there had to be several repetitions of the dream encounter. Any fear or flight at the time of the initial waking vision would deprive the novice of the spirit help he wanted. And any direct revelation to another person of his experience would deprive him of the power it conferred. In practice, however, the occupation a man took up would suggest the kind of spirit he encountered, and if it did not, he could make oblique allusions to it in the miming that was part of his dance and in his spirit song.

All special occupations were inspired by spirit encounters. Canoe makers, as we have seen, had woodpeckers for their guardian spirits, warriors had hornets, hunters had wolves, shamans had mythical serpents, clairvoyants had owls, and fishermen had salmon, cod, and various birds that preyed on fish. Those whose guardians did not give them specific vocations would receive dancing power, which had little practical value except to confirm one's position as a participant in the winter festivals and therefore confirm that one was a socially accepted — if not a privileged — person; and many kinds of spirits could offer such power. Relations with the spirit did not end with first encounter; spirit wolves would lead hunters towards game, and when a canoe maker went to work in the woods the sound of the hammering woodpecker would encourage him. Such encounters were regarded as materializations of the guardian spirit and signs of its continuing benevolence.

Even though the initiate was not expected to describe his guardian spirit experience or reveal the spirit's identity, there was a public aspect to the experience, manifest in the dance with its accompanying song, which, like all possessions of this kind, had to be validated by public performance accompanied by the presentation of gifts to witnesses. In this way, individual experience was incorporated into the collective experience at the winter dances, which among the Fraser Delta people and those of southern Vancouver Island continued throughout the winter on such a scale that the partitions would have to be taken out in the great houses where the dances were held, so that there would be enough room for the audience and for the performers stamping their way around the fires to the tune of drum and rattles and for the people singing in chorus each dancer's spirit song. (These winter gatherings go on today with surprisingly little change, and in my Epilogue I give the impressions of a modern outside observer.)

The winter dances were usually sponsored by individual house heads who acted as patrons for the occasion, but at the same time a kind of dance society did emerge. It lacked the elaborate and prestigious gradations of the Kwakiutl secret dancing societies and it was not adapted, like those of the Haida, to strengthen the social hierarchy. It appears to have been — and still to be — an informal grouping of initiates intent on inducing the experience of the spirit quest in those who had not received it spontaneously. Individuals — young men or young women — were seized, forcibly secluded, starved and kept from sleeping, and often rendered unconscious by various means, so that a trance state could be induced in which they would hallucinate and receive visions of guardian spirits.* Anything they uttered on such occasions would be remembered by the listening initiates so that it might later become the basis of the novice's spirit song. This kind of conscription into ecstasy seems hardly in keeping with the original idea of departing into the solitude of the wilderness and acquiring a guardian through one's

*Among many groups of Indians in South, Central and North America, the visions of the spirit quest are often induced by ingesting hallucinogenic substances such as peyote, and Siberian shamans use the fly agaric and other fungi as aids to ecstatic experience. I have found no evidence for the use of such substances among the Coast Indians, either among shamans or spirit questers. Nor did the Coast Indians prepare fermented drinks, though they did — at least in the Queen Charlottes — grow a form of tobacco, to be pounded and chewed with seashell lime.

own ascetic efforts, but it does represent the beginnings of a tendency to socialize spiritual experiences, which, as we shall see, was carried much further among the more northerly peoples of the Coast.

Parallel to the guardian spirit quest with its essential concept that, however the spirit was encountered, its gifts were made to the individual and could not be transmitted by inheritance or in any other way, there was among the Salish a complex network of hereditary ritualism generally referred to as *siween*. (There were of course local dialect variations of the term.) *Siween* applied to a variety of ritual observances which were essentially magical in character, involving spells and rites intended to bring about desirable results or to eliminate undesirable conditions. The application of *siween* was highly specialized to cover all the crises likely to arise in Salish life except those very specifically involving the shaman, whose province was notably circumscribed by these rival ritualists with their small areas of power.

Midwives, with their magical aids to easy or safe childbirth; people who prepared a corpse for burial and took it out of the house through a hole made specially in the back wall; men who performed the first salmon rites; men or women who conducted purification rites after puberty or who protected parents from the perils of childbirth: all these possessed *siween*, as did people who knew the powers of medicinal herbs and the women who knew the carefully guarded secrets of how to induce abortions. *Siween* was a power that could be inherited, since it depended on the knowledge of some fragment of ancient lore, embodied in propitiatory incantations and acts that could easily be taught, and including elements of practical psychology and sometimes of primitive pharmacology. The ritualist had his sign of office — a rattle of deer hooves — and his socially privileged position; like the shaman, he expected payment for his services.

Thus, along with the craft specialists and the psychic technicians (shamans and clairvoyants), who derived their power from individual inspiration, we see among the Salish a widely diffused body of hereditary knowledge (for there was hardly a family that did not contain an expert whose powers in some small area were useful to the community) that reinforced the feeling, implicit in the spirit quest, of a universal accessibility to the supernatural, or rather, since these peoples did not make the kind of distinctions we make, to the natural world permeated by spirit as conceived by the animist mentality.

CHAPTER EIGHT

The Raven's Kin

It is when we travel north up the Coast, to the northeasterly tip of Vancouver Island, to the deep fjords that penetrate the coastal mountains north of Bute Inlet, and when we follow the intricate channels of the Inland Passage up to Prince Rupert and the Queen Charlottes and Alaska, that we reach the peoples who produced the art that made the Coast Indian tradition one of the great achievements of world art. The Kwakiutl created an expressionist art of great vigour and fantasy, in which many critics have detected a Dionysian quality that seemed also to inspire this people's elaborate ceremonials. The northern tribes — the Tlingit, the Tsimshian, and the Haida — created a more controlled and at the same time a more decorative kind of art. At times, with the Tsimshian, it verged on naturalism in its realistic portraitures, and at other times, with the Haida, there was a sweeping baroque grandeur about its more ambitious examples; if we are to accept *Dionysian* as a reasonable analogical definition of Kwakiutl art, then the complementary adjective of *Apollonian* might as appropriately be applied to the art of the more northerly peoples, since it was a reflection of a social system that depended on the unchangeability of tradition, and yet — like Apollo himself — had its own areas of darkness.

At present it is of the northern tradition that I am writing; in the following chapter I shall discuss the social structure and ceremonial patterns that produced the somewhat different art of the Kwakiutl.

What strikes one immediately in trying to reach the roots of northern Coast Indian art is that there is very little in the way of a changing natural environment that might explain such a profound difference as existed during recent centuries — and perhaps long before — between the vigorous and competent artistry of the Tsimshian and the meagre artistry of the Salish. For, in most respects, the environments of the Salish and the Tsimshian were essentially similar. Both lived in temperate climates: the coastal regions around Prince Rupert, like those around Vancouver, are under the warming influence of the Japanese current, and over both of them the rain forest flourishes. The Salish had one great river, the Fraser, rich in salmon and sturgeon runs, but the Tsimshian had two great rivers, the Nass with its vast run of oolichan, or candlefish, whose oil production was the envy of the whole Coast, and the Skeena, where the salmon ran so abundantly that the Gitksan, one of the branches of the Tsimshian people, could maintain a lavishly endowed culture more than two hundred miles from salt water — the farthest inland probing of the Coast civilization. Across the waters of Hecate Strait from the mouths of the Nass and the Skeena, the archipelago of the Queen Charlottes balanced Vancouver Island lying across the Gulf of Georgia from the Fraser

The Haida village of Skedans, about 1880,
with housefront poles and memorial poles.

estuary; and the island-shielded and inlet-bitten Alaskan coast going northward repeated the coast going northward from the Fraser, with the main difference that at the very top end of Tlingit territory, around Yakutat Bay, the great glaciers of Mount Elias chilled the winter air so that the people had to dress in skins and wear moccasins like the Athapaskans inland over the mountains. And all the way from Puget Sound to Yakutat Bay the same natural abundance of animal life and forest cover prevailed, except that in the far north of the region the giant cedars vanished, so that the Tlingit above the Stikine had to rely on inferior woods like spruce for their houses and poles, and to import from the Haida their large canoes and their cedar bark fibre for textiles.

If one cannot explain the vigour of northern art by any dramatic change in the environment or in the kind of abundance it offered to the fisherman and the hunter and the Stone Age carpenter, it is equally impossible to give it an explanation in terms of the innate characters of the peoples involved. It is true that in physique the Haida and the Tlingit, and to a lesser extent the Tsimshian, were visibly different from the

Salish and the Nootka. They were taller by the rather striking average of four inches, and Haida warriors six feet tall were by no means uncommon. They were also somewhat paler in complexion than the peoples farther south; and Captain Dixon, more than a hundred and eighty years ago, commented on the delicate skins and red cheeks of the young Haida girls. But if these physical characteristics differentiated the northern tribes from the Coast peoples farther south, they did so only in a way that seemed to demonstrate the resemblances between the northern tribes and the Athapaskan interior peoples with whom, as I have already shown, legend and language seem to link at least the Haida and the Tlingit. Yet no basis at all for an artistic tradition of such splendour can be found in this relationship, since the Athapaskan peoples — especially the Sekani, Carriers, and Chilcotin, who inhabit the interior of British Columbia — have shown themselves among the least originative of North American peoples, whether in terms of visual art or of technological inventiveness.

There is indeed good reason to believe that the Tlingit and the Haida gained their matriarchal system of inheritance, and even the rudiments of their elaborate patterns of clans and crests, from the Déné group, for they share these basic elements with people of the stock — and particularly the Carriers and the Sekani — who still follow a fishing and hunting life in the interior. It is even possible that the Tsimshian, though belonging to a different language group, had lived so long in the area between the Rockies and the Coast Range that their social patterns had become adjusted to the regional norm even if they had not already been organized in matrilineal clan groups. Yet it is also evident that, whatever the Haida or the Tlingit or the Tsimshian brought with them to the Coast in the way of social innovations which they superimposed on the simple patrilineal patterns of the Old

Haida and other early Coast peoples, they did not bring with them the art by which we now know them best. It evidently developed on the Coast out of a special set of social circumstances, and those circumstances appear to have been involved in the opportunities which an unaccustomed economic abundance offered to those who wished to gain personal and group glorification within a clan society.

The art was in fact the ultimate efflorescence of that working upon each other of a surplus economy and a clan-dominated competitive value system that encouraged conspicuous display disguised as conspicuous generosity, and in the process liberated an extraordinarily widespread aesthetic capability. And so, though we can respond at first glance to the appeal of this art, to understand it we have to understand the society that produced it.

In material ways, except for the high art it produced, that society was basically similar to those of the Nootka and the Salish. The Gitksan, with their inland situation and the great mountain ranges and forests overlooking the Skeena, may have been more involved in trapping and hunting than most Coast peoples; the Haida, who had little game on their ice-razed islands, may have hunted for little but bear, and because of the shortness of their streams, have relied more on their rich catches of halibut and black cod than on salmon. But the essential basis of the culture still remained the produce of sea and river that could be caught in such abundance that it would ensure five months of productive winter leisure and, as a bonus, offer the means of trade to bring in from the peripheral regions the luxuries that heightened the quality of daily living, at least for the men of title, and enhanced the ingenuity of artistic production.

It is sufficient to give one example of the abundance that prevailed even in these northern waters: the great oolichan fishery of the Nass

A club used for killing fish. The Haida ornamented even quite commonplace implements.

River, controlled by the Coast Tsimshian and their Nishka cousins, which not only provided the Tsimshian peoples themselves with the nutritious relish that made all their winter dried food more palatable, but also gave them a surplus that made them rivals of the Tlingit and the Chinook among the great traders of the Coast.

The oolichan is a kind of smelt, *Thaleichthys pacificus,* about nine or ten inches long, which is so full of oil that when dried and placed upright it will justify its other name of candlefish by burning from snout to tail with something less than a hard gemlike flame. It runs in the Nass about the middle of March, and continues for about six weeks; a similar run exists in other rivers, including the Fraser, and the Stikine and Taku in Alaska, but the oolichan oil of the Nass has the same kind of reputation among Indian epicures as the caviar of the Caspian has among European gourmets; in flavour and clarity alike it is unexampled.

In aboriginal times, when the seal hunters announced the approach of the first shoals with their attendant crowds of gorging creatures — from killer whales down to harbour seals, and from eagles down to crows — the Tsimshian and the Nishka would hold their annual feasts of friendship and their peace dance to wipe out all mutual grievances, and having cast eagle's down on each other's hair, would be prepared for the

149

Killer whale motif on a hat made of spruce roots.

weeks of work that awaited them. As the fishing went on, people from other groups, particularly the Haida and the southern Tlingit, would appear, but they would be allowed only to watch and to trade, never to fish in the reaches belonging to the Tsimshian peoples.

Once the first oolichan had been welcomed reverently, with rites similar to those for the first salmon, the slaughter would begin and many methods would be used: the fish rake, whose use for catching herring among the Nootka we have already noticed; dip-nets; and an ingenious bag-net which seems to have been invented in fairly late times, not long before the European traders arrived, by a girl who had been watching a bullhead or sculpin swallowing fry. The bag-net in fact resembled a bullhead, having a wide mouth facing downstream and a narrowing body made of nettle fibres, with the end tied shut. When enough fish had crammed themselves into the bag, the wide end would be closed off, and the narrow end, trained into a canoe, would be opened to dump the catch. It is said that at the height of the runs a bag-net haul might run as high as two tons of fish.

Once caught, the fish were taken ashore in baskets and dumped into large pits where they were left for a few days to ripen — in other words, to rot — which it was thought helped to liberate the oil. Having passed the beaches of India where the curious fishy condiment known as Bombay Duck dries as it decomposes, I have at least some slight idea of the miasmic stench that must have hung over the river banks, to the delight of the Indians who thought of it as the smell of prosperity, and to the discomfort of early European travellers. To one of those travellers — no less than the celebrated missionary, William Duncan — we owe a description of the process of rendering which they followed, a description that does not lose in vividness because it betrays an active Victorian squeamishness:

> I found each house had a pit near it, about 3 feet deep and 6 or 8 inches square, filled with the little fish. I found some Indians making boxes to put the grease in, others cutting firewood, and others (women and children), stringing the fish and hanging them up to dry in the sun; while others, and they the greater number, were making fish grease. The process is as follows: Make a large fire, plant four or five heaps of stones as big as your hand in it; while these are heating fill a few baskets with rather stale fish, and get a tub of water into the house. When the stones are red hot bring a deep box about 18 inches square (the sides of which are all one piece of wood) near the fire, and put about half a gallon of the fish into it and as much fresh water, then three or four hot stones, using wooden tongs. Repeat the doses again, then stir the whole up. Repeat them again, stir again; take out the cold stones and place them in the fire. Proceed in this way until the box is nearly full, then let the whole cool, and commence skimming off the grease. While this is cooking, prepare another boxful in the same way. In doing the third, use, instead of fresh water, the liquid from the first box. On coming to the refuse of the boiled fish in the box, which is still pretty warm, let it be put into a rough willow-basket; then let an old

A painted Haida housefront, photographed by R. Maynard in 1884.

woman for the purpose of squeezing the liquid from it, lay it on a wooden grate sufficiently elevated to let a wooden box stand under it; then let her lay her naked chest on it and press it with all her weight. On no account must a male undertake to do it. Cast what remains in the basket anywhere near the house, but take the liquid just saved and use it over again, instead of fresh water. The refuse must be allowed to accumulate, and though it will soon become putrid and change into a heap of creeping maggots and give out a smell almost unbearable, it must not be removed. The filth contracted by those engaged in the work must not be washed off until all is over, that is, until all the fish is boiled, and this will take about two or three weeks. All these plans must be carried out without any addition or change, otherwise the fish will be ashamed, and perhaps never come again.

Some of the Indians actually used old canoes for the rendering of the fish and trod the mush, like grapes, before the final breast-pressing process began.

The Tsimshian and the Nishka always had a great surplus of oolichan oil, and this was traded up the Skeena to the Gitksan villages, whence it was carried on men's backs in leakproof wooden boxes over the grease trails to the peoples of the interior; they provided cinnabar, obsidian blades and hides in exchange, notably the elk skins which were either used in double ply for armour (two thicknesses could stop a stone-headed arrow) or as a jacket to wear under the quite elaborate armour of wooden slats, which the northern peoples used, often crowned by carved wooden helmets bearing the clan crests,

This frontlet for a Haida chief's diadem is made of maplewood and abalone shell.

At Haida feasts oolichan grease was offered in carefully carved and finished dishes.

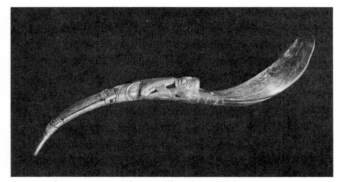

Spoons for ceremonial use—like this Haida spoon—were carved from the horn of the mountain goat.

in the same way as a mediaeval knight's casque would often wear the crest of his lineage. One of the Fort Simpson clans claimed the monopoly of the Skeena River grease trade, and its line of chiefs — the Legaics — became so rich that they began to arrogate to themselves the absolute and exclusive role of royalty in dealing with clan members and clan property, a role that did not come to an end until William Duncan with his threats of eternal damnation reduced the last of the Legaics to a quivering penitent.

The Haida, who had no oolichan runs in their islands but who consumed large quantities at their feasts as well as in daily living, would bring their great canoes to trade. The Haida canoes probably represented the technological as distinct from the aesthetic high point of northern craftsmanship, and in this region they enjoyed the same repute as Nootka canoes in the south. The Haida canoes were even more capacious and elaborate than those of the Nootka. The larger craft, used for transporting merchandise or for long-distance warfare, were made of giant cedars and some were seventy-five feet long, which meant that they were at least as long as some of the smaller vessels used by American traders. In beam they were often as much as seven feet, and this width, extraordinary for a dugout canoe, shows how skilfully they were stretched, after being hollowed by the adze. Such a canoe could carry forty men and two tons of freight. They were substantial enough to cross in relatively calm weather the considerable stretches of unsheltered water between the Queen Charlottes and the mainland channels, and would often travel down to Victoria for trading or make the eight-hundred-mile journey to Puget Sound for slave raiding. One of the Tlingit tribes, after their village had been bombarded by an American warship and their chief killed, actually made a revenge voyage in a Haida canoe down to Washington Territory, as it then was, killed and beheaded the local customs officer at Port Townsend in compensation for the death of their kinsman, and then set out for home.

As Norman Newton has suggested in *Fire in the Raven's Nest* (his study of the decline of the Haida culture under the impact of European pressures), such voyages through tortuous channels with many hidden perils from reefs and tide races, undertaken by people who did not belong to these waters and who had no charts, required a great deal of navigational skill (certainly as great as that of the Polynesian canoe voyagers) and probably a considerable astronomical knowledge. It seems likely that on such missions much of the voyaging would be done at night, and I would imagine that — like the Gilbert Islanders in the South Pacific — the Haida and the Tlingit knew how to navigate by the stars and perhaps by an accurate memory of the patterns of currents and the sets of tides transmitted by old men who had previously sailed the waters between Haida and Salish territory. When one considers that most anthropologists deny that sails were used in aboriginal times (though many Indian informants insist that sails of mats and of thinly split cedar planks were actually used before the white traders appeared) such long voyages are all the more remarkable.

In terms of design, the feature that made the Haida canoe so distinctive was that, while the Nootka added a separate and detachable prow piece, the Haida carved a separate stern piece as well, which contributed in the larger craft to a sweeping grandeur of line, always enhanced by the painted designs of the crests of the chiefs who owned them. However, most canoes were much smaller, craft of twenty to thirty feet long being used for ordinary travelling, and even smaller and lighter boats for fishing and for hunting seal and dolphin.

The great Haida canoes which took months to complete, and the well-organized co-operative toil during the oolichan runs, are only two examples which proclaim the great industriousness of the northern peoples. Like many primitive folk, they had a work ethic of their own, and few people were more despised than the lazy man who failed to do his share of the necessary work and relied for his food on the fact that the members of his household would never refuse him, because it would shame them unendurably if he were to go and ask for food at another of the houses belonging to his clan. Yet, like the peoples of many other nonurban cultures, the Coast Indians tended to relate their work to cyclic needs. When there was nothing urgent to be done, they relaxed and appeared to be idle; since the Victorian missionaries firmly believed that "Satan finds some evil still for idle hands to do," one of their first efforts — fortunately unsuccessful in the long run — was to turn the Indians (as Duncan did in his model Tsimshian settlement at Metlakatla) into imitations of model English workingmen, toiling diligently six days every week and worshipping just as diligently on Sunday. But even in pagan days, when there were important tasks in their proper seasons (like catching and preserving fish during the annual runs, or providing the means of comfortable shelter or transport, or preparing the goods needed for trade or for festivals), the northern Indians would work long hours without complaining, and they did it voluntarily, since the craftsmen — unlike the craftsmen of ancient Greece and Rome — were never slaves, nor were

153

The Gitksan village of Kitwancool in 1909 with the "Hole in the Sky" pole at the extreme left. Already the building structure had been influenced by European styles and the poles were standing free of the houses.

the hunters or fishermen with their sacred roles, but always honoured freemen, the relatives — albeit distant — of the chiefs; the slaves did only menial tasks.

Because of this attitude, life in the northern villages took on a relative opulence, compared not only with the peoples of the mountainous interior to the east but even with the southern Coast people, who did not have the same flair for converting abundance into a kind of elegance. Early travellers tended to complain of the untidiness of Nootka houses and to describe with condescension the ramshackle character of the great, rambling, Salish collective dwellings. But the houses of the northern peoples aroused mainly admiration.

It is true that the summer fishing villages were untidy places, since the processes that went on — like the rendering of oolichan already described, or the cleaning, drying, and smoking of salmon, or the preserving of clams — left a great deal of decomposing garbage, largely because of the taboos against disposing indiscriminately of the offal from animals who had been kind enough to allow themselves to be killed and eaten.

But the winter villages were a different matter. Food would be transported there in preserved form: the oil stored in flasks made of kelp bulbs; the dried salmon and halibut and black cod and herrings bundled or hung from the rafters among the wreaths of smoked clams; the dried fish roes and seaweed cake, the steamed and desiccated camas tubers, the slabs of dried salmonberries, salal berries, soapberries, the sheets of hemlock bark half-bread, all stuffed into great wooden chests; and the dried crab apples wrapped in leaves and stored in dry corners or preserved in fish oil. The canoes would be drawn up on the beaches and carefully covered against bad weather. And the people who had gone naked or at best covered with a coat of grease to foil the summer flies and mosquitoes (unless they were chiefs for whom it was shameful to be seen nude by slaves) would have assumed their winter garb, which for everyday outdoor wear meant sea otter skin, bearskin or even rabbit skin robes on a cold day and cedar bark raincapes and rain hats for wet weather, and indoors a togalike mantle of cedar bark weave for the men and a similar garment plus a kilt of the same material for women. (Except in the far north of Tlingit territory, none of the Coast peoples customarily used any footwear summer or winter, since the constant damp quickly rotted the buckskin moccasins that were obtained from the Athapaskans.)

What I have described is, of course, merely everyday garb. When festivals were called there was ceremonial garb, intended to display and to enhance the standing of every person taking part, and even when there were no festivals the heraldic ornamentations of the house where a man lived would reflect his pretensions.

Although there were local variations, the houses of the northern peoples were very similar in their general principles of design. They were all gabled houses, built of timbers hewn by stone or later iron adzes, and planks split by horn wedges from great trunks of red cedar. Philip Drucker, in his *Cultures of the North Pacific Coast* (1965), gives a description of the construction of a Tsimshian house which cannot be improved upon as a guide to the architectural principles according to which the gabled houses of the north were built:

Tsimshian chief in 1903, wearing Chilkat blanket and head-dress and surrounded by his ceremonial regalia.

Four square cornerposts were slotted to receive the 'plates,' or side beams. They also supported the paired plates that formed low gables at front and rear. Subsidiary posts, usually elaborately carved, supported the typical double ridgepole, and often still other posts and beams divided in span between the paired ridgepoles and the side-plates. Sills were morticed into the bases of the counterposts at front and sides; upper sill faces and the undersides of roof plates had matching slots into which planks were fitted vertically to form the walls. Roofing consisted of double rows of overlapping planks. An ingeniously suspended plank smokehole cover could be rotated on a horizontal axis to one side or the other of the central smokehole to keep out wind and rain.

Houses were a little more than square, fifty by fifty-five feet being average size and proportions. A central pit, approximately five feet deep and thirty feet square, formed the main living space, where women cooked at the central fireplace and people ate or lounged. One or more sets of steps led into the pit, which was usually lined with wide cedar-plank retaining walls. Some houses had narrow platforms around the principal pit, serving as subsidiary steps and benches. . . . The upper platform, at ground level, served for storage and for sleeping space.

On that level, at the end of the house facing the doorway (usually an oval hole in the portal post) there would be a cubicle of carved and painted wood where the chief and his immediate family would sleep. The other family groups in the house would usually improvise partitions out of the carved and painted boxes which held their personal belongings. Reed mats, cedar bark blankets and fur blankets would serve as bedding; cedar bark mats would be hung around the walls to keep out the draught; there would be cooking boxes, feeding dishes and other utensils scattered around the hearth of sand and stones in the centre of the house; but the only furniture in our sense of the word would probably by a wide seat with a carved back perched without legs on the edge of the platform, on which the chief would sit tailor-fashion like a Tibetan incarnate lama on his lion throne.

This form of house, which is also made by the central Coast peoples (Kwakiutl, Bella Coola, northern Nootka, and at least the Comox among the northern Salish) appears to have been very ancient in the region radiating from the Skeena River - Nass River triangle. Tsimshian and Gitksan legends both claim that such houses, called *da'aq*, already existed in the mythical land of Temlaham in those days before men had offended the animals and had brought upon themselves first of all the Flood and later the earthquake fury of the mountain goat spirits. The antediluvian houses of Temlaham were said already to have painted front walls and carved door posts with oval doorways, and two or more terraces below ground level. Indeed, some legends even tell of vast houses with ten such terraces where hundreds of chiefs could be feasted. No archaeological searches have yet discovered traces of ancient Temlaham, or indeed of any ancient destroyed villages in the area where Temlaham is most often thought to have existed beside the upper Skeena, but recent finds

around the harbour of Prince Rupert have revealed the sites of houses of the same shape and not far off the same size as the great houses of the northern peoples of historic times. Some of these house sites date back more than four thousand years, to about 2500 B.C.; the house style, perhaps in a simpler form, may be older in the area than the peoples originating in the interior mountains who were making such buildings when the first Europeans came.

Apart from the skilful way in which he would find everything made, considering the limited range of available tools, there are two things that would be likely to strike a stranger who might be carried back into such a house at about the time, two hundred years ago, when Perez encountered the Haida. He would, if he were a curious and open-minded man, learn sooner or later that the house had not been built by the man's own family or clan, but by people of his father's clan. (This would lead him to the discovery of the whole matriarchal system of inheritance by which the house would pass not to the chief's son, but to his oldest sister's son.) And he would notice that almost every object he picked up that had a workable surface would be carved or painted with designs that at first seemed bewilderingly various, but among which he would detect certain recurrent elements. These elements, he would soon find, represented the crests that belonged to his host or, to be more exact, that belonged to the house and were displayed by his host.

The Haida were especially devoted to this profligate use of crests. As Edward Sapir remarked more than sixty years ago, in an address delivered to the Royal Society of Canada in 1915, when the old Coast Indian order appeared to be completely moribund:

> Crests are shown or utilized in different ways. They may be painted on movable boards used as screens or otherwise, painted on the outside of the

house or along the bed platform, carved on the house-posts or beams, or on memorial columns, or on the outside house-posts popularly known as totem poles, tattooed on the body, painted on the face during feasts, represented in dance-hats, masks, staffs, or other ceremonial paraphernalia, woven in ceremonial robes, referred to in clan legends, dramatically represented at potlatches in performances based on such legends, referred to in songs owned by the clan or clan-chiefs, and in individual or house names. . . . So accustomed have the West Coast Indians, particularly those of the north, become to the representation of crest animals in carving and painting, that they reproduce them even in objects that are not as a rule connected with the exercise of privileges. Among such objects the beautifully decorated ornamented dishes, boxes, batons, spoons, rattles, clubbers and gambling-sticks that are so often admired in ethnological museums.

It is after his long — but still not entirely complete — list of the uses to which crests were put by Coast Indian artists at the request of their patrons, that Sapir makes a couple of remarks that seem to me of central importance to the subject:

> We see how the elaboration of the crest system has fostered among these Indians the development of plastic art. It has also been suggested, and I believe with justice, that the tendency to artistic and dramatic representation in turn reacted upon the development of the crest system, a development that was strengthened by the ever-present desire for new privileges and for novel ways of exhibiting the old ones.

Now the system of crests was, as Sapir suggests, most strongly developed among the three northern peoples of the Coast. It spilled down to the Kwakiutl and the Bella Coola, but was never as important in stimulating activity among them as the winter dance complex; it hardly appeared at all among the Nootka and the Salish. But among the Haida, the Tlingit, and all branches of the Tsimshian it was woven intimately into the whole pattern of social organization which characterized the matriarchal society of the north.

One can describe that society by beginning with the concrete and particular — the house and its inhabitants — or by beginning, as I shall do, with the general and nebulous, the great division of each northern people into a number of exogamous sections or, as the Indians sometimes called them, "sides." Some anthropologists have named them *moieties*, but that fits only incompletely, since although the Haida and the Tlingit had two divisions, Raven and Eagle, and Raven and Wolf respectively, the Tsimshian had four: Eagle, Wolf, Killer Whale, and Raven on the salt water, and Eagle, Wolf, Frog, and Fireweed among the Gitksan. Others have used the term *phratry*, applied to clan divisions in ancient Greece, but again the word is not exact. Drucker has preferred to use the word *clan*, but this again in simple terms is not entirely satisfactory, since the social unit we are talking about includes actual clans, which often have different or extra crests of their own and which are local units, whereas the so-called phratric system is so widespread that a Raven man of the Yakutat Bay Tlingit could not marry a Raven girl from the region of Ketchikan almost three hundred miles to the south, even though he had never seen her or her people and could not possibly have any close blood relationship with her. Perhaps, to avoid the inexactitude of *moiety* and *phratry* and the inadequacy of *clan*, the analogical situation of the extended family might be evoked to invent the term *extended clan*.

The extended clan had no formal existence in the sense of organization or structure. There were never any gatherings of all the Eagles or their representatives; there were no chiefs who spoke for the extended clan as a whole. Yet its existence was real and strong, in terms of the

Two Tsimshian carvings. The human figure (*left*) was probably used in shamanic rites. Its overt phallicism is unusual in Coast Indian art. The rattle (*above*) shows Raven with the moon in his mouth.

Eagle chief died among the Haida, it was the Ravens, his father's people, who would conduct all the practical arrangements for his funeral (just as Ravens had made his cradle when he was born) and later be rewarded at the memorial potlatch that his Eagle successor would give. When a Raven wanted a new house built, Eagle chiefs organized the craftsmen, and having taken formal responsibility, received presents at the house dedication feast and themselves paid off the workmen. Similarly, a Raven chief would take the nominal responsibility for carving and erecting an Eagle chief's pole, even though the actual work might be done — as everyone knew — by a famous carver of the region (sometimes even a carver outside the tribe, for many Tlingit poles were carved by Tsimshian craftsmen and a number of the finest Gitksan poles are by men from the Nass River). Finally, the duality created by the extended clan system provided perhaps the two most essential elements in a society given to conspicuous competition for honours — a set of permanent rivals and a set of permanent spectators. For, whenever to validate a privilege a chief of the Eagles gave a potlatch, his guests, if he were a Haida, would always be Ravens, and their witness would provide the validation.

Thus, the extended clan had a real existence

origin myths and migratory histories of the various extended clans, in the taboos that prevented marriage between their members, and, most positively, in the unwritten rules of reciprocity which meant that the two halves not only mingled through marriage but also supported each other in many functional ways. When an

but no organized existence. The clan, on the other hand, was a concrete and organized phenomenon. It consisted of a number of houses of the same "side" within a village, each containing an extended family related to the families in the other clan houses. There might be several Eagle clans within a village, each having its own crest or crests in addition to the eagle; Sapir quotes the case of a Haida Eagle clan at Skidegate which had six other crests: the mythical sea wolf, the dogfish, the weasel, the sculpin, the halibut, and, strangely enough, the raven crest of the opposite extended clan. Such subsidiary crests were generally regarded as having been obtained by ancestors of the clan of the house through spirit encounters, but the right to use them could also be obtained in other ways — through marriage, through mutual giving, or even by the extermination of a clan and the seizure of its crests in war.

There was an informal system of authority which emerged out of the house and clan organizations within a village, but it was a very loose kind of authority, for in few cases among the Coast peoples did the word "chief" in its ordinary sense really apply, and most of the languages had expressions that were very close to the Salish "real man." The head of a Haida extended family directed rather than owned the property of the house. It was he who apportioned the use of hunting and fishing grounds, who acted as custodian for the names and privileges that belonged to the house and transferred them to his relatives at appropriate feasts, who served as the ceremonial head of the extended family, displayed its house crests on appropriate occasions, and took every opportunity, through the right use of surplus goods accumulated by him and his kin, to enhance its standing in relation to other houses.

Within each clan group of several houses, the head of the most prestigious house became by

Kitwancool's "Hole in the Sky" pole is one of the oldest housefront posts still standing on its original site. It is at least ninety years old.

tacit recognition the clan chief, and within a village the heads of the various clans formed a kind of informal council, and the head of the wealthiest of them in material and immaterial goods became the village chief. Although, if it were a large village, the two "sides" might be visible in the arrangement of the houses in two rows — one for Ravens and one for Eagles or Wolves — there was no actual political structure of the extended clan within the village. The shadowy ladder of authority that did exist went from house to clan to village, which suggests that an exogamous division into two clans at village level was the original pattern, which became complicated as the original simple clans split by migration; significantly, house and clan names, as distinct from crests, often do not relate to patron spirits but to places of origin, some of which are identifiable locations in other parts of the Coast from those in which the villagers now live.

On a village level the roles of the clan and house chiefs were even slighter than in their own family groups, since no chief could interfere in the affairs of another house. Even trading was a matter for individual houses, since the accumulation of property for potlatches and other ceremonials depended on it, though there were occasions when local groups would co-operate to defend trade, as the Tlingit clans of the Chilkat tribe did in 1854 when they marched hundreds of miles inland to destroy a Hudson's Bay Company post on the Yukon — Fort Selkirk — which had been founded six years before and had been diverting much of their trade with the Athapaskan peoples. The Tlingit, in fact, were much more inclined to co-operate in any kind of warfare than either the Haida or the Tsimshian. They worked together on fortifying their villages in the early nineteenth century, and the Sitka tribe had a citadel inhabited by thirteen hundred people on a clifftop to which the only approach was by defiles in which log barriers had been placed to make access difficult. There was a double palisade of logs about fifteen feet high and three feet thick, and inside the palisades an earth embankment which protected the houses from shelling by warships. The organized aggressiveness of the Tlingit prevented the Russians from ever imposing their authority effectively over southeastern Alaska; the tribes fought several pitched battles against the intruders and in 1801 actually destroyed the Russian fort at Sitka, while ships trading in Tlingit waters took exceptional precautions against attack until well into the nineteenth century.

Traditional warfare tended to be a matter of clans rather than villages, and among the northern peoples themselves it was usually a matter of revenge for some real or fancied slur on the clan's honour. There was no impartial means of law enforcement and in fact no code of law among the Coast Indians; perhaps there were no concepts of justice or equity as we understand them. Crimes were actions that in some way or another harmed a clan, rather than an individual, and harm could include the causing of shame; it was for the harmed or shamed group to exact rectification rather than punishment. Where a member of one clan was killed or injured by a member of another clan, the *lex talionis* in its Indian form went into operation. A death must be wiped out by the death of a man of equal rank in the offending group; to punish the actual murderer was of less importance than to even the scores in terms of rank, and if a commoner killed a high-ranking chief, the offending clan must put up a man of equal standing for sacrifice.

If this form of settlement were agreed upon, it would be a ceremony of high drama, in which the chief who offered himself for death would come out of his house in full regalia, singing his crest songs and flourishing a club or spear; he would, however, only make a pretence of fighting and would allow the warrior chosen as executioner to kill him. A chief who made such a sacrifice was highly regarded, since he had died to redeem the honour of his clan; the actual murderer was not killed, but his position was considered so shameful that he became a virtual outcast. Lesser injuries than death, and offences against dignity, were usually settled by payment of *wergild*, and sometimes this was accepted even in the case of death, in which event the actual murderer might find himself handed over as a slave by his clan in part payment of the compensation.

Whichever way compensation was made, the end of the affair would be a peace dance at which gifts were exchanged and the past was regarded as erased. If, however, the offending clan refused to make any compensation, this was regarded as a *casus belli*, and the offended clan would watch its opportunity to make a surprise attack to even the score; since this usually meant that many more people were killed than was necessary in terms of strict compensation, the result would be the start of a vendetta that might continue for years. Usually such attacks were carried out by clan war parties, but there were times — if the chances of plunder seemed tempting — when a number of clans might unite in a larger expedition, though this did not happen as frequently among the northern peoples as it did among the Nootka. On such a war expedition the ordinary chief would usually delegate his authority to a war chief who would be a warrior by vocation, and the expedition would be accompanied by a shaman to recommend auspicious times and directions for the attack and to steal the souls of the enemy so that their bodies would be easier to kill.

There were certain other offences for which death was usually the penalty. Incest was one of them, and theoretically this meant any sexual relationship with a member of the same phratry or extended clan, no matter from what village he or she came. It would be the members of the offender's own clan who would act in this case, and usually also in the case of sorcery, which was almost always proceeded against on a shaman's accusation and ended with the presumed offender being tied up and left on a beach for the tide to drown or being strangled by having his neck pressed between two logs. Because of such

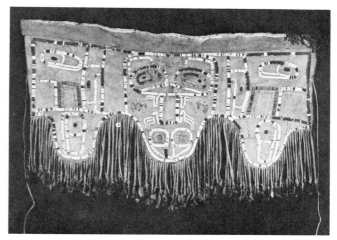

Caribou hide dance-apron with fringe of deer hooves.

powers, the shamans were much feared, particularly among the Tlingit, for not only could they bring the accusation of witchcraft, against which there was no effective defence, but they could — it was believed — steal one's soul or inject sickness into one. In addition, shamans in this region often assumed an almost political role by acting as advisers and agents of the chiefs, and thus they added magic to temporal power. Although there were a few chiefly shamans, most were of commoner rank, and it was only in alliance with the chiefs that they could play a part in the system of authority as it developed among the northern peoples.

Neither among the Tlingit nor among the Haida, nor among the Tsimshian was there any clearly established form of political organization beyond the clan and the village. Haida villages acted as completely autonomous units (in so far as they had any internal unity, which did not always happen) and the Tlingit villages were often at war with each other. Certainly nothing like the Nootka confederacies, in which one chief enjoyed a kind of paramountcy as hereditary ceremonial head and spokesman of the league, existed anywhere in the north, though certain

A Tsimshian *amhalait*, or chief's head-dress ornament, from the Nass River.

tem, by the time the anthropologists began to take notice of it, had certainly been affected by the gathering together of the nine lower Skeena villages (a good two-thirds of the Tsimshian people) at Fort Simpson, which became a veritable town of four thousand people, undoubtedly the largest settlement to exist in historic or prehistoric times among the Coast Indians. The chiefly ranks within the former villages, with which everyone was familiar, were disrupted by this gathering of the clans in which there were scores of people of noble rank with prestigious names and crests who had to be worked into the pattern for the mass potlatches that began to be held. In the attempt to sort out the relative ranks of every claimant, there is no doubt that some chiefly lineages rose far higher than they would have done in their own small villages, and arrogated to themselves a kind of royal rank; they were supported in this by the tendency that arose among the Tsimshian, once they had gathered together at Fort Simpson, to think of themselves as a nation in a way they had never done before, a development that did not happen among the more remote Nishka and the Gitksan, who remained in their villages and maintained an almost ferocious local autonomy.

In any case, it must never be forgotten that the ranking system which played so great a part in the thoughts of the northern peoples was ceremonial rather than political. It was not a matter of class in the European sense or of caste in the East Indian sense. Nobody except a slave could be an outcaste, since, in theory at least, all the people who lived in a house were blood relatives and all the members of one clan in a village were in some remoter way kinsfolk. It was because of such tenuous links that in the later nineteenth century, when the smallpox plagues had destroyed many chiefly families, people who were generally regarded as commoners were able, once they had gathered enough goods to give the

lineages among the Coast Tsimshian enjoyed a degree of prestige outside their clans and their villages that led early authorities to talk of a "royal" class among the Tsimshian, in some way higher than the "noble" class they had detected among other peoples.

The ranking system did indeed become extremely complex among the Tsimshian, and there are said to have been two houses so exalted that to avoid marrying beneath themselves the chiefs of one clan always married the chiefs' sisters of the other clan, and vice versa. However, the peculiarities of the Tsimshian ranking sys-

necessary potlatches, to lay claim to vacant titles and very often to be accepted. It makes good sense, then, to discard the concept of a rigid class stratification of nobles and commoners, and to think of Coast Indian societies as pyramids of rank, with nobody exactly equal to anybody else because everyone's collection of names and privileges was somewhat different from his neighbour's. The gap between those at the top and those at the bottom was evident, but once one had descended below the chiefs and their heirs, the great middle ground became nebulous, and younger nephews or cousins of the chief were hardly distinguishable in the respect they commanded from the commoners who had their own special prestige as carvers, canoe makers, shamans, or warriors. Indeed, such commoners might themselves very well be the grandnephews or younger nephews of chiefs, too distant in normal times to be regarded as noble, but never too distant to have a claim in times of disaster.

It was as the great testing ground for pretensions to rank that the potlatch assumed one of its main functions in the northern societies, and so much depended on what was seen at the potlatch through the vital and vigilant eyes of witnesses (which was the formal function of the guests) that it is probably best to attempt some kind of visual imaging of what happened at such times.

A chief might decide to hold a potlatch for a number of reasons, though in every case the exhibition of privileges and the validation of titles to them would be involved. The importance attached to specific types of occasions varied among the three northern peoples, the Tlingit having a special preference for the mortuary celebrations following the death of a great chief. But the most common occasions for a potlatch were: the giving of ceremonial names to children (the names were possessions of the house, and one Gitksan house — to give an example — pos-

Two Gitksan women of Kitwanga in ceremonial dress.

sessed thirteen chiefly names and thirty-eight names of lesser importance); the puberty celebrations of girls, usually accompanied by piercing the ears and lips for rings and labrets; the ceremonial depositing of the ashes or bones of a dead chief; the erection of a memorial or heraldic pole, which among some groups took place four years after a chief's death and served to restate claims to crests and legends; and a new chief's assumption of his predecessor's rank, name, and privileges. In aboriginal times potlatches appear to have been given at quite long intervals, and a chief who could add seven rings to his crest hat to celebrate an equivalent number of potlatches was thought to have fulfilled his obligations adequately. Indeed, because of the trouble and expense involved, a great potlatch would be used for many subsidiary purposes, such as the granting of minor titles and privileges, and the naming and ear-piercing of the children of lesser clan members, all of which would be regarded as having been validated by the feasts and gifts provided for the major occasion.

Before a chief decided to hold a potlatch, he would gain the co-operation not only of his house kin, but also of the houses of the same clan and of other clans within his village belonging to the same phratry or extended clan. The guests would be members of the opposite clans, and if it were a major potlatch, chiefs from other villages would also attend. Once the time for the festival had been settled, the chief's messengers — usually his nephews — would go out, weeks before the date. They would paddle to the beach of the strange village, wearing ceremonial dress and carrying carved orators' staffs, and as soon as they were noticed they would shout out their message, so that it immediately became public. Then they landed and were taken to the house of the invited guests, where they were kept for several days, being feasted and repeating their invitation until it was accepted. No chief ever declined a potlatch invitation; that would have been an unpardonable insult. But it was thought undignified to accept immediately, and every important chief expected to be asked several times.

If the guests came from distant villages, they would set out in good time, since to be late for a potlatch was another great offence. They would usually camp a short way from the potlatch village on the night before the feast began, so that they could put on ceremonial dress. In the morning they would paddle up in their great painted war canoes, with the masked chiefs performing their crest dances in the bows and the paddlers singing their songs. Before landing, the visiting dignitaries would make speeches lauding their hosts, and the latter would reply with welcoming dances and orations. Then the guests would step ashore, in European times to the firing of muskets and in early days to the beating of planks and drums.

As the visiting chiefs entered the house of their host, the dress they displayed would begin with a kind of diadem, with a frontlet of finely carved maplewood inlaid with abalone and bearing the face of a man — sometimes with a bird's beak — or the figure of an animal, and intended to portray the clan's most potent guardian spirit, in human, semihuman, or animal form; a fillet of cedar bark — reddened for sacredness — would hold the frontlet in place, and the crown would be garnished with ermine skins hanging down to the shoulders and a ring of upright sea lion whiskers, which during dances or at other crucial points of the ceremonial held a mass of white eagle's down that the movements of the chief scattered among his guests or hosts as an earnest of peace or friendship. Among the Tlingit these diadems were often replaced by conical wooden crest-hats, also decorated with shell, ermine, and sea lion whiskers.

The chief's main garment would probably be one of the elaborately beautiful Chilkat blankets, invented by the Tsimshian but in historical times made only — and very laboriously — by one group of the Tlingit who had access to a supply of the necessary mountain goat wool. Boldly executed by women weavers from man-designed pattern boards, the designs of the Chilkat blankets showed in black, white, green, and yellow the crest animals and birds of the particular chief, their identifiable features broken up and rearranged to make a pattern filling the whole pentagon of the blanket, which was really a deep-fringed ceremonial cape, often accompanied by a dancing apron designed in the same way and fringed with rattling deer hooves. In post-contact times Chilkat blankets became very scarce, and chiefs would often have to be content with button blankets, made of blue or red broadcloth (and often of both united in appliqué patterns) and decorated with pearl buttons sewn on in such a way as to represent the appropriate crest or crests; with such a blanket, the dance apron would often be fringed with tiny metal bells or with thimbles crowded together to give a tinkling sound. Every chief carried in his hand, almost as a sign of office, a bird rattle, carved out of two pieces of wood which were bound together after small stones had been placed in the hollow; the finest of these were the intricately-carved raven rattles made by the Tsimshian, which were in demand everywhere on the Coast.

As the guests in their regalia entered the potlatch house, a speaker with his staff awaited them inside the oval doorway: a man knowledgeable in the titles and genealogies of the Coast, since he must call without error the ceremonial name of each guest. The host chief would stand at the top of the house, in front of a screen carved with his crests, and invite the guests to be seated where they "always belonged." Then an usher, usually one of the chief's nephews, would lead the guest to the seat allocated to him. This was always a tense moment, since where a man sat reflected on his rank relative to the other guests, and the host had to take into account not only hereditary standing, which was fixed, but potlatch standing, based on patterns of giving, which fluctuated. A chief shown to a wrong seat would protest, and if it had been a mistake the host could placate him with a small gift and a more honourable place; but if the mis-seating appeared to be deliberate, such as a place in the corner of the room for a high chief, then it was an insult, and the offended guest would depart in anger and a vendetta might very well ensue to wipe out the insult.

Assuming that there were no hitches at this early stage, the potlatch would usually continue for four days, the generally accepted minimum, though generous chiefs would keep their guests for a week or more. Every day there would be speechmaking, carried on in the elaborate and redundant Coast style of oratory, and there would be feasting, with the younger brothers and the classificatory nephews of the host chief (i.e. all the male relatives of the same age group in the house) serving the guests. Dried salmon would be toasted before the great fire in the centre of the house and offered on individual wooden dishes, the highest-ranking guest always being served first. Oil would be provided to dip the fish in, and then would follow other courses, often brought on in gigantic feast dishes shaped as crest animals or birds. There would be shellfish of various kinds, seaweed, fish roes, and berries in oil, the meal usually ending with a kind of foamy mousse made from snowberries whipped up in oil and flicked into the mouth with a special flat spatula. Carved spoons of wood, or mountain goat and mountain sheep horn, would be used in eating some of the other courses. Nobody was excluded from this feasting, and the houses would be packed to partake of the host's generosity, but the women and the children were expected to remain inconspicuous and silent; a matrilineal society is not necessarily a matriarchy, and women did not often play ceremonial roles among the Coast Indians.

On the first day, the host clan would perform its dances, to the tune of box drums and of boards raised above the ground and beaten with batons. The masks of the dancers would reproduce the house crests, and the songs and actions would tell the legends of how they were acquired. On the second day there might be similar dances by the guests, displaying their crests. Later, as the potlatch went on, there would be actual dramatic performances, miming the supernatural experiences of the host clan, in which a variety of elaborate masks would be used, some of them — especially among the Tsimshian — characterized by a kind of inspired realism and obviously meant as portraits, and others being transformation masks which would split apart at some crucial time in the miming performance (accompanied always by drumming and the appropriate songs) to reveal the humanoid spirit behind the original animal face. Like most American Indians, those of the Coast were given to mimicry, and often these dramas of ancestral spirit quests would be interspersed with comic performances in which the dances represented the despised peoples of the interior, or the Coast Salish, or, in historic times, the European intruders, towards whom the attitudes of the Coast peoples were curiously ambivalent, compounded of admiration, envy, and mockery. The potlatches would also be occasions for conjuring competitions between shamans, who took advantage of the fitful lighting provided by the central fire to perform sleight-of-hand tricks, and who seem, on occasion, to have undertaken some of those extraordinary feats of mind controlling flesh, like walking through burning embers, which we now know — from evidence gathered in many parts of the world — can in fact be performed by people in a state of ecstasy.

A potlatch, in other words, was first-rate entertainment, and the hosts probably paid as much attention to the quality of their food and the ingenuity of their dramatic inventions as they did to the proper exhibition of their crest privileges. Nevertheless, there was always the serious business of the occasion to be gone through, the ritual acts to be performed, the privileges to be asserted, the names and titles to be assumed, and the status to be implied, all before witnesses whose acquiescence served as a validation. On the fourth day, or whatever the last day might be if the feasting was prolonged, would come the culmination of the potlatch, the presentation of the gifts.

If the honour of the guests was at stake at the beginning of the potlatch, now it was the honour of the host that was to be judged by a company of ceremonial experts. Once the order of seating was accepted, the order of receiving gifts was established, which meant automatically that as the host chief stood beside the gifts piled at the head of the house, or — better still — out on the beach because the house could not contain them, the guest with the best seat received the biggest gift and so on down the chain of rank to the commoners who received some tiny present, perhaps even only the fragment of a blanket, because they too acted as witnesses in validating the privileges claimed by the host. As long as the guest received his gifts in the right order, and received more than anyone below him in rank, he did not suffer in any way. It was the host's reputation, not the guest's, that was imperilled when gifts were too small and the potlatch was not one of those that resonate in men's memories. His hereditary privileges, indeed, had been validated by witnessing and giving, but in a subtle way the prestige of his crests and his clan would be diminished; one encounters constant references in the lore of the northern Coast peoples to crests that were once potent but lost their power and sank into being the lesser crests of houses related to the original one.

The potlatch ended, always, in a curiously but perhaps symbolically unceremonious way. As the nephew-ushers under the chief's direction presented the gifts, the guests feigned indifference, and allowed their kinsmen to accept on their behalf. Then they bundled everything into their canoes and started for home; this time there were no speeches, no dances, no songs of departure to match the songs of welcome. The purposes of the potlatch had been fulfilled; to dwell on them would be to invite misfortune. Like the ancient Greeks, the Coast Indians before history had a lively sense of the perils of *hubris*. So the guests sailed away without departing songs, and the house was left stripped of its material wealth, yet — if the potlatch had been well managed — enhanced in reputation.

Out of this society, dominated by concepts of rank and symbolic privilege, emerged the art of the northern peoples which in the first century or so after the arrival of the Europeans was produced on such a copious scale that, reflecting on all the great collections which exist in Europe and North America, one can only be astonished at the productivity of the small population — much less than a hundred thousand in the 1770s and falling rapidly throughout the nineteenth century — that made all these extraordinary artifacts. And I use the word *extraordinary* with deliberation, because an ordinary work of Coast Indian art hardly exists; the carvers of masks and rattles and poles and shamans' puppets were craftsmen highly conscious of their spirit-blessed role, and though they worked within what seemed from the outside to have been narrow conventions of design and execution, they retained the individuality of vision of true artists and never made two works — or at least two good works — that were exactly alike.

The art of the three northern peoples and that of the central Coast peoples — the Kwakiutl and the Bella Coola — have indeed a great deal in common, and there are times when it is difficult, without some exact knowledge of provenance, to distinguish a northern Kwakiutl from a Tsimshian piece. Yet there are certain inclinations in which the two areas differ, and the principal of these — a great expressionism of manner among the Kwakiutl and at the same time a great emphasis on three-dimensionality — tend to react upon each other. The Haida carver, for example, when he is making a feast dish which commemo-

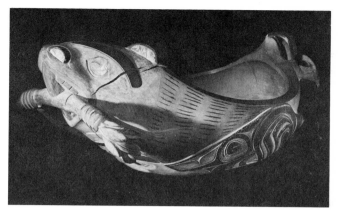

The movement of a swimming beaver is effectively captured in this Tsimshian food dish.

rates the house crest, will tend to apply the crest in relief to an object whose round or oval shape has already been determined, whereas the Kwakiutl will make a sculpture of the animal and adapt it for use as a bowl. Similarly, in the case of the northern poles, even though the carving may be deep and bold, as it often is in Haida work, the semicircular shape of the pole contains the design within its curving surface, except that occasionally some prominent feature, like the beak of a raven, eagle or hawk, or the fin of a killer whale, may project frontally. The Kwakiutl tend to be concerned more with the form to be represented in its own three-dimensionality, to sculpt deliberately beneath the original surface curves of the material, and to add freely in all directions, with wings and limbs of considerable dimensions often dowelled onto the main sculpted block of wood; in carvings like the Kwakiutl thunderbirds the idea of applying design to an existing natural form has completely vanished, and what we perceive is an autonomous sculptural creation expressing an imaginary vision.

Such autonomous creations were not of course entirely absent from the arts of the northern peoples, particularly the Tsimshian, so that once one has made a few general remarks about

167

Gitksan pole at Kispiox.

the northern style, it is possible to divide its products into various categories according to formal character but also largely according to purpose.

Essentially the art was figurative without being representational in a naturalist manner; it was not an abstract art in the conventional sense, nor was it based on geometrical forms, in spite of the fact that the artists were highly conscious of geometrical spaces and the need for designs to be adapted to them. All forms were based on nature and derived from human beings, animals, and birds, or from mythical beings which, like the heraldic animals of mediaeval Europe, often combined the characteristics of one or more animal species. Plant forms were rarely used, and what often appear to the uninitiated observer as geometrical shapes are usually stylized natural forms, like the rectangles with rounded corners which by convention sometimes represent eyes and sometimes joints. The subject matter of the northern art was limited; most often it was the crest animals that were represented, though the poles and often the big house-end screens favoured by the Tlingit would represent adventures of ancestors with mythical or magical beings; since the tales were not general knowledge but the property of the clans, and the carvers were taken into the confidence of the chiefs who erected the poles, it is not always easy even for a modern Indian to interpret the poles.*

The task of interpretation is complicated by the fact that each animal or being has its recognized attributes and need not be represented by more than one of them: the beaver, for example,

* Indispensable sources of many of the stories connected with the poles are the two books which Marius Barbeau prepared, after long journeys on the Coast, for the National Museum in Ottawa, *Totem Poles* (two volumes) and *Totem Poles of the Gitksan*. Barbeau's speculations on the recent origin of pole carving are unconvincing, but the explanations of the iconography which he collected are invaluable for our understanding of the poles,

by his broad tail (or merely some cross-hatching to suggest it); the killer whale by his dorsal fin; the raven by his straight beak. Such economical representation was only one aspect of a general willingness to distort or dismember an animal form in any number of ways, so long as the crest still remained recognizable to the initiate. As I have already suggested, the general concept of dismemberment, like the concept of transformation embodied in some of the masks and the concept of penetrative vision embodied in designs in which the internal structure of animals was made visible, derived ultimately from shamanistic doctrines; these artistic features are to be found in many parts of the world where shamanic cults exist. What distinguishes the Coast Indians is their adaptation of these practices for purely formal purposes. Thus, one often sees the double profile of a wolf joined by the feet to fill the square side of a box, or a bear split down the middle like a kipper and spread out on either side of his backbone to cover a pentagonal house front, or a raven distorted out of all recognizable shape, except that his beak and talons can usually be recognized in the pattern, so as to fill the curved space of a conical crest hat. At other times — and this is always the case in the Chilkat blankets and often so in carved and painted screens — a pattern may be created entirely out of various detached members of an animal arranged symmetrically over the given surface. Added to these practices, which in obvious ways anticipate the methods of modern western painters (like Picasso in Europe and Shadbolt in Canada), there are other symbolic

Among the Tlingit the bones of the dead were preserved in elaborately painted boxes.

devices which complicate the carvings of the northern Coast peoples; for example, wisdom or potency may be suggested by placing conventionalized faces where eyes or genitals would normally be carved, or in the palms of hands.

It is possible to make a distinction in the work of northern artists — which will become more pronounced when we reach the Kwakiutl — between work done for heraldic purposes to perpetuate the crests of clans and houses, and work done for dances and for shaman's regalia. The dances were either those performed at potlatches to present clan or house legends, or performed at the winter ceremonials of the so-called secret societies. The secret society rituals of the northern peoples appear to have been acquired from the northern Kwakiutl by chiefs who changed them into new privileges (so that initiations too became house possessions determined by heredity), and they did not assume the kind of semiautonomous modifying role in the culture which they did among the Kwakiutl. But they did produce a wealth of artifacts, mainly masks, and the demands of dancers and shamanic ritualists created a style in the north that in an almost literal sense was a magic realism.

as well as preserving a great many of the fascinating ancestral tales that were passed on from generation to generation during the winter nights in the great houses. A more elaborate formal analysis of Coast Indian art styles than is possible in the present book is given by Bill Holm in *Northwest Coast Indian Art: An Analysis of Form* (1965).

Tlingit grave house. Funeral ceremonials formed an important part of Tlingit ritual life.

What one notices about the crest-dominated type of art among the Coast Indians is the essentially conservative framework within which the artist operated, even though he did so with a versatility that made every good work a unique piece. It was a framework, an iconographically defined concept of form, that was extraordinarily adaptable so that the handle of a horn spoon, less than two inches long, will contain the same figures in the same proportions to each other as a pole forty feet high, and yet the aesthetic effectiveness of the work is not diminished by the extreme diminution of scale. But the fact remains that the artist who specialized in crest paintings and carvings worked in a limited range of recognized symbolic forms and followed closely the requirements of a chiefly patron.

The carver of masks and ritual objects, on the other hand, was expected to display originality and ingenuity, which seem to have been regarded as signs of inspiration, of possession by spirits of special potency. The standing of the carver of masks was, for this reason, often considerably higher than that of the pole carver. The Tsimshian, for example, divided their carvers into the *ukgilyae*, who made only secular objects linked with the crest complex, and the revered *gitsontk*, who carved the masks within which, during their performances — whether commemorating clan legends or performing secret society rituals — the dancers were held actually to become the beings they represented. Many of these masks, representing mythical beings, were works of sheer fantasy, while those that projected the everlasting Coast theme of transformation, were often mechanically ingenious. At the same time, perhaps the most remarkable of the Tsimshian masks remain the delicately carved pieces, realistic and imaginative at the same time, which were intended as portraits.

The tools and techniques the artists used were simple: an elbow adze for rough-hewing the piece; a D-adze for the finer cutting, which for better control was always done towards the carver; curved knives and sharpened beaver teeth for the finer details; bone drills where holes were needed; fine sandstone or sharkskin for ultimate smoothing; stone mortars to mix vegetable and mineral colours into a kind of fish-egg tempera; diagonally cut brushes of bristles and vegetable fibres. The artists were quick to adopt Western materials where they might be incorporated into existing ways, such as iron for tools and the more brightly coloured paints provided by the traders, but the techniques and even the tools remained the same, iron being merely substituted where stone was once used. For some of the more conventionalized shapes, like the ovoids and the blunted rectangles that appear so often as space fillers, the artist might use little stencils of birch bark, but the line he then painted would fluctuate so eloquently in thickness that there seemed nothing mechanical about the final result; and the design as a whole, though it usually seemed to fit its space with almost mathematical exactitude, would be applied directly to the surface to be decorated, without the use of rulers, compasses, or any mechanical aid, and without any independent sketch being used as a model. This kind of direct application of a design, which the artist seems to conceive spontaneously and to hold in his mind all the time he is working, is vouched for by many observers of Coast Indian artists at work, in the present days of the culture's revival no less than in the past. It is an aspect of a happy combination of mechanical capability and aesthetic precision that can perhaps best be understood if we end with an illustrative example: the making of one of the wooden boxes which were among the technological triumphs of the Coast culture and of which the Haida probably made the finest examples.

The artist-craftsman who set out to make a box would take a thin cedar plank large enough to form the four sides of the box he planned; he would trim and smooth it with adze and abrasives to the right size, shape, and thickness. At three points he would cut across it a V-shaped groove or kerf. Then the plank would be steamed until it could be bent at the three corners. The ends of the plank, which would come together to form the fourth corner, would be bevelled and then joined either by neat spruce-root stitches or with pegs. A solid bottom would be prepared and slotted so that the box could be fitted in and pegged into place. In the more elaborate boxes, for storing precious items, a lid would also be supplied. Well-made boxes often fitted so neatly that no caulking was needed even if they were used for storing somewhat fluid substances. All this was done without squares or measuring instruments, and afterwards the artist would proceed with his decoration in paint or in low relief, or sometimes in both, with equal disdain of intermediary preparations and equal sureness of eye. It is hard to think of a people in whom the natural aesthetic sense was so abundantly existent, and stimulated rather than curbed by the presence of controlling formal conventions.

Masked dancers of the Kwakiutl winter ceremonial.

CHAPTER NINE

The Winter Dancers

The Kwakiutl are a scattered group of tribes speaking related dialects and possessing certain cultural similarities that distinguish them from other peoples of the Coast. The word *Kwakiutl*, meaning "beach on the other side of the river," in fact applies strictly only to a single group, one of the four tribes from northeastern Vancouver Island who came together in a very loose confederacy when Fort Rupert was founded in 1849; but the name of this group, which attained the highest rank in the joint ceremonials at Fort Rupert, has been universally adopted by non-Indians to describe all the linguistically related peoples. Apart from northern and northeastern Vancouver Island, these peoples inhabit the deep coastal inlets from Bute Inlet in the south up to Douglas Channel. More than two hundred miles as the raven flies separate the northernmost group, the Kitimat, from the Euclataw at Campbell River, and through the tortuous channels of the Inland Passage by which canoes must travel the distance is much greater. Kwakiutl territory includes few stretches of ocean beach, like those of the Nootka or the Haida, and it contains no rivers as important as the Fraser, the Skeena, or even the Bella Coola have been to other Coast peoples.

So, essentially, the Kwakiutl were a people of salt-water channels, of the deep fjords where mountains meet water that are so characteristic of the coastal regions of British Columbia north-ward from Burrard Inlet. Yet, strangely enough, the Kwakiutl believed that they lived on the shores of a great river. The extraordinary tidal currents that flow in their territory may have been partly responsible for such a belief, which hauntingly echoes the ancient Greek concept of the River of Ocean; but it may also give us at least a hint of Kwakiutl origins, a suggestion that they came to the Coast by way of a river, and applied a concept to which they were accustomed to the otherwise somewhat incomprehensible behaviour of the tidal currents in the channels on which they lived, in comparison with the more open seas they encountered travelling between Queen Charlotte Strait, which divides Vancouver Island from the mainland, and Fitzhugh Sound which is the southernmost entry into the Inland Passage. If they did come originally by river, the Fraser seems the obvious possibility, and this reinforces the theory, based on linguistic similarities, that the Kwakiutl and the Nootka are related, however distantly, to the Salish; the resemblances between aboriginal Kwakiutl and Salish styles, and the evident links between the guardian spirit quest and the Kwakiutl winter ceremonials seem to reinforce such speculations.

However, the migration must have been far enough in the past to leave no trace in the memory or the myths of any of the Kwakiutl peoples, who regard their territory as their primeval home, and trace their origins through the

173

numayms or lineages (the word means roughly "one kind") to mythical ancestors who, as Boas puts it, "appeared in a specific locality by coming down from the sky, out of the sea, or from underground, generally in the form of an animal, took off his animal mask, and became a person."

As they appear in history, the Kwakiutl are divided into three fairly distinct language groups. The Southern Kwakiutl inhabited Vancouver Island and the mainland coast and intermediate islands between Bute Inlet and Smith Inlet. On Rivers Inlet lived a somewhat isolated intermediate group called the Wikeno. North of them, speaking a markedly different dialect from the true Kwakiutl, were the Heiltsuk, or the Bella Bella, and still farther north, in Douglas Channel, were the Haisla, whose language, it has been said, stands in about the same relation to Southern Kwakiutl as English does to Dutch. Obviously there must have been many centuries of separation to bring about such a considerable difference in speech patterns.

Kwakiutl territory bordered on that of a number of peoples, and certainly in historic times — and probably long before — there were cultural spills from one area to another. The Haisla had once held coastal territory almost as far as the Skeena, but the Tsimshian pushed down so far as to establish control of the seaward end of Douglas Channel; and even in the territory remaining to the Haisla, the intermingling of the two peoples must have been considerable in the centuries before European contact, since the names of the two major villages, Kitimat and Kitlope, are Tsimshian rather than Haisla. To the south, Kwakiutl territory marched with that of the Nootka on western Vancouver Island and the Coast Salish on both the island and the mainland; and here, in historic times, the Euclataw, the southernmost and perhaps the most warlike of Kwakiutl tribes, pushed south into Salish territory and established villages at Cape Mudge and Campbell River. To the east, a considerable enclave was cut into Kwakiutl territory by the presence of the Bella Coola, the Salish-speaking people with a very interesting culture of their own who inhabited the valleys of the Bella Coola and Dean rivers and the shores of salt water on Dean Channel and North Bentinck Arm, which they held somewhat precariously, under constant threat of raids by the Bella Bella. Since they were so closely linked regionally and culturally with the Kwakiutl, I shall discuss the Bella Coola at the end of this chapter.

Outside influences, it should be emphasized, may have been strong on the edges of Kwakiutl territory, but many of the villages were far up protected inlets, which was one of the reasons why the Kwakiutl as a whole came under direct European influence less early than people like the Nootka, the Haida, and the Tlingit. The first Europeans to encounter them appear to have been Vancouver and his men, though by the time he reached them in 1792 they had already received European goods by Indian trading routes and were quite obviously aware of the existence and the mortality of white men. The people who lived in the remoter villages up the long inlets had few European visitors and even few visits from other Indian peoples until comparatively late in the nineteenth century; and in winter, even during the present century, the most distant villages were so cut off that illegal potlatches were regularly performed in them without fear of visits from police or the Indian Agents. While none of the Kwakiutl at any time in the nineteenth century was quite so free from interference as the Gitksan, who were not visited by Europeans until the first Hudson's Bay Company trader appeared in the later 1860s, it is fair to say that Kwakiutl culture remained reasonably unaffected by outside influences until after 1849, when Fort Rupert was established.

Up to now I have been writing of the

Kwakiutl as if they were in some sense united, and both culturally and linguistically they were indeed, to use their own term, "of one kind," but without being in any true way homogeneous, since customs and ceremonials varied considerably within the Kwakiutl area. There was also a substantial amount of intermarriage between the various groups, Haisla, Heiltsuk, and Kwakiutl, motivated largely by the desire to acquire ceremonial privileges that had the effect of enhancing one's rank. But there was never any kind of political unity among people who spoke the various Kwakiutl dialects, or even among people who spoke the same dialect, and when their villages did go to war (which seems to have happened less often than their avowed esteem for the warrior virtues might suggest) it was almost as likely to be against another Kwakiutl village as against the Bella Coola or the Salish, though the Euclataw were certainly tempted by the passivity of the Salish to attack them rather frequently in furtherance of the slave trade that they carried on with the northern peoples.

Except in the special post-contact situation of Fort Rupert, with its loose confederacy of peoples, the largest political unit among the Kwakiutl was the village, which, according to the estimates that Boas made, comprised in aboriginal times between five and eight hundred people. The winter site of the village would often give its name to the tribe that inhabited it, and there would be a degree of co-operation between the six and eight numayms of which the village consisted. Often that co-operation would extend to warfare, but it was most clearly displayed during the winter ceremonial season, the season known as Tsetseka, which one Kwakiutl chief has interpreted as meaning "Everything is not real."

During Tsetseka, when the people abandoned their ordinary work-season names of spring and summer (the Bakoos season), the structure of the numayms, with their normal system of ranking, would be replaced by the rule of the secret dancing societies and the officials who controlled their traditional protocol. In practice this did not mean a great shifting of power, since the men and women who assumed prominent roles in the dancing societies had to be wealthy enough to make the lavish gifts needed at initiation, which meant that they would probably be the high-ranking people, who in their normal season guises enhanced their rank by the giving of potlatches and the purchase of privileges through marriage. But it did mean that for one season of the year the Kwakiutl villages were under at least a kind of unified government, and there is no doubt that the all-village involvement, either as initiates or as spectators, in the winter dances — where the ceremonial ranking structures cut right across the numaym structures — made for greater village unity than existed among most of the other Coast peoples.

The numayms themselves were groups of kinsmen arranged according to hereditary rights over positions of ceremonial standing. It is possible that at one time the numayms may have originated as no more than extended families (though Boas suggested that they in fact represent the fragments of archaic village groups), but by historical times they had become clusters of houses with their inhabitants, and in each group of houses there was a series of positions or chiefly roles; each of these positions commanded an ancient name, and a "standing place" or "seat" which determined its rank. The men — and more rarely the women — holding these positions were regarded as the nobility of the numaym; they would not necessarily be closely related, since they had descended by different lines from a common ancestor, and the younger sons of a position holder were really no more than commoners with expectations; if enough people died off — and in some areas this hap-

 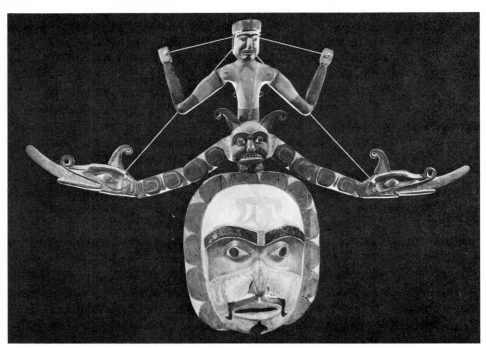

Kwakiutl grave effigy from Kitimat (*left*). Kwakiutl mask (*right*) with movable parts operated by strings.
The mask represents the sun, the Sisiutl (two-headed snake), and the sun's humanoid manifestation.

pened after the smallpox epidemics of the nineteenth century — almost anyone within a *numaym* could lay a plausible claim to a title on the basis of remote ancestry, provided only that he could gather enough goods to validate it in potlatch.

We can get some idea of the size of the Kwakiutl nobility from the information Franz Boas gathered at the end of the last century from George Hunt and his other Indian informants: that "among the thirteen tribes of the region extending from Fort Rupert to Nimkish River and Knight Inlet, there were 658 seats," which means about fifty noblemen per village. Now the total number of the Kwakiutl at the beginning of the historic era was probably not much more than twelve thousand, and if one remembers that the figures Boas presents do not include the northern Kwakiutl groups or the Euclataw, it is

likely that he is talking of a population of less than eight thousand even at its prime, among whom one can assume that little over twenty-five hundred were males of sixteen years old or more; this means that one male adult in four held noble rank, and that many more had expectations that were often fulfilled, particularly when the older men decided to give up their titles to younger men. Such ranking positions in the *numaym* were distinct from any credit a man might gain from potlatches, any crests he might obtain by marriage, purchase, exchange or conquest from neighbouring groups, or any ranks within the dancing societies which he might acquire by initiation during the Tsetseka season, though of course these enhanced his name and his standing place. Far indeed from being a rigid class structure, Kwakiutl society even in aboriginal times appears to have had a notable mobility,

A Kwakiutl bridegroom and party set out to seek his bride, with a masked dancer in the prow singing the songs of his lineage (*above*). On return to the groom's village, the newly married couple stand on a platform at the back of the canoe while a member of the groom's family sings a song and the paddlers beat time (*below*).

and perhaps — here as elsewhere — the only really rigid class division was that between freemen and slaves.

The highest ranking man in a *numaym* was its chief, who looked after the common clan property with the help of other noblemen, acting in a rather informal council. In the village the ranking was by *numaym* rather than by individual rankholder, and at potlatches and other secular celebrations the nobles of each *numaym* would sit together in the place collectively due to them by rank. The other *numayms* would take up the less prestigious blocks of seats, but the comparative ranking of individuals would not come into question. The man with the highest rank in the leading *numaym* was tacitly recognized as the village chief, though his role would in practice be ceremonial rather than political.

The way in which ranks were inherited depended on which Kwakiutl villages were involved; comparing the Haisla and the Heiltsuk with the Southern Kwakiutl, one sees a very interesting example of cultural transition in actual operation, for the northern groups had acquired from the Tsimshian even before the historic age the custom of arranging inheritances and marriages according to an exogamous and matrilineal class system, whereas with the Southern Kwakiutl a system nearer to that of the Salish and the Nootka prevailed, with inheritance generally regulated by patrilineal primogeniture, though some kinds of property could pass by either route.

There were no profound economic or technological differences between the Kwakiutl and neighbouring peoples like the Tsimshian, the Bella Coola, or the Coast Salish. Salmon and oolichan, with a few less important fishes and other seafoods, were the main basis of their subsistence and also of the surplus on which they depended for more extravagant manifestations of their culture. Every *numaym* had its berry-picking grounds and its hunting preserves, but both were limited by the density of the first-growth rain forest that flowed down to salt water, clogged by deadfalls and underbrush, and overshadowing the very beaches. The red cedar, as everywhere else on the Coast except for the northern Tlingit region, was the great provider of wood for houses and fibre for a utilitarian fabric, which the women prepared by pounding the inner bark of the tree with a beater not unlike that which Polynesian women use when they prepare, from the inner integument of the paper mulberry, the bark cloth known as *tapa*; the main difference, which negates the suggestion of a southern Pacific influence, was that while Polynesians glue thin films of bark together, the Kwakiutl women turned the fibre into yarn and wove it on a primitive loom that must have come from Asia. Houses were, almost without exception, the large gabled buildings we have already encountered among the northern tribes, the fronts covered with great paintings of thunderbirds, killer whales, or other appropriate crests, and the entry to the house often cut through a tall portal post as massive in proportion as the remainder of the dwelling, which could often hold hundreds of people — a whole village — when the owner decided to make it available for the performance of a winter initiation ceremony or a similar festival.

The Kwakiutl dressed — or neglected to dress — very much like other Coast Indian peoples, often naked on a summer's day, but garbed as elaborately as a Tibetan high lama for a potlatch or some other festive occasion. Explorers usually saw the Kwakiutl fully dressed, since welcoming an interesting stranger was always a ceremony; and as the years went on, the chiefs gathered a miscellaneous collection of British and American naval and military garb which they might wear when they travelled to Victoria, or to impress the less sophisticated of the interior peoples, or to make a missionary feel at home — as when, among the Haida, the future Bishop Collison saw in his first Christmas congregation a high chief dressed as a rear admiral, a younger dignitary decked out in a belled jester's garb of many colours, and an old shaman wearing a surplice to complement his ritual horned head-dress. For purely indigenous occasions, the Chilkat blanket or the button blanket, with the diadem adorned with abalone and ermine, was — among the Kwakiutl as elsewhere — the proper evening dress. To accompany such garb there were appropriate adornments. Unlike the Haida, the Kwakiutl did not go in greatly for tattooing, but they painted their faces in charcoal and vermilion on a foundation of animal grease according to appropriate crest patterns, and while they agreed with the Salish that the kind of heads which the ancestors had transmitted to men were not of the best design, they improved them not by flattening them but by binding them tightly so that they assumed the becoming shape of a backward-tilting sugarloaf.

In all such basic matters the Kwakiutl did not depart greatly from the coastal norm; they shared the abundance of their neighbours, and in the summer they set about gathering and preserving its products with the same methods and the same degree of application. In the winter season they utilized the surplus with equal energy, to such a degree that the Kwakiutl winter ceremonials are more celebrated than any other on the Coast, and Kwakiutl ceremonial art has a special kind of eloquent vigour that — alone among the Coast styles — at times verges on the excess of emphasis. There is no doubt that everything the Kwakiutl did in the winter season of ceremonial — at least in historic times — was grandiose and expansive, but one can debate whether it justified Ruth Benedict's celebrated strictures in *Patterns of Culture*, with their suggestion that such phenomena as the competitive potlatches

A Kwakiutl wolf-man transformation mask from Alert Bay.

and the Hamatsa dances reveal the existence of a "megalomaniac and paranoid trend." On the contrary, a good argument could be put that the Kwakiutl in fact used such ceremonials for exorcising the violence of their own society and that occasions of this kind represented a sublimation of more barbaric earlier customs.

The development of the potlatch among the Kwakiutl during the second half of the twentieth century was sensational. Helen Codere, in her investigations of this complex of customs and its links with vanishing warrior cults, has shown quite clearly that in both cost and complexity the Kwakiutl potlatch expanded radically after 1849, when the Hudson's Bay Company post was established at Fort Rupert and the four local tribes who went to live there started a system of competitive feasting, which eventually embraced all the southern Kwakiutl tribes. This system was fuelled by the new sources of income that came from the fur trade, from the establishment of the canneries which provided work and also bought fish, and later from the opportunities of unskilled employment in Victoria, all of which brought cash and goods flowing into the villages and — since much food was gathered in the old way — provided an unparalleled excess of resources for conspicuous spending during the winter. In her investigations of recorded family histories, Codere has found that the largest potlatch among the Southern Kwakiutl prior to 1849 was one in which 320 Hudson's Bay Company blankets were given away, probably a slighter affair than the potlatches being given by the northern peoples at this period. But in 1869, twenty years later, there was a Kwakiutl potlatch where goods to the value of 9,000 blankets were distributed, and in 1895 one in which the value of 13,000 blankets was given away.

In 1921 the last of the great potlatches was held, in defiance of the law, and it exceeded all its predecessors. At this feast, likely to be remembered as an epic event as long as the Coast Indians retain any sense for their own culture, the Mounted Police dramatically arrested the host, Chief Daniel Cranmer of the Nimkish tribe at Alert Bay, and seized twenty-three coppers and other regalia which are still retained in the Museum of Man in Ottawa. Before they arrived, Dan Cranmer had given away to his three hundred guests, during the six days of the feast, the equivalent of thirty thousand blankets, which it had taken him eight years of hard work, careful trading, and money lending at high interest to accumulate. Apart from thousands of actual Hudson's Bay Company blankets, the goods given away included canoes and motor boats, pool tables and oak trunks, violins and guitars, sewing machines and gramophones, bedsteads and bureaus, washtubs and crockery, cash scattered everywhere for the scrambling children, and on the last day a thousand sacks of flour. Dan Cranmer came out of prison broke but unrepentant. He had given the greatest of all the Coast potlatches, and thirty years later he said: "Everyone admits that that was the biggest yet. . . . In the old days this was my weapon and I could call down anyone."

One has only to consider the profligacy of the gifts and the chief's sentiments to understand without too much explanation what the potlatch became for the Kwakiutl during the seven decades from 1849 to 1921, when it collapsed as an institution less because of legal prohibition than because of the Depression. It was no longer a matter merely of a feast on the occasion of some important life event, with gifts to the witnesses so that a title or a ritual could be validated. The competitive element had become dominant. The privilege became less important than the feast that validated it, and rival chiefs competed to the point of bankruptcy and — sometimes — even of suicide in order to remain ahead of their rivals. To "call anyone down" became the ultimate aim, and a great deal of ritual hostility entered into the potlatches, expressed on such occasions as the grease feasts, in which vast quantities of oil would be burned, and canoes and other property cast into the flames, while, to keep face, the guest chiefs had to sit scorching beside the fire until the challenging chief chose to put it out.

It is easy to read megalomania and paranoia into all this, but the interesting fact is that the memories of those who saw or took part in such contests do not suggest vindictiveness so much as the kind of pleasure in a hard-won victory that we expect in our own culture from a successful sportsman. And, indeed, the great potlatches of the years between 1849 and 1921 did take on a great deal of the quality of sporting events, with the chiefs as performers and the guests as critical and appreciative spectators. It is hard in any other context to understand the institution of the rank of Eagle which Kwakiutl chiefs granted to a man completely outside the ranking structure who nevertheless gave splendid potlatches. Such potlatches validated no traditional titles or privileges, but they showed splendid initiative and generosity, and for this the chiefs were quite willing to grant the Eagles what they wanted —

precedence in the receiving of gifts — in the spirit of good amateur sportsmen granting the occasional superiority of a professional.

During this period, to destroy property became an even greater sign of grandeur than to give it away, and the lore of the potlatches is full of stories of slaves killed — or liberated (which was also a destruction of property) — or of thousands of sacks of flour cut open and thrown into the sea. The most bitter contests arose around the ritual giving, selling, and destruction of coppers — curious escutcheonlike objects engraved with crest emblems — which acquired an artificial value because of their involvement in the potlatches. Nobody knows quite how old a feature of the Coast culture the copper really is. The Russian fur trader, Lisiansky, reports having seen Tlingit chiefs in 1804 accompanied by slaves who carried and beat copper shields which were obviously signs of prestige, and it is possible that the earliest emblems of this kind were made of metal brought from the Copper River in Alaska and hammered into shape. It is true that the oldest coppers now in existence appear to have been made from the kind of copper which in the eighteenth century was used for sheeting ship bottoms, and which the Spaniards began to trade to the Indians in the 1770s. But the interesting fact is that the Spaniards found the Indians immediately wishing to obtain sheet copper, which suggests they already had a use for it; and it really seems unlikely that the very peculiar shape of the copper — with its pentagonal top and rectangular lower portion, its T-shaped central ridge and its engraved crests — could have evolved out of nothing in the twenty-odd years between the very occasional visits of Spanish ships with small quantities of copper for trading, and Lisiansky's appearance in 1804. We are left with the conclusion that as a crest emblem the copper, which is shown on some quite well-worn petroglyphs, is in fact con-

A Kwakiutl copper.

siderably older than the earliest specimens in museums may suggest.

Coppers played special roles in naming ceremonies, were often included in marriage settlements, and were always displayed at the climax of a potlatch. To give a copper at a potlatch was a challenging gesture; it complimented the receiver only if it were known that he could return an equally valuable copper, but it shamed him if this turned out to be impossible. Selling a copper was another kind of challenge, since the buyer was always obliged to pay appreciably

Thunderbird, Sea Wolf, Sisiutl, and carvings of a dead chief's coppers honour his grave at Alert Bay.

more for it than had been paid at the time of the previous sale; and there are coppers in existence that have a potlatch value of as much as sixteen thousand blankets.

> Still more feared [says Boas] is the breaking of a valuable copper. A chief may break his copper and give the broken parts to his rival. If the latter wants to keep his prestige, he must break a copper of equal or higher value, and then return both his own broken copper and the fragments which he has received from his rival. The latter may then pay for the copper which he has thus received. The chief to whom the fragments of the first copper are given may, however, also break his copper and throw both into the sea. The Indians consider that by this act the attacked rival has shown himself superior to his aggressor, because the latter may have expected to receive the copper of his rival in return so that an actual loss would have been prevented.

More often, however, a broken copper would be restored by rivetting together the fragments, and such a copper would gain in value as a sign that its owner had destroyed property. All these performances with coppers were acts of high drama, and the chief who was giving or destroying one would assume for the occasion the mask of Tsonkwa, the wild woman of the woods, who in Kwakiutl myth was the terror of small children (whom she was reputed to eat) but also the bringer of wealth.

The vast expenditures on giving inevitably affected Kwakiutl economy during the great period of the potlatches. It is true that only surplus goods and money were being used for potlatch purposes, but the surplus was now greater both absolutely and proportionately to income, so that by far the major part of the wealth that found its way into Kwakiutl hands immediately went into circulation in the potlatch circuit. But as competitiveness grew, the urgent needs of individual potlatchers tended to exceed their immediate incomes and so large-scale usury appeared. Careless writers, like Ruth Benedict, have spread the impression that potlatch gifts had to be doubled when they were returned. The absurdity of such a supposition becomes evident if one considers a potlatch gift of a thousand blankets; seven potlatches later the appropriate return gift would be swollen to sixty-four thousand blankets, twice as much as was given at the largest potlatch yet known. In fact, if the return gift were only marginally greater than the original gift, that would be quite sufficient to save face. What did happen was that men — particularly young men — who were badly in need of money or goods to put on an acceptable potlatch would borrow from a man who was gathering goods for a potlatch some years ahead. The rates of interest for such loans were high, and did in fact often amount to a hundred percent a year.

By the last decades of high potlatching, there was certainly an air of compulsiveness about the efforts which the chiefs and their *numayms* would put into saving for a potlatch and staging it, but one wonders whether — except perhaps in degree — it was much different from the obsessive attention many people in our culture devote to competitive sports and to the gambling commonly associated with them. The Coast Indians, too, were enthusiastic gamblers, and would lose and win a great deal at the guessing game of *lahal*, which was played to the tune of songs and drumming before audiences, and certainly gamesmanship played its part in the late great potlatches. But so also did strategy, and there is a great deal of merit in the arguments of those, like Helen Codere and Franz Boas before her, who have pointed out the extent to which the potlatch became a substitute for warfare. This was evi-

dent even to the Kwakiutl themselves, and Boas quoted a statement made by one of the participants in a potlatch at Fort Rupert in 1895:

> When I was young I have seen streams of blood shed in war. But since that time the white man came and stopped up the stream of blood with wealth. Now we are fighting with our wealth. . . . We do not fight now with weapons; we fight with property.

The whole oratory of the later potlatch, and particularly of the competitive potlatch, was studded with warlike images with references to the giving of property as a means of overcoming one's rivals, who were also one's ritual enemies.

The role of certain forms of nonlethal but highly competitive activity as a substitute for warfare has long been known. It was when internecine conflict declined in the feudal countries of mediaeval Europe that the sham warfare of the tournament became popular. Wild rustic games like shinny, in which whole villages played against each other, were obviously ritualized combats; and in some of the South Pacific islands, Samoa particularly, the missionaries found a rough early form of cricket (which is still played there) extremely helpful in diverting from actual warfare the hostile feelings among the local tribes that survived conversion.

There is no doubt that war on the Pacific Coast had virtually come to an end by the early 1860s — it ended later in the interior — and that there was no major warfare among the Kwakiutl after the later 1850s. This may be attributed partly to the increasing presence of British gunboats on the Coast and to the different attitudes towards Indian wars that developed after the fur traders were replaced by the colonial administrators in Victoria. Yet there is little doubt that, in terms of warfare, the peoples of the Coast were themselves undergoing a transition at the time the Europeans arrived.

Although it is hard to speculate on what happened in prehistoric times, there is some reason to suppose that at an early period on the Coast the various peoples may have been given to head-hunting and cannibalism on a large scale, and that the taking of heads in warfare pursued for other reasons, and the ritual cannibalism of the Hamatsa ceremonials during the winter dances, were relics of such a time. But by the late eighteenth century, actual cannibalism was as distasteful to the Kwakiutl as it would have been to an Anglican who carried out the ritual cannibalism of symbolically consuming the body and blood of Christ.

In a similar way, though warriors were theoretically honoured among the Kwakiutl, it seems evident that most other people regarded them with fear and distaste, as unpredictable bullies. There was no cult of heroism on the Coast like that which would send the prairie Indian singing to the death that faced him. Coast Indian warfare was always stealthy and shamefaced, with real courage displayed only on occasion by the defenders; and despite all the bold talk which warriors made on departing from their villages they would often be content with slaughtering some unfortunate traveller they had encountered or — as on one known occasion — with collapsing a tent on some sleeping fishermen and stabbing them through the canvas so that there were heads to take home and boast about.

All this led warriors to be somewhat less than admired, and it is possible that an introduction to European ideas of boldness and heroism may have helped to destroy what standing they had and to reveal them, even to their own people, as cowardly assassins rather than heroic fighters. Certainly, they seem to have done much less than they boasted of, for the Coast Indian society would never have been so prosperous or so settled in its village life, or so developed in its ceremonial and technology, if surprise raids had been as frequent as the oral accounts assert. All in all, one must agree with H. B. Hawthorn's remark that for the Coast Indians in general, war was "more a horrifying concept than a practice." No wonder that, in exchange, they were happy to take up the war of property, fought with words in the battlegrounds of their own great houses with the wealth-piled beaches before them.

Everywhere on the Coast, the winter was a time when the world of spirits and that of everyday nature drew closer. It was a time when mythical beings were thought to walk the earth invisibly, and when men re-enacted their encounters with the spiritual world. In the Kwakiutl villages, as summer faded into autumn, the people gathered and sang the personal songs of those who had died since the last ceremonial season, while the relatives wore special mourning masks. Then there followed a period of saturnalia called Klasila, when the people relaxed after the summer's labours of fishing and food preserving, displayed their family masks and dances, and feasted light-heartedly, until at the end of four days a forbidding masked figure named Gakhula appeared, exhorted the people to remember that this was a serious season and went away. Shortly afterwards the spirit whistles began to sound in the woods, and the people dispersed to bathe ritually and prepare themselves for Tsetseka, the winter ceremonial season.

What happened during Tsetseka clearly derives from an inspired combination of a number of archaic Coast cults. First, and basic to the whole complex, there was the guardian spirit quest, which we encountered among the Salish as an individual search but which here has become institutionalized as the process of initiation into a secret order patronized, as it were, by collective guardian spirits. Next, there is the heritage of traditional Eurasian shamanism,

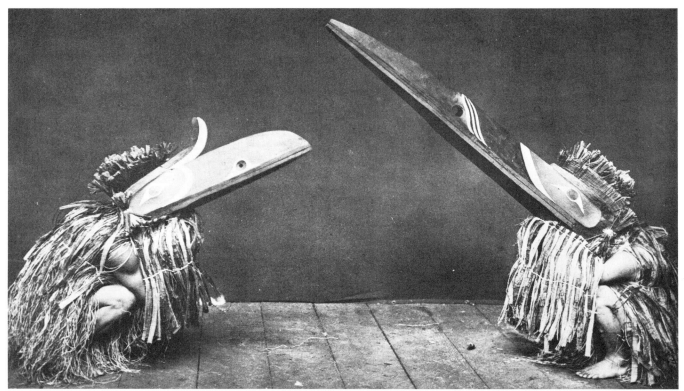

Several kinds of massive bird masks were used in the Hamatsa Society dances. The supernatural Raven, on the left, was one of these birds and the Hokhokw, on the right, was another. The heavy masks were attached to the body with harnesses and the beaks could be made to open and shut with a clanking rhythm in time with the dance.

which in the winter ceremonial of the Kwakiutl shows itself, strangely enough, in the performances of the dancing order that is dedicated to the war spirit, Winalagilis, but in fact concerns itself with miraculous healing, fire-walking, the use of the magical quartz crystals, and death-and-resurrection after dismemberment, all of them elements of the essential shamanic myth. Next — though of prime importance in the hierarchy of the dancing orders as they appear in historic times — there is the Hamatsa Society, under the formidable patronage of Baks-bakualanu Xsiwae, the "Cannibal from the North End of the World," who presides over the ceremonial invisibly, with his breath whistling

(through wooden whistles blown by mortal men) from the hundred mouths that stud his body; this ritual is said to have originated among the Heiltsuk (Bella Bella), from whom the Southern Kwakiutl acquired it by warfare and murder, and it appears to be the derivative of a cannibalistic warrior cult.

But the winter ceremonials as they were actually performed bore roughly the same relation to their spirit quest, shamanic, and warrior-cult originals as the tragedies of Aeschylus did to the dances in honour of Dionysus, out of which the whole splendid tradition of the Greek drama arose. As in Greek drama, the original primitive elements were secularized in the Kwakiutl

Whistles represented spirit voices but seldom did they also portray spirits, as this Kwakiutl one does.

winter dances, absorbed into the chiefly ranking system, and turned into a splendid dramatic event that glorified the important lineages and provided the populace with the kind of entertainment that still, in the late twentieth century, astonishes and moves not only the heirs of the Kwakiutl but also, when they have a rare opportunity to witness it, the descendants of Europeans as well.

Already in 1895 Boas gives us, in *The Social Organization and Secret Societies of the Kwakiutl Indians*, the essential basis of the winter dancing orders as they had developed at the beginning of the historic era:

> The object of the whole winter ceremonial is first, to bring back the youth who is supposed to stay with the supernatural being who is the protector of his society, and then, when he has returned in a state of ecstasy, to exorcise the spirit which possesses him and to restore him from his holy madness.

In fact, as one learns from the accounts of Indian chiefs who have gone through initiation to the Hamatsa Society, the initiate does not go through the self-imposed rigours of the guardian spirit quest; he does not go out for long periods in the wilderness and eventually induce the trance that brings him his familiar. On the contrary, he becomes an initiate in this highest-ranking society mainly because, as part of his lineage possessions, his father owns the right to initiation; the father will be a hamatsa, but since the memberships of the societies are strictly limited, he must retire so that his son may take the place, and it is very likely that at this point he will actually sponsor the expensive ceremonials. Although a retreat into the wilderness is theoretically prescribed and is indeed simulated, in fact the young initiate is usually secluded at the back of the building being used as the dance house for the hamatsas, and there he is instructed in the ways of miming possession so

Winter ceremonial dance showing Kwakiutl power boards. The boards were used in the dance of the war spirit.

that he can appear in the flickering firelight before the assembled initiates and spectators, pretend to be in ecstasy, simulate the eating of human flesh, perform every action so exactly that the most experienced observers cannot see a flaw in his dancing, and finally be subdued and brought back to sanity; in all of this the audience participates, half-incredulous and half-believing, and in the meantime achieving,

through the vicarious purgation of emotions, the true Aristotelian catharsis.

There is no need for me to describe the intricate and fascinating details of the Hamatsa ceremonial, which have been told often by chroniclers from Boas in the 1890s and Curtis in the Edwardian era, down to the present time. It is clear that, through simulated terror and relief, the people who witnessed gained a very similar

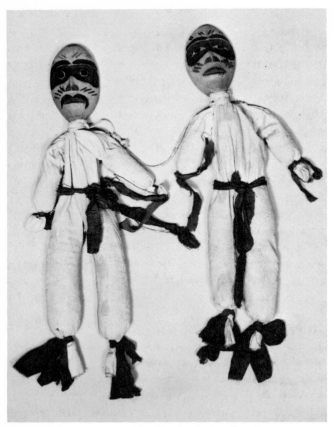

These puppets are used for illusionistic effect in Tokwit dances during Kwakiutl winter ceremonials.

halfway point between spontaneous possession and institutionalized simulation of possession in the informal winter dance societies that would often seize people who had not succeeded in their guardian spirit quest and induce a trance experience through forcible and artificial means. The Kwakiutl went further, in that the trance experience appears to have been consciously simulated and its accompanying actions learnt by rote. The Kwakiutl, in other words, had progressed further than the other peoples of the Coast in the direction of transforming individual spiritual experience into the socially approved collective experience of a church, as highly dramatic as those of Rome or Constantinople at the height of their ascendancy. The drama of the Mass: the drama of the Hamatsa Society. Quite apart from the common element of ritual cannibalism, each represented a secularization of the true spiritual impulse and each achieved a notable level of aesthetic achievement, which is the collective equivalent of individual spiritual insight.

In this context one cannot neglect the superb stagecraft of the Kwakiutl, in whose service some of the most remarkable artifacts in the Coast tradition were produced. The dances of the Hamatsa Society itself had a kind of grim austerity; its ecstasies were simulated with the minimum of theatrical apparatus and were the more effective for this reason, as the novice clad in simple boughs whirled in his frenzy, as his naked woman assistant danced before him with a tempting desiccated corpse in her arms, as the dancers bearing the great masks of mythical birds six feet long span on their haunches like Cossacks and clanked their great beaks in menacing chorus, and as the snarling grizzly bears kept silence with their frightful presence. But there were other dances whose range of conjurors' devices would have delighted a Houdini. This was especially the case in the Tokwit dance, when a

emotional release to that which the Athenians experienced when watching the shocking stories of Agamemnon and Oedipus, or the Elizabethans experienced when witnessing the agonies of Macbeth and Hamlet — facing a world of primitive spirituality with which they were too sophisticated to cope, as one suspects some of the Kwakiutl were already too sophisticated to cope with the natural starkness of a true quest as the Salish still followed it.

But there are some important aspects of the Kwakiutl winter ceremonials that still remain to be noted. First of all, in discussing the spirit dances of the Salish, I already noted a significant

girl was beheaded, stabbed with spears, burnt in a box, and went through many other cleverly simulated torments which at the same time delighted and mystified the uninitiated audience. Other characters flew about the house, supported by invisible strings, or operated flying magical figures, while many of the crest masks that were displayed at this time simulated miniature killer whales with moving fins and tails, or birds that flapped their wings, or creatures with telescopic noses that could extend half across the house. Others were ingenious transformation devices in which the face of one creature would slowly open, as the tempo of the drumming changed, to reveal a quite different creature, or in which the rays of a sun mask would reform themselves into the tail of a whale. Tsetseka was indeed a time when "everything is not real." It was also a time when the particular mechanical talents which distinguished the Kwakiutl from the other Coast people had full scope to develop outside the limited area of shamanistic gimmicks, and many of the products of the artists' ingenuity have in their fantasy a beauty that far excels any mere conjuror's adeptness that they also reveal. It is an interesting other side to a Kwakiutl art that in the larger sculptures tends to an emphatic kind of naturalistic vigour, deriving from an archaic style whose roughly grotesque grave-figures and potlatch welcoming-figures showed a striking resemblance to those of the Salish, and seemed to link backwards to the early megalithic style that at one period may well have dominated the artistic production of the whole Coast.

There is a final, social aspect to the Kwakiutl winter ceremonials that should not be overlooked. It has often been said that when the Tsetseka season began, the whole summertime order was overthrown, but this should not be understood in terms of a subversion; there was no question of the humble being exalted or, as in

Crabs with moving legs, operated on spool rollers, scurried over the floor during the Tokwit dances.

the ancient Greek mysteries, of slaves becoming the ritual equals of their masters. What happened was, first, that everyone abandoned secular summer names and adopted the winter ceremonial names to which they were entitled. The conduct of affairs lapsed out of the hands of the chiefs of households and *numayms,* and was taken over by a group of ceremonial officials consisting mostly of senior members of the dancing societies, who had retired from active roles and who made sure protocol was observed and appointed proctors and other officials to maintain order; in addition each dancing society had its officials with their various ceremonial functions.

The *numayms* no longer existed; they had gone underground with the summer names, whose use was penalized. Instead, the people were organized into two groups: the Seals, initiates and novices of the eight dancing societies, with the Hamatsa at their head; and the Sparrows, the noninitiates who were graded into ten groups according to age and sex, from girls and boys (who had their separate societies) to young women and men, and then to the old women, and at the top the chiefs and the high chiefs who had retired from the Seals and reverted to the Sparrows. The Seals behaved truculently to the Sparrows, who teased the Seals, so that the

This Kwakiutl figure, which welcomed guests at potlatches, is almost twice human height.

serious business of the festival was constantly interspersed with simulated conflict and with sheer comedy at the feasts that punctuated the dances.

What happened was not a breakdown of the Kwakiutl social order, since nobody without hereditary rank was ever allowed into the exclusive membership of the Hamatsa Society, and few people without rank could in any case have afforded the expensive initiations into the ascending line of lesser dancing societies that were prerequisites for entry into the Hamatsa. More important, for a whole season — with the temporary eclipsing of *numaym* and family — the Kwakiutl were able to relate to each other in a new order that horizontally embraced people from every lineage. It was the season when, despite the ritual quarrels between Seals and Sparrows, the village was most clearly a unity, and it is characteristic of Coast Indian society that such a unity should be achieved in a ceremonial rather than a political context.

The Bella Coola were the smallest in numbers of the peoples of the Coast. As we have seen, they were an offshoot of the Salish and had come down into the river valleys they lived in, so long ago that no memory of the migration remained. The Bella Coola had survived largely by developing intimate relationships with neighbouring peoples that had preserved them but had also profoundly modified their culture. More than any other Coast people they intermarried with other linguistic groups, especially with the Bella Bella and with the Kwakiutl group on Rivers Inlet known as the Wikeno. They traded with the Athapaskan peoples of the interior, the Carrier and the Chilcotin, and the ease with which Mackenzie found his way in and out of Bella Coola country in 1793 suggests that on this, their mountain frontier, relations were good. Such alliances and business connections gave at least a partial protection to a people who were never more than two thousand in numbers and who were divided among forty small villages not easy to defend. At the same time, this unusually developed pattern of outside contacts meant that the Bella Coola tended to imitate the techniques of their neighbours and to acquire crests and ceremonials from them as marriage gifts.

Yet though there was perhaps no group whose lives united more strands of the Coast culture, the Bella Coola were still a curiously isolated people, encountered almost accidentally by Mackenzie, too far away from the main canoe routes to be much endangered by the aggressions of the northern peoples, and little noticed by the maritime fur traders or even the early explorers by sea; it was the Bella Bella, not the Bella Coola, who told Mackenzie of their encounter with Vancouver. And in a number of very interesting ways the Bella Coola remained a people unlike the others.

The difference emerged in the style of their villages, which, because of the narrowness of the river valleys, were often built on piles out over the water, perhaps in this perpetuating an older Coast style; they had small dugout canoes especially designed for the rapid waters, and their fishing was largely a matter of weirs and traps in narrow streams, so that, as Mackenzie found, they were particularly concerned over the pollution of their waters. They even appointed river guardians whose duty it was to make sure that nothing was done to offend the migrating salmon and oolichan on which the Bella Coola depended if they were not to starve in isolation; the guardians could kill people they found throwing refuse into the river (and apparently did so without hesitation).

In spite of their close relationship with the northern Kwakiutl groups, the Bella Coola never adopted the pattern of matrilineal phratries that some of those peoples had already taken over

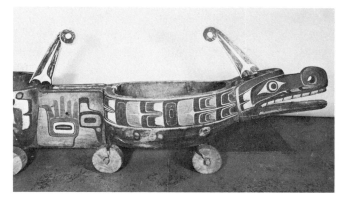

In their feast dishes (*above*) the Kwakiutl often gave sculptural solidity to the shapes of animals. The figure at top is part of an articulated and wheeled feast dish, which is twenty feet long and is made in the form of Sisiutl, the two-headed serpent.

from the Tsimshian. In fact, more than anything except their language, their social pattern was distinctly Salish in character. It was based on the ancestral family. The myth of the ancestral family was in turn linked with the intriguing cosmogony which Thomas McIlwraith thirty years ago found still very much alive in the traditions of some of the Bella Coola lineages.

Perhaps because they were a small, threatened people, the Bella Coola seem to have

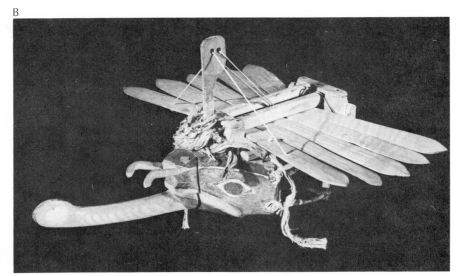

A. This carved house post, representing a sea monster, was collected from the Kwakiutl village of Koskimo in 1956 and stood in the grounds of the University of British Columbia before being installed in the Museum of Anthropology there in 1976. *B.* A Kwakiutl wind mask with movable wings. *C.* A carved Kwakiutl box, used as a coffin.

worked out their cosmogony somewhat more carefully and reassuringly than other Coast peoples, unlike the Haida, for example, whose views of the basin-shaped skies and the Shining Being above seem vague and inconsistent, and the Kwakiutl, who appear to have had almost no conception of a supreme being at all. The Bella Coola seem to have evolved, as imperilled peoples often do, the view of an originating being — called Alkuntam — who was not necessarily creator of the universe but certainly maker of men and animals. It was Alkuntam (behind whose house grows the great shamanic tree filled with the owl manifestations of the souls of men) who sent to earth the ancestors of the forty-five original Bella Coola families, all in animal guise. As soon as they arrived on earth, the ancestors emerged as men from their animal garb, which they sent back to Alkuntam's paradise, retaining only the right to use the animal cloaks as their crests. It is fitting, in view of the technological achievements of the Coast Indians, that in one version of the Bella Coola origin myth Alkuntam is shown commissioning four heavenly carvers to create the models of all human and animal races.

Alkuntam was a sky god in the shamanic tradition. The sun was his canoe, and when he entered it in the daytime he wore a shining golden cloak whose lining was the silver of salmon, and at the season when Alkuntam reversed his cloak the salmon filled the rivers.

The ancestral families founded by Alkuntam formed the basis of Bella Coola society, and incidentally proclaimed the antiquity of their villages, for every one of the forty-five ancestral couples is said to have founded a village, and by the time of contact with the Europeans forty villages remained. In fact, through marriage, migration, and merger, larger villages did appear, and there was a tendency among the Bella Coola to spend the summers in their original fishing

This Bella Coola bear mask admirably shows the bold expressionism typical of so much carving.

and berry-picking sites, but to congregate in winter at places like Bella Coola itself and Talion on North Bentinck Arm, where the long dark winter months could be enlivened by feasting or by the activities of the Kusiut Society, a somewhat more informal version of the Kwakiutl dancing orders, in which the privileged stratifications of Coast Indian society were so relaxed that it is said slaves could be admitted — and sometimes were — provided their owners were indulgent enough to make the necessary gifts.

But among the Bella Coola, as among the Coast Salish, a tendency to cluster in winter for the sake of comfort and company did not lead to the emergence of an elaborate social order. The ancestral families were not formed into clans or phratries; inheritance was important, in that the ancestor's most direct heir was always accorded respect if not authority (which existed among the

Although the original house has gone, the house posts (Raven and Bear, and Raven and Beaver) still stand.

eight such groupings, but like the great Chinese clans, it remained, even in dispersal, a powerful social nucleus.

The art of the Bella Coola is easily distinguished, even though in many respects it followed the general style of the Coast between Alert Bay and the Skeena. There were poles in considerable variety and many crest masks, as well as the customary equipment of wooden utensils, which if not as elaborately carved as those of the northern peoples, were still made with care and true proportion. Fewer poles were erected than among the northern peoples, since Bella Coola crests — being those of individual families rather than clans — tended to be simpler; and the masks, except for those of a few mythical beings who appeared to celebrate such occasions as the emergence of spring, tend to represent the animal guises under which the ancestors descended from Alkuntam's heaven.

Perhaps it is because they are not bound to the myths of large clans that Bella Coola carving and painting are not so formalized as those of the northern peoples and at the same time do not project the sheer melodrama of Kwakiutl art at its excessive extreme. When one looks at Bella Coola masks, perhaps the first impression is one of a rather rustic solidity. The features — especially the eyes and eyebrows, and often the nose — are emphasized to the verge of caricature; there is a bulging solidity to all this flesh expressed in wood; the colours tend to be dense and somewhat hot. It seems a less patrician art than that of the northerners or even the Kwakiutl, and this may be an exact impression, for the aristocracy among the Bella Coola were less securely defined than among any other Coast people except their fellow Salish, and so perhaps among them, as among the Salish with their simple emphatic funereal sculptures, we see the nearest thing among the Coast Indians to an art that is not only primitive but verges on the popular.

Bella Coola only in the most tenuous way), but he never became the head of his lineage until his wealth-gathering capacities had been tested. Four or five successful potlatches were usually sufficient to establish the head of an ancestral family as the ranking chief of the winter village he inhabited, though it was a role with no political authority and hardly any ceremonial relevance. Essentially, the ancestral family remained the basic unit of Bella Coola society; it might not necessarily be attached any more to a specific territorial locality, and individuals through marriage might be able to claim stakes in as many as

Part IV

Fallen splendour. A pole at Kitwanga on the upper Skeena River.

CHAPTER TEN

The Transformers

The myth of the Transformer was deeply rooted in the consciousness of the Coast Indians. They shared it with the Siberians. For both peoples, the Transformer — and the Trickster also — was Raven. They shared it in a different way with the Indian peoples of the interior, for whom the Transformer-Trickster was Coyote. All were peoples in whom the concept of a creator deity was never strong and whose view of the supreme being in the heavens was at best ambivalent; such a being was not always benign, any more than life itself is, and often kept from the lesser beings the very gifts that might ease their lives and bring them a modicum of happiness. Such benefits arrived most often as gifts of the Transformers, for it was Raven who changed the sublunary world by presenting men with gifts like fire and the light of the heavenly bodies, which in his guise as Trickster he stole from the supernatural beings who directed the universe with little care for the welfare of men or animals. Yet the Transformers themselves were also ambivalent, since only by cunning did they secure the gifts they passed on to other beings, and in all other ways they retained the rapacious nature of ravens and coyotes. Nobody ever believed that their feats as Prometheus-beings had been motivated by benevolence; they were feats carried out for the excitement that success would bring, and if anyone benefited, that was merely a lucky bonus for which the Transformer might exact his price.

When the Europeans appeared in their midst two centuries ago, some of the Indian peoples of British Columbia saw them as manifestations of the Transformer. We have already seen how Simon Fraser was greeted as at least a companion of Coyote, and how the northern peoples imagined the first white-sailed ships they saw to be Raven returning. And in their own ways the newcomers did fulfil the mythical roles attributed to Raven and Coyote. If they did not bring the gift of fire, they brought other gifts that were as double edged. They transformed the human world of the Coast as radically as ever Raven did. And as tricksters they dealt in illusions, so that the benefits which at first seemed to be flowing in to the Coast peoples when the early sea traders arrived were almost all in the end seen as hollow at best, and at worst as deadly.

The aboriginal culture was no more ideal than any other human culture. To those within the magic circle of blood and crest it offered a nourishing mixture of freedom and support, sustained by myths whose reality was regularly and dramatically re-emphasized in art and ceremonial. But towards anyone outside the magic circle, towards the slave or the stranger met by chance, it could be as brutal as any culture the world has known. Perhaps there were not the great holocausts of slaughtered prisoners that took place in the Aztec capital of Tenochtitlan, but the difference was mainly numerical; there were far fewer Haida or Kwakiutl or Tlingit sacrificers, and far fewer potential Salish victims, than there were Mexicans of either kind. Yet for the one slave crushed under a Tlingit chief's house post, the degree of agony was no less than for each of the thousands of victims whose hearts were torn out on the great pyramid in the annual sacrifice to the war god Huitzilopochtli.

Yet, as we have seen, the culture of the Coast Indians flourished precisely because there were long periods of peaceful leisure when raiders did not come, and the degree of common culture that did develop suggests a world where violence was as often rhetorical as it was actual. The obvious areas of difference — shapes of houses and canoes, different forms of harpoons, hafted hammers among the northerners as against hand-held ones in the south, more emphasis on crests in the north and on individual guardian spirit quests in the south, matrilineal as against patrilineal inheritance, and even the varying manners of art — all these were enough to prove that the culture was not homogeneous, but certainly not enough to deny an underlying unity that could not have emerged merely out of a common environment. Despite their obstinately sustained linguistic differences, we have to assume that the peoples of the Coast were in productive contact over a very long period before the Europeans arrived, and we may also assume that one of the reasons for this contact was the combination of a highly developed culture with barely developed political concepts. Culture tends to unite; politics tends to divide.

Even in historical times we have seen the flow of influences within the Coast Indian culture in ways that cannot be attributed to European influence. It was not, for example, until fairly well into the nineteenth century that the Hamatsa dance spread through conquest from the northern to the southern Kwakiutl, and the same complex was spreading northward — wholly accepted by the Tsimshian but only partly by the

This photograph, taken by E. S. Curtis before World War I, shows the move from traditional to modern, with thunderbird figures in front of clapboard cottages and bird crests on long houses built of sawn lumber.

Haida and hardly at all by the Tlingit — when the influence of the missionaries checked what otherwise would almost certainly have been an acceptance by all the northern peoples (naturally within their own crest-dominated framework) of this very exciting dramatic complex. Cultural borrowings were often facilitated by marriage contacts between the various dialect divisions of peoples like the Kwakiutl, the Tsimshian, and the Tlingit, but also, in the case of peoples like

E. S. Curtis took his famous photographs during the twilight years of the classic Coast culture. Here he has combined the traditional cedar bark cape and spruce root hat with silver bracelets made with alien techniques but engraved with ancient Haida patterns.

known more about each other and about the world immediately surrounding them than early ethnologists were inclined to assume. Even the institution of slavery — as in the ancient world — was a channel of contact between peoples, for the slave often brought with him some technique that was a little better than that used in his master's house, and the slave who was ransomed often took some similar gift home to his own people. Even war played its part in the diffusion of the culture.

I emphasize this theme of the dynamic unity of the native culture because the immediate result of European contact was merely to increase the impetus of an existing development within the Coast Indian world. In other words, whatever was productive in the gifts of the new Transformers was used by the native culture precisely because it was a dynamic culture and open to vital new elements. It was the negative elements which the culture could not absorb that led towards its destruction.

There are really four phases to be observed in the relationship between the Coast Indians and the invading culture. First, there was the period of the fur trade, which began with the discovery in 1779 by Cook's sailors that sea otter skins could be sold for vast profits in Canton, and which ended when the creation of the crown colony of Vancouver Island in 1849 put an end to the trading hegemony of the Hudson's Bay Company on the Pacific Coast.

The colonial period included the early gold rushes to the Fraser Valley and Cariboo; the beginning of settlement in southern Vancouver Island and the Fraser Delta (and over the border around Puget Sound); the metamorphosis of Victoria from a trading post into a miniature capital, and the appearance of other small towns like New Westminster; and the coming of the missionaries — all events that had disastrous effects on the Indians and their culture. This was also

the Bella Coola and the northern Coast Salish, with neighbours of other linguistic groups.

Trade, extending southward down the whole coast and inland up all the great river routes, not only linked the Coast peoples with each other but also sustained relations between them and peoples outside the area, such as the Eskimos and the Aleuts to the north, the Athapaskan and Interior Salish peoples to the east, and the Chinook to the south; techniques and ideas as well as material commodities passed along the trade routes. The Coast peoples seem to have

the period when the really drastic reductions of Indian populations became evident.

In 1871 — following on the American acquisition of Alaska in 1867 — British Columbia entered the confederation of Canada. Colonial rule had ended in the whole area inhabited by Coast Indian peoples, and there followed in both Canadian and American territory a period of paternalistic rule with an accompanying policy of acculturation, symbolized in Canada by Sir John A. Macdonald's banning of the potlatch, so that the decline in population — which continued apace — was soon accompanied by a loss of spirit caused by the difficulty of sustaining an indigenous culture belonging to a dwindling native group among an actively hostile majority of strangers. This was the time when it came to be widely accepted that the Indian peoples of the Coast, as well as their culture, were dying out.

The fourth period has been the present era, which followed the reversal of population trends that became evident between the two world wars. It has been marked by a recovery of self-pride among the Indian peoples, leading to politically radical demands for a recognition of aboriginal land rights and also to a marked revival of some visible aspects of the culture, notably art and ceremonial, during the past two decades.

The fur trade period itself splits apart rather naturally into two sections. During the first forty years or so, after the pioneering voyage of Captain John Meares to Nootka Sound in 1785, the little ships of the "King George Men" and the "Boston Men" competed up and down the coast with such vigour that in some seasons as many as two hundred boats appeared and the sea otter was hunted almost to extinction. After the Hudson's Bay Company pushed northward and established Fort Langley on the Fraser River in 1827, the great fur-trading corporation squeezed out the individual traders and established a working monopoly in collusion with the Russian-American Company of Alaska. Neither the individual traders nor the companies' representatives were interested in changing the cultural or social patterns of Indian life. They were there merely to carry on commerce and did not wish to see any change in the flow of salable pelts. The Indians proved sharp bargainers and took full advantage of competition between the individual sea traders; when the company used its monopoly to regulate prices, the Indian chiefs seized control of the middleman trading between the Coast and the interior tribes, and many of the Tlingit and Tsimshian clans made considerable fortunes. During the whole fur trade period an extraordinary flow of trade goods reached the Coast, including not only manufactured articles from Europe, pigments and other goods from China, and metal items specially made by the ships' craftsmen to meet the current demands of the local Indians, but also native wares which the trading captains could transport more quickly and in larger quantities than was possible by the slow canoe routes of native trading. For example, the elk skins traded by the Chinook from the Rockies and used by the northern Coast tribes for armour began to appear in larger quantities from the 1780s onwards, and it is thought that much of the deeply coloured abalone shell which appears in Coast Indian diadems of the early nineteenth century was actually bought by American sea traders from the Indians in California and carried north by them. On occasion, the "Boston Men" even became involved in the coastal slave trade, buying at the mouth of the Columbia children captured from Oregon tribes and shipping them up for sale to the Haida and the Tlingit.

For the first generations at least, this great influx of goods into the territory of the Coast Indian peoples only changed their cultures in directions that were already established. As we have seen, the acquisition of iron tools did not

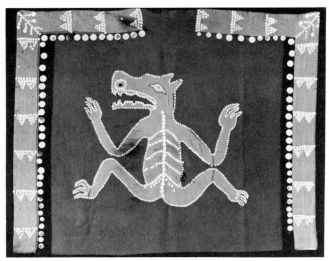

After the appearance of European traders these button blankets, made of imported cloth and pearl buttons, replaced the traditional woven blankets.

mean a technological revolution, since the Coast peoples were already familiar with metal, even if they had previously seen it only in small quantities, and they merely reproduced in iron the kind of tools they had already been refining for millennia in stone and jadeite and antler. This meant that work was more quickly done, more artifacts were made, and they were made more quickly, but the styles in which they were made remained astonishingly constant, though the scale may at times have been somewhat magnified. The great mass of European goods gathered by trading actually found its way into the ceremonial circuit. Until long into the nineteenth century the Indians still lived on their customary diet based on dried fish and oolichan grease, obtained in traditional ways; and for everyday use they did not begin to wear European clothes until after the 1850s. But they did often use European cloth for ceremonial robes, and they turned the cheapest type of Hudson's Bay Company blanket into an item of currency; the blankets passed backwards and forwards at potlatches in vast bales, and when they were not being given away they were usually stored for the next feast, only rarely being utilized as garments or as bedding. Other types of goods were later acquired for the same purpose, and to this day, at Indian potlatches, one recognizes the kinds of property that are never put to practical use but travel on from feast to feast, and often return in the end to the original giver, since the Indians have no objection to the circulation of presents. The new kinds of goods did not mean that the basic pattern of the potlatches changed; they merely became larger, more numerous, and more competitive.

But there were other consequences of the arrival of the Europeans which brought not only changes in some aspects of the potlatch, but also changes that cut at the very foundations of the Indian way of life. For the sea traders brought not only better tools and more goods for giving; they also brought alcohol, new and deadly sicknesses, and firearms.

The Indians of the North Pacific Coast never discovered the processes of fermentation, so that they did not even have equivalents of the beers which the Aztecs made out of agave juice and the Incas out of chewed maize kernels, nor, as I have said, do they appear to have used any kind of plant for hallucinogenic purposes. Their ecstasies were achieved through physical privations and solitude; it was a process of getting bushed rather than getting drunk. When the Indians were offered alcohol by the first explorers, they rejected it with disgust, just as they rejected cheese, whose taste they found sickening in comparison with the rank whale oil which they sometimes used. But gradually they were persuaded to accept, until the regale of rum became a regular feature of the trading process, as it was everywhere in Canada.

Perhaps, by missionaries especially, the role of alcohol in what happened to the Indian peoples of the Coast has been exaggerated, but there is no doubt that after Victoria became a populous and raucous frontier community for a brief while in 1858, many of the northern peoples in particular would travel hundreds of miles south in their great carved canoes to obtain liquor freely, and would return with their craft loaded with dubious concoctions made by the local merchants. The consumption of alcohol tended to mar the ancient dignity of feasting procedures and to exacerbate the passions of competitiveness in potlatches, particularly in places where the Indians were gathered in large communities and status rivalries were already strongly felt. Drinking among the Tlingit actually added to the general North American vernacular, for deserters from American ships taught them to brew a concoction from molasses, which they called *hootchenoo*, whence derived the word *hooch* that became so familiar throughout the United States during the era of prohibition.

No doubt some Indians did die of alcoholism, but more of them undoubtedly died from the firearms which they were already buying in quantities by the 1790s. It would be decades before the hunters of the Coast abandoned their powerful sinew-backed bows for the inaccurate muskets distributed by the traders. But even poor firearms turned out to be advantageous in the small-scale warfare to which the Indians were addicted, since if they were no more effective in hand-to-hand fighting than the traditional clubs and daggers used in ambushes and night attacks, they were much more terrifying and often deadly in the close quarters of ambushes. Certainly they gave the Indians who possessed them a considerable tactical advantage. They enabled the Euclataw, after they had seized Cape Mudge and Campbell River from the Comox Salish, to turn for a while into pirates threatening the narrows through which the northern canoes had to pass on their way to Vic-

By the early twentieth century mass-produced factory goods were being used as gifts at potlatches.

toria, and there is little doubt that the virtual extermination of such small Athapaskan peoples as the Tahltan and the Tsetsaut was due to the fact that their rivals, the Tlingit and the Gitksan respectively, who coveted their hunting grounds, had more firearms. Thus the arrival of the white men made Indian warfare more deadly, and for a brief period more frequent, than it had ever been before; more people died from guns than had died in the past from clubs or from the curious two-tipped daggers made from Asian iron which the Indians used before the white men came.

But the effects of alcohol and firearms might easily have been absorbed by the Indian culture without in the end destroying it. The sicknesses

201

introduced by Europeans — and deadly to people who did not know them and had developed no antibodies — were disastrous. It is possible that smallpox reached the Coast with the first contact between the Spaniards and the Haida in 1774; Captain Portlock in 1787 found that there had already been an outbreak among the Tlingit some years before and in 1794 Captain Bishop gathered similar reports of an epidemic among the Kaigani, the Haida of Prince of Wales Island.

Venereal diseases arrived with Cook's sailors in 1778, and were spread by the crews of the sea trading vessels that came in later decades, since — as the Spanish captains somewhat primly noted — the "King George Men" and the "Boston Men" were alike quite willing to accept in trade the services of slaves whom the chiefs prostituted. But the contraction of venereal sicknesses probably reached its height in Victoria from 1858 onwards, when the northern tribes would bring women down by the boatload for the purposes of prostitution. Almost invariably these were slaves; tales that the chiefs prostituted their wives and daughters for trading goods are quite untrue, though in later years, when commoners began to potlatch extravagantly so as to gain rank, some of these ambitious men did indeed sell the favours of their female kin to gain the goods they needed. However, the prostitution of slaves was just as detrimental to the Indian peoples as that of chiefs' daughters would have been, since the slaves were often the concubines of the chiefs and so disease would spread through a whole community.

Syphilis did kill some Indians. It and other venereal diseases rendered others infertile and contributed towards the very low Coast Indian birth rate during the latter half of the nineteenth century. But infectious rather than contagious diseases were the great killers. Smallpox swept the Coast again in 1835-36, but the most disastrous epidemic of all was that which struck in 1862; brought on one of the ships that sailed from San Francisco, it attacked the Indians who were encamped outside Victoria and was carried north by the panic-stricken survivors who fled before the plague. By the time this epidemic had burnt itself out whole villages of people had died, about a third of the native population of the Coast had been eliminated, and there were only half as many Indians in the region as had been there when the Europeans came. Other epidemics followed, and the ease of travel which the ending of Indian wars during the 1860s had brought about, contributed to their spread; the Indian communities had barely begun to recover from smallpox and to benefit from vaccination when the worldwide outbreak in 1918 of what became know as Spanish influenza reduced them further, so that by the 1920s — the general low point numerically of the Indian populations in this area — there were about a quarter as many Indians on the Coast as there had been a hundred and fifty years earlier in the 1770s. Fewer than six hundred Haida remained, a twelfth their original strength; they had abandoned all the outlying island communities and gathered in the two remaining villages of Masset and Skidegate. A similar concentration had been forced on the Bella Coola, of whom, in 1929, only 249 remained, a tenth of their strength when the white men, those terrible Transformers, came.

Europeans had introduced to the Coast Indians two of the classic Victorian sins, booze and prostitution. But the Indians, being natural men, had no sense of sinning, and the role of the missionaries was to make up for this deficiency. There is no doubt that the missionaries consciously utilized the misfortunes and demoralization of the Indians in the latter part of the nineteenth century to draw them into the fold and to destroy at least the more visible aspects of their traditional culture.

William Duncan was the most celebrated of

the missionaries to the Coast Indians. There had been one or two Catholics before him, and some Russian Orthodox priests had made converts among the Tlingit and established tiny native congregations that survive to this day. Duncan was an Anglican lay preacher, a young man of humble birth and narrow education, but of forceful character and a strong intelligence. Sent out by the Church Missionary Society, Duncan reached Victoria in 1857. Shortly afterwards he was allowed by a reluctant governor, James Douglas, to make his way north to Fort Simpson, where the Tsimshian villages, clustered around the Hudson's Bay Company post, offered the largest concentration of Indian people in the area. There Duncan carefully learnt the Tsimshian language, and began to preach in the various great communal houses. He secured the support of the powerful Legaic, head of the strongest and wealthiest clan, and because of the competitiveness that had entered into the situation at Fort Simpson, all the other chiefs had to invite Duncan to preach because they would have lost face if he had not appeared in their houses. But Duncan was too intelligent to imagine that his sermons were more than counters in the Fort Simpson game of chiefly prestige, and he saw that even while they welcomed him, the Indians continued to call in their shamans, to hold their potlatches, and to indulge in the grisly Hamatsa Society dances which they had acquired only recently from the Haisla of Kitimat; he even believed — and one can only guess whether or not he was right — that from the gallery of Fort Simpson he had seen naked hamatsa novices tearing apart and eating the body of a slave woman.

Duncan always claimed that the social experiment historically linked with his name — the model mission village of Metlakatla — was suggested to him by members of his congregation, who felt that they could only become true Christians if they were detached from the pagan ways of their brethren. But this was precisely the philosophy of the Church Missionary Society — to begin by gaining the confidence of a people, and then influence their desires until they willed their own change and could be left to follow their destinies as model Christians. One suspects that the main native contribution to the scheme was merely the suggestion that the mission would gain immense prestige if it were established at the channel of Metlakatla, the old winter gathering site of the Tsimshian tribes before they resorted to Fort Simpson; Duncan planned everything else.

He certainly went all the way, when he led his followers out of the Babylon of Fort Simpson, to detach them completely from the pagan past. They were expected to wear European clothes, to keep regular hours, to police themselves, to work in the industries that would make them as self-sufficient as possible; to abandon the old communal dwellings, which seemed so promiscuous to Christian puritans, in favour of individual family dwellings. They were expected *not* to indulge in a good many pagan activities which Duncan's disapproval automatically graded as sins; these included "the Demoniacal Rites called Ahlied or Medicine Work; Conjuring and all the heathen practices over the sick; Use of intoxicating liquor; Gambling; Painting Faces; Giving away property for display; Tearing up property in anger or to wipe away disgrace." One notices the clever intermingling of sins acquired from white men, such as drinking, with the original Indian cultural complexes that Duncan was really intent on destroying, such as the potlatch, the activities of the shamans, and the winter dance complexes. Unlike some other missionaries, who urged their congregations to destroy every artifact connected with the pagan past, he had nothing against totem poles or the system of crests as identifying badges of social groups; he

A potlatching Kwakiutl chief and his attendants. The gifts on display show the transition from native to imported products. The woven hats are traditional; the silver bracelets on poles are made by Indian craftsmen using acquired silversmith skills; the enamelware and blankets have been bought from white traders.

entered Confederation in 1871, Duncan tried to turn the Indians into Christians at the expense of their native culture — the culture that identified and sustained them — and thus in his own way contributed to the long period of demoralization that emerged from the great failure of spirit which marked the last decades of the nineteenth century.

Duncan inspired his followers at Metlakatla to build a vast neo-Gothic church of painted wood garnished with filigree fretwork; it became known as "Duncan's Cathedral" and was reputed to be the largest ecclesiastical building of its time west of Chicago. Within the church, on each side of the Lord's Table (for Duncan never spoke of anything as papist as an altar!) he allowed two large poles bearing the crests of the local clans to be erected. But the symbolism of the poles was negated, since Duncan denied the rest of the culture by seeking to suppress the potlatch and the shamanic rites (including the winter ceremonies of the dancing societies) which helped to give significance to the lives of the Indians. By acceding to the demands of the missionaries and of many Indian converts, and legally banning the potlatch, the winter society ceremonials, and the Salish guardian spirit dances for almost seventy years, from 1884 to 1951, the Canadian government in turn aligned itself with the forces of acculturation.

Even without such open attacks on the Indian culture, it would probably have declined for other reasons. As white settlement spread, as the appearance of canneries on the coastal inlets was followed by commercial fishing, the economic basis of Indian society began to shift. Unlike many other Indian groups, those of the British Columbian coast never surrendered their lands by treaty, which did not prevent the lands over which they had once hunted and picked berries being alienated. In fact, the policy followed in the crown colony and later under Confederation

was observant enough to recognize that the poles were never worshipped as idols, and he realized that if he showed some respect for the crest system he stood a better chance of retaining the friendship of the powerful Tsimshian chiefs and of being able to influence their followers.

In his little Christian Utopia, whose fascinating story is too long and complicated to be told here in all its entirety, Duncan did enable a good many Indians to survive physically during the disintegration of their culture in the later nineteenth century. Yet there is no doubt that like most of the other missionaries (the Catholics were actually a little wiser than the Protestants in matters of interfering with the native culture) and like the Indian Agents responsible to Ottawa who came on the scene after British Columbia

was that land not already surveyed or scheduled as an Indian reserve could be pre-empted by a white man, and surveyed land could be bought, but not by Indians. Without their consent, the Indians were left merely the reserves allocated to them, and perhaps the only fortunate aspect of the situation was that winter village sites and the sites of summer camps were usually preserved. But this did not prevent white and later Japanese fishermen from trespassing with the support of the law on what had formerly been Indian fishing grounds, or catching the fish offshore long before it reached the river estuaries. As a consequence, the fish runs were rapidly diminished and the Indians were forced themselves to become commercial fishermen. At the same time, the extermination of fur-bearing animals had destroyed the primary means of obtaining trade goods, for only peoples far from the coast, like the Nishka and the Gitksan, continued to trap profitably. Many Indians abandoned traditional occupations altogether and began to take wage employment in sawmills or logging camps, or seasonal employment on the farms of the Fraser Valley or around Puget Sound.

By the beginning of the present century the Coast Indian still lived on his traditional sites, though the decline in population meant that the remoter villages were abandoned and the people of different clans and areas tended to cluster in common settlements. Many had their commercial fishing boats, often mortgaged to the canneries or the packers; others worked for wages in local industries; yet others survived on minimal welfare payments; and a few still tried obstinately to sustain a subsistence existence based mainly on foods their ancestors had used (though most Indians had come to like bread and sweet foods, and many made a gesture towards agriculture by growing potatoes on the old shell middens.) They were also nominal Christians, though often their Christianity was mingled

Curtis's photograph of a Kwakiutl chief shows the transition of the very regalia. The rattle, orator's staff, Hamatsa headband and neckband are traditional —but not the button blanket or Western clothes.

with traditional elements, as in the Indian Shaker Church among the Salish, with its holy dancing and its deafening handbell ringing. They now lived in individual houses as nuclear families, held their property individually rather than communally as in the past, and either abandoned their potlatches and spirit dances or carried them on in secret. The crests and songs were remembered by the older people, and even by the young the lines of descent in clans and ex-

This pole, a fine example of recent Gitksan carving, stands outside a chief's house at Kitwancool, the most remote village on the upper Skeena River.

to external influence helped to keep their particular form of the Coast culture vigorously alive long after it seemed to be dead elsewhere). The impetus of missionization meant that by the 1880s native ceremonial patterns ceased to spread (so that the Hamatsa complex never reached the Tlingit or the southern Salish), and the discouragement of the potlatches that validated them made pointless the carving of totem poles and of the masks and rattles associated with the display of privileges on such occasions. In other words, the social motivations of most kinds of Indian art vanished, and since it was essentially a social art, that meant its decay. It is true that early in the nineteenth century a trade in Indian art objects sold as curios developed, and it found expression particularly in miniature wooden totem poles and in model canoes. But these had little of the vigour and none of the meaning of works made for actual use in the Indians' ceremonial life, and the same applied to the debased craft of carving in a soft black slate known as argillite which developed in response to traders' demands. Some works in this material, notably those of the famous and, in my view, overrated Charles Edenshaw, displayed a modicum of virtuosity, but there is a meretricious slickness to most argillite work, in spite of the attempts by connoisseurs, who do not understand the Coast Indian traditions, to inflate its value. It was made for trade, and at best for the collector trade, and had no significance within the culture, nor does it have any meaning within the culture's current revival.

It is difficult yet to write in any conclusive way on the changes that have taken place within the last two decades in the situation of the Coast Indians. By the end of the 1920s, as I have already suggested in my Introduction, the direction of the population graph had begun to change dramatically, and in numbers the Coast Indians have by now almost reached the level of the years

tended clans was not forgotten, any more than the inherited names. But this did not mean a great deal in everyday life, and the times when the people spent a working summer gathering the wealth to be spent over a ceremonial winter seemed to have passed away.

Undoubtedly all these circumstances combined to produce the great decline in Coast Indian art that became evident from the mid-1880s onwards on the coast itself (though very much later among the Gitksan, whose noted resistance

during the late eighteenth century when the dreadful white Transformers appeared among them. This has not meant that the deserted villages have been resettled or that the Indians have returned in any numbers to traditional ways of living. Indeed, there has been a tendency for them to compete more energetically in the white man's world, and every year more young Indians are attending the universities of the Northwest Pacific area. There have been also the political developments on which I have also touched earlier, but in the context of this book they are relevant mainly to demonstrate the upsurge in vitality, mental as well as spiritual, among the Indian peoples of the Coast during recent years.

It is an upsurge that has not been without its effects on native arts and culture. Young Indian artists have begun to relearn the methods and the aesthetics of their predecessors. Some of the work they do, particularly in argillite carving, in silver jewellery, and in such newer media as the serigraph, is directed at tourists or collectors and suffers from the same lack of conviction as the earlier argillite carving. Some of their work is public art, in the form of poles that are commissioned by governments or other authorities, and here, in the hands of contemporary artists, of whom Mungo Martin was such a notable link with the great past, there have been examples of carvings as strong and as imaginative as those of the artists who lived within the tradition. Perhaps this is precisely because of the public nature of such commissions, since the art of the Indians was, as we have seen, a public as well as a social art, dependent on ceremony, nourished by acclamation.

This is why the other interesting work that Indian artists on the Coast have been producing recently is linked with the revival of ceremonial that has taken place since the withdrawal twenty-five years ago of the ban on the potlatch. Of the masks, rattles, and other ceremonial ob-

No traditional houses survive, but recently this replica of a Kwakiutl house was erected in Victoria by Kwakiutl craftsmen who inherited the ancient art.

jects now being carved, some indeed find their way onto the tourist market and some are immediately withdrawn from active meaning by museum purchase. But others are being used again by peoples like the Kwakiutl and the Gitksan and the southern Salish, among whom the ceremonial tradition has never been lost. What that tradition still means it is hard to tell, except in the old Indian way of witnessing its validity through one's own presence, and that is why I end this book not with an ordinary summary but with the description of an encounter that I now remember as a true epiphany.

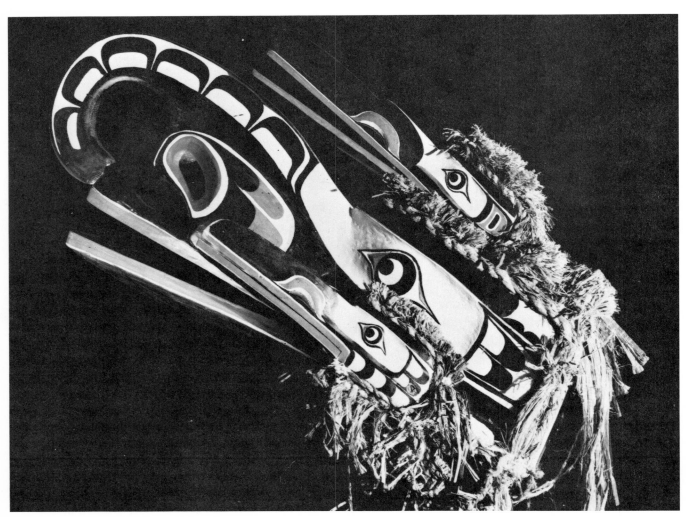

This version of a crooked-beak mask, carved by Mungo Martin in 1953, is a fine example of modern Indian art.

A Witnessing

Midden Bay is not a name you will find on the maps, but it represents a real place, a Salish village on the frayed eastern coast of Vancouver Island, facing the Gulf of Georgia. It was not easy to find on the cold and misty December night when we turned off the Island Highway fifty miles or so north of Victoria and followed the winding side road around placid coves and then into a forest where the only landmark we had been given was an Indian cemetery at a crossroads. We found the cemetery — white wooden crosses gleaming suddenly out of a tangle of brown bracken — but turned the wrong way and ended in the cul-de-sac of a sluggish development: roads roughed in, tumbling billboards, a couple of derelict trailers. We retraced our way to the cemetery, took another direction, and knew we were on the right road when the hardtop ended and we began to bump over the potholes of a decaying gravel road. We passed Indian houses, slowing to avoid children and pups dashing into the gleam of the headlights, and came down to the water's edge, the black bay sucking at the banks of mingled soil and broken oyster shell that betokened an ancient settlement, the houses lit with bare bulbs, cars parked along the ice-glazed earth road around the beach. Behind the houses loomed a long dark building — no windows but sparks spurting out from the three wide openings in the corrugated iron roof. We nudged our Volkswagen in between the big, battered old cars and the new station wagons, and as we turned off the engine the hard thud of the drums beat in our ears. The spirit dances had begun.

When the Indian Act of 1951 was passed, and the infamous clause prohibiting potlatches and spirit dances was finally removed from the statute books, an injustice that had lasted as long as most living Coast Indians could remember was furtively rectified. This did not mean that the ceremonies started up again, for they had never come to an end, but at least nobody risked going to prison for performing them. Nor did it mean that potlatches and spirit dances came into the open. Experience had taught the Indians of the Pacific Coast the wisdom of keeping their customs to themselves. Even today, twenty-five years after the ban was lifted, many people who live quite close to Indian villages have no idea that the traditional ceremonials have returned to assume once again their centrality in the pattern of native life. The woman who kept the lodge where we would be returning to sleep the morning out traded regularly with women from Midden Bay for their Cowichan sweaters and other craftwork, but she was quite unaware that dances went on regularly there — sometimes two or three times a week — throughout the winter. We had come to know of them only by chance, and it was by oblique arrangement that we received a barely stated invitation from a chief's wife who was herself an initiate. We were to turn up, and if anyone questioned us, we were to mention her name; she would be there, but it was clear she did not intend to sponsor us in any open way. And it might be a good idea, the message went, if we left our cameras and tape recorders at home.

Thus, by the time Inge and I pulled open the heavy wooden door of the dance house at about eleven o'clock that December night, we had a good idea how important a part spirit dances had resumed in Salish life. Even so, we were not prepared for the scene that greeted us. The house was made of sheets of plywood nailed on a frame of rough cedar; it was somewhat over two hundred feet long and more than fifty feet wide. Six-tiered bleachers of worn planks ran along two sides and both ends, and these were well occupied. In the long open floor of the house three great fires blazed, six-foot logs piled crisscross in squares to the height of a man so that they became gigantic cubes of flame and embers, out of which the smoke and sparks drifted up to the smokeholes and billowed around the house, occasionally half-blinding one. At least another hundred people — men with tambourine-shaped drums in their hands — stood on the trodden earth floor, so that altogether there must have been between eight and nine hundred people there. (We were afterwards told that as winter involvement and attendance increased each year the house became more crowded, so that by the end of March between fifteen hundred and two thousand people might be present, coming from villages all over southern Vancouver Island and even from the lower Fraser valley and from the State of Washington over the border.)

We stood diffidently just inside the doorway, waiting, as seemed appropriate, to be recognized. A man almost as big as the King of Tonga, with a drum in his hand and his face painted black with a mixture of charcoal and grease, came forward, said we were welcome, and led us to the bleachers on the right of the house, nearest the door; the chief's wife never made herself known. We climbed to places on the top bench and saw at once that the house was divided between the initiates with their black faces and their attendant family groups on the left-hand side of the room, and the noninitiated spectators and witnesses on the other. A few smartly dressed Indians from the United States were sitting next to us in our little strangers' enclave; we were the only white people there.

The drumming had just ceased when we entered, but as soon as we sat down there was a kind of coalescent flowing of the men on the floor towards the initiates' bench. A black-faced girl with a tartan blanket slung over her shoulders began to stand up, assisted by women on each side of her, and all at once, with a spontaneity which I afterwards learned was more apparent than real, the drums began to beat in a distinctive rhythm, and the song — the girl's personal spirit song — emerged (that is the only word that really expresses the process) in a kind of surging chorus, as she started the dance that the spirit had given her, which would take her around the hall and the great fires. She danced with her torso bent forward, gaze fixed on the ground as if in trance, disregarding the spectators, her hands extended, and fingers weaving in patterns that reminded me of the *mudras* of Asian dancing. In her dance she was followed by a little cluster of attendants, members of the extended family to which she belonged, the women raising their hands upward and addressing strange high-pitched calls to the spectators, as if appealing to us for witness, and as they went they handed out silver quarters to the drummers — for every participant in any Pacific Coast Indian ceremony must be rewarded.

As the dancer spun round the third fire at the

head of the house, the drums thudded more loudly, people in the bleachers joining in with their own drums and keeping the rhythm, until there must have been two hundred drums beating and the sound reached a thunderous crescendo that seemed to carry the singing on its crest and filled the house with an extraordinary atmosphere of occult power, which we felt even on that first dance and more intensely on each occasion as the evening went on. Finally the girl danced back to her place on the bench and sank down on it, wailing loudly. It was the spirit calling from within her, and as she wailed, the spirits of the women around her were activated, and they gave strange mewing calls like seagulls.

The drums and the singing had ceased as abruptly as they began, as if some invisible conductor had waved his staff. All suddenly became relaxed, the crowd of drummers dissolved into pairs of men chatting as they strolled over the floor, children clambered over the bleachers, women wandered off into a little room in the corner of the house and came back with paper cups of coffee and pieces of home-made cake as if it were a church social. And then, out of all this casualness, there came another sudden gathering of the drummers, the next black-faced girl rose from her place, a different song surged up, and she made her turn of the room. Five women danced in this way; the drum and song rhythms were similar, and so was the general shape of the dance, yet in each case the hand movements and the stance, like the song, were quite distinctive, expressing each dancer's special spirit helper, and I was reminded of the Samoan women's dance, the *siva*, which is regarded as the supreme expression of any woman's personality.

Inevitably, as all this went on, we were apprehensively assessing the attitude which these hundreds of Indians engaged in their native ceremonies might display towards us, strangers and aliens as we were. Those from south of the border, among whom we sat, were friendly enough, but though they were also Salish they shared neither the dialect nor the dance traditions of the Cowichans, so that they were almost as much outsiders as we were. And we had heard, as one does everywhere in British Columbia these days, of militancy among the native peoples. The lodge keeper had told us how, only a month before, the people of Midden Bay, incited by "agitators from the States," had closed off all the local roads in pursuit of their land claims. And yet, though we stayed among them until far into the morning, we were aware of no special feelings towards us of any demonstrable kind. Certainly nobody made any gesture of hostility, and later we were in a special way included in the events enacted that evening. For most of the people, we seemed to be merely members of the crowd of witnesses, and we were careful to do nothing that might draw us out of the anonymity of such a role.

The men's dances were perhaps more closely traditional than those of the women. The women had worn no distinctive garments and used no ceremonial instruments. But as the dances went on the black-faced male initiates sat shaking their rattles, which among the Salish are staffs about three feet long, carved and painted, with crests on their tips (I noticed the head of a bald eagle and that of a serpent) and half way down rings of mussel shells (once it would have been deer's hooves) that give a thin, dry clatter when they are shaken. When a man's turn came to dance, he would give his rattle to an attendant who plied it as he followed the dancer around the fires. The men dancers wore embroidered dance leggings and jackets of dark blue serge, from which hung dozens of little bone appendages in the form of miniature paddles. They danced with knees and elbows rigidly angled, performing a percussive stamp and nodding their heads up and down vigorously; the most vigorous were those who wore wigs of human hair that came down over heads and shoulders, almost to their waists, like great candle-snuffers with tufts of feathers at the tops, and completely blinded them so that their attendants had constantly to push them away from the fires. These were initiates possessed of warrior spirits. When the men returned to their seats, they too wailed, but the spirits aroused in the men around them growled like bears.

These were all men and women who had actually gone through initiation and performed their novice dances at some time in the past; they were now validating their status as full-fledged spirit dancers. But all at once, in the middle of the men's dances, an uninitiated girl was spontaneously possessed. She was sitting among one of the families on the dancers' side of the house when she sank wailing into a trance and was immediately lifted and carried over to the spectators' benches, neutral ground. Women clustered around her, speaking to her, stroking her, wailing softly, until a strange, tall figure appeared and knelt before her. He was an old man with the asexual look of those elderly actors who play young women in Kabuki, his grey hair long, plaited around his head, tied with bits of red ribbon. It was too far off to see what this ritualist actually did, but it appeared to be some kind of communing with the spirit, for he made passes, and then raised his head and twice gave a strange falsetto cry, after which he immediately threw a blanket over the girl's head.

She remained under that blanket for the rest of the night, for a bit of stifling is considered a good thing in such situations, and when her family left early in the morning she was led out, still completely covered, for her protection but also for those of others, since supernatural forces were hovering around her. Her initiation would begin at once, and while she was kept for days in seclusion on a meagre diet, her attendants would listen to the spirit speaking through her in cries out of which they would compose the song that henceforward would be hers alone. People who are conscripted, as it were, into the fellowship of dancers often have to go through severe hazings, as they did in pagan days, but those who are spontaneously possessed are treated with special gentleness.

Now began the part of the ceremonial without which none of the dances we had seen would be regarded as valid. The only way of validation is through giving on the part of the initiates' families. Men and boys began to come into the house carrying cardboard cartons, which were piled in a long row in front of the initiates' benches. Then, one by one, the family groups began their round of the bleachers, the black-faced dancer making the gifts, and an elder in each group, expert at the gradations of rank, pointing out each recipient.

Blankets were — in keeping with tradition — the principal gifts, and a person's status was made evident by the kind of blanket he received. High rank (which usually means you have made rich gifts in the past) merited five-point Hudson's Bay Company blankets; low rank (which means meagre giving in the past) merited only hideously flowered flannelette sheets. We ranked at the level neither of blankets nor of the silk scarves with rhinestone jewels knotted in the corners which formed the second round of gifts. Still, we were witnesses, our presence helped to validate the dances, and we were rewarded during the later rounds, when crockery and fruit were given out; we had to accept, for refusal of a gift would have publicly shamed the dancer and his whole family, and ourselves as well. Gift after gift was sent up, hand over hand, to our place at the top of the bleachers; when we counted them afterwards, we found that we had collected one gold-and-white cup and saucer, one large rose-patterned ironstone plate, one glass mug, one

Pyrex dish, four oranges, and fourteen apples. Such gifts indicated that our presence and our behaviour had been accepted. They also gave some means of judging the quantity of goods changing hands that night, for we were only minor recipients among the three or four hundred people who sat on the spectators' benches. One gigantic woman sitting just below us went out with three large cardboard cartons filled with her presents, and the combined families must have spent several thousand dollars in such gifts alone.

Nor were these the only transfers of property, for every occasion like this is used as an opportunity for the public settling of ceremonial debts, and the floor was taken up for at least an hour, while the families went round with their gifts, by men making orations in ceremonial Old Salish as various obligations were straightened out by the handing over of prominently displayed bundles of bills, whose amount was always declared on spread fingers raised high for everyone to see. Several hundred dollars changed hands in this way in addition to the gifts made to the witnesses on the right-hand benches.

It was after the giving that two isolated dances took place, and these in their different ways were the most moving episodes of the night. A small boy led in a young man in a strange garb of jerkin and leggings of grey and white wool, with many tassels, and head-dress coming down over the face, rather like that of the warrior dancers except that it also was made of much-tasselled grey and white wool. He carried a tasselled spear jingling with shells on whose point someone had struck a big red apple.

He was a novice dancer in a state of possession, and according to Salish beliefs a highly dangerous figure who had to be watched carefully lest he go berserk and start attacking people with his spear. This young man, however, did nothing but wander vaguely around the floor until the drums began to beat; this threw him into his dancing frenzy, and he covered the circuit of the house twice in a series of extraordinary sightless leaps, like some blind primitive Nijinsky, bouncing up and down with knees and feet tightly together, as if he were made of rubber, and giving a great deal of trouble to his small attendant who had to keep him from jumping into one of the fires. At last he sank down on a bench at the far end of the house, well away from the actual initiates, and there the spirit wailed in him like a wolf for a good hour before he finally settled into a silent trance. Nobody took any notice of all this. It was obviously what a respectable traditionally minded young man was expected to do in Salish society.

This performance of a young man beginning his career of spiritual possession was balanced by the other late dance, which clearly marked an end. An ancient woman had been sitting in the middle of the dancers' bench, and now she was being helped to her feet by her daughters and granddaughters. She was almost skeletally fragile and dressed in a pink sequinned gown and a rhinestoned headband with a few white eagle feathers stuck in it, as if she had got ready for one of Pierre Berton's early Hollywood films on the Canadian West; her cheeks seemed to have been dusted with wood ash, for they had an unnatural greyness. She was so weak that she had to be supported in her slow walk, and all that remained of her dance was the continual movement of her hands and fingers in the gestures that expressed her spirit. Yet it was in one way the most dramatic dance of the whole night, for the drummers came down out of the bleachers to join those on the floor and make an avenue of sound through which the old dancer progressed, with hundreds of voices shouting out her song, and her attendants scattering handfuls of coins among the drummers and the singers. It was obviously a farewell, for we felt no doubt that this was the old woman's last dance, and that she and everyone else knew it. But it was also the kind of assertion of continuity, for here was a person who had been a child in the last flourishing of the old native culture, and by supporting her in her dance the rest of the people were not only proclaiming their continuity with the past but also celebrating the revival of the old ways.

Somewhere past three in the morning the crowds on the bleachers began to thin as people set out on the way home to other villages, and we went out with them. We were elated by what we had seen, above all by what we had heard and felt in the vast vibrations of sound that surged about the great house. The Salish contend that attendance at the spirit dances can cure many sicknesses that are in some way or another psychosomatic. But it seemed to us not merely a matter of individual cure, but of the cure of a whole people from the alienation of those intermediate generations when they lived between two worlds, their native culture almost completely destroyed and the culture of the white man temperamentally alien to them.

It seemed as though time had taken a spiral, and now these Coast Indians were in possession again of the heart of their culture, the spirit dance cult, which expressed their collective Salish identity, and at the same time emotionally supported each individual as the old communal Indian life had done. Quite apart from the sense of occult power produced by the drumming and the singing, one recognized a feeling of confidence and pride among the hundreds of people gathered in the dance house. Here they were in their own world, secure, and that was perhaps why they could accept the two of us without either the shy embarrassment or the nervous hostility that so often mars relations between Indians and whites. It was a sign of the reverence with which the people of Midden Bay regard their revived pagan ceremonies, that — despite cynical forewarnings by local whites — we saw no one in the great house who was either drinking or even mildly drunk, and when we went outside there was none of the drinking in cars that accompanies white dances in Vancouver Island village halls.

Next morning we went down again to Midden Bay to see in the daylight what the village looked like. It was little different from other Vancouver Island Indian villages. The cemetery at the crossroads was a rough field where gaudy, plastic flowers were the only decorations. The houses looked ill maintained, the gardens grew only rubbish, and if it had not been for some expensive station wagons and pick-up trucks, one would have thought Midden Bay one of the poorest places in Canada. This was not really so, for the Indians here were relatively prosperous, many of the men earning well from fishing and most of the others having regular work in the local sawmills. It was merely that they had different ideas on how money was well spent; that night of ceremony and giving suggested to me that they might be right.

Bibliography

The titles which I list below do not represent all the works I have consulted during the last two years of study, but they are those which in hindsight appear most germane to the book that has emerged. I have confined myself, except for one thesis and three important special issues of magazines, to published books; the articles which have given hints on special aspects of Coast Indian life and history are too numerous to be listed within a reasonable space, but those who are especially interested in such pieces would do well to consult the excellent "Bibliography of the Arts and Crafts of Northwest Coast Indians" by Ian L. Bradley, which appeared in the Spring 1975 issue of *B.C. Studies, Vancouver*, and the equally useful "Select Bibliography of Anthropology in British Columbia" by Wilson Duff and Michael Kew, published in 1973 in the same journal.

Adams, John W. *The Gitksan Potlatch*. Toronto: Holt, Rinehart and Winston, 1973.

Anderson, Bern. *Surveyor of the Sea: The Life and Adventures of Captain George Vancouver*. Toronto: University of Toronto Press, 1966.

Arctander, John M. *The Apostle of Alaska: The Story of William Duncan of Metlakahtla*. New York: H. Revell Co., 1909.

Artscanada. Special Issue: "Stones, Bones and Skin: Ritual and Shamanistic Art." Toronto, Dec. 1973-Jan. 1974.

Averkieva, U. P. *Slavery Among the Indians of North America*. Translated from the Russian by G. R. Elliott. Victoria: Victoria College, 1966.

Barbeau, Marius. *Alaska Beckons*. Toronto: Macmillan, 1947.

———. *Haida Carvers in Argillite*. Ottawa: National Museum of Canada, 1957.

———. *Medicine Men of the North Pacific Coast*. Ottawa: National Museum of Canada, 1958.

———. *Totem Poles*. 2 vols. Ottawa: King's Printer, 1950.

———. *Totem Poles of the Gitksan, Upper Skeena River, British Columbia*. Ottawa: King's Printer, 1929.

Barnett, Homer G. *The Coast Salish of British Columbia*. Eugene: University of Oregon Press, 1955.

———. *Indian Shakers: A Messianic Cult of the Pacific Northwest*. Carbondale: Southern Illinois University Press, 1957.

B.C. Studies. Special issue: "Archaeology in British Columbia: New Discoveries," edited by Roy L. Carlson. Vancouver, Fall-Winter, 1970.

Begg, Alexander. *History of British Columbia*. Toronto: William Briggs, 1894.

Benedict, Ruth. *The Concept of the Guardian Spirit in North America*. New York: Kraus, 1964.

———. *Patterns of Culture*. New York: Houghton Mifflin, 1934.

Boas, Franz. *Kwakiutl Ethnography*. Chicago: University of Chicago Press, 1966.

———. *Primitive Art*. New York: Dover Publications, 1955.

———. *Race, Language and Culture*. New York: Macmillan, 1940.

———. *Religion of the Kwakiutl Indians*. 2 vols. New York: Columbia University Press, 1930.

———. *The Social Organization and Secret Societies of the Kwakiutl Indians*. Washington: National Museum, 1895.

Bolton, Herbert E. *Fray Juan Crespi, Missionary Explorer on the Pacific Coast, 1769-1774*. Berkeley: University of California Press, 1927.

British Columbia Heritage Series: Our Native Peoples.
1. *Introduction to Our Native Peoples*. Victoria, 1966.
2. *Coast Salish*. Victoria, 1952.
4. *Haida*. Victoria, 1952.
5. *Nootka*. Victoria, 1966.
6. *Tsimshian*. Victoria, 1966
7. *Kwakiutl*. Victoria, 1966.
10. *Bella Coola*. Victoria, 1953.

Carlson, Roy L., ed. *Salvage '71: Reports on Salvage Archaeology Undertaken in British Columbia in 1971*. Burnaby: Simon Fraser University, 1972.

Carr, Emily. *Klee Wyck*. Toronto: Oxford University Press, 1941.

Carter, Anthony. *This is Haida*. Saanichton: Agency Press, 1968.

Clark, Ian Christie. *Indian and Eskimo Art of Canada*. Toronto: Ryerson Press, 1971.

Clutesi, George. *Potlatch*. Sidney, B.C.: Gray's Publishing, 1969.

Codere, Helen. *Fighting with Property: A Study of Kwakiutl Potlatching and Warfare, 1792-1930*. New York: J. J. Augustin, 1951.

Cook, James. *The Journals of Captain Cook* edited by J. C. Beaglehole. 4 vols. London: Cambridge University Press, 1955-67.

Craven, Margaret. *I Heard the Owl Call My Name*. Toronto: Clarke, Irwin, 1967.

De Laguna, Frederica. *Under Mount Saint Elias*. Washington: Smithsonian Institution Press, 1972.

De Menil, Adelaide and Reid, William. *Out of the Silence*. Toronto: New Press, 1971.

Dixon, George. *A Voyage Round the World*. London: George Goulding, 1789.

Dockstader, Frederick J. *Indian Art in America*. Greenwich, Conn.: New York Graphic Society, 1961.

Drucker, Philip. *Archaeological Survey of the Northwest Coast*. Washington, D.C.: Government Printing Office, 1943.

———. *Cultures of the North Pacific Coast*. San Francisco: Chandler, 1965.

———. *Indians of the Northwest Coast*. New York: McGraw-Hill, 1955.

———. *The Northern and Central Nootkan Tribes*. Washington: U.S. Government Printer, 1951.

Drucker, Philip and Heizer, Robert F. *To Make My Name Good: A Reexamination of the Southern Kwakiutl Potlatch*. Berkeley: University of California Press, 1967.

Duff, Wilson. *Histories, Territories and Laws of the Kitwancool*. Victoria: B.C. Provincial Museum, 1959.

———. *Images Stone B.C.* Saanichton: Hancock House, 1975.

———. *The Indian History of British Columbia*. Vol. 1. *The Impact of the White Man*. Victoria: B.C. Provincial Museum, 1964.

———. *The Upper Stalo Indians of the Fraser Valley, British Columbia*. Victoria: B.C. Provincial Museum, 1952.

Duff, Wilson; Holm, Bill; and Reid, Bill. *Arts of the Raven*. Vancouver: Vancouver Art Gallery, 1967.

Eliade, Mircea. *Rites and Symbols of Initiation*. New York: Harper Torchbooks, 1958.

———. *Shamanism: Archaic Techniques of Ecstasy*. New York: Pantheon Books, 1964.

Fields, D. B. and Stanbury, W. T. *The Economic Impact of the Public Sector Upon the Indians of British Columbia*. Vancouver: University of British Columbia Press, 1973.

Ford, Clellan S. *Smoke From Their Fires*. New Haven: Yale University Press, 1941.

Fraser, Douglas. *Primitive Art*. Garden City, N.Y.: Doubleday, 1962.

Garfield, Viola E. and Forrest, Linn A. *The Wolf and the Raven*. Seattle: University of Washington Press, 1948.

Garfield, Viola E. and Wingert, Paul S. *The Tsimshian Indians and Their Arts*. Seattle: University of Washington Press, 1950.

Goddard, Pliny Earle. *Indians of the Northwest Coast*. New York: American Museum Press, 1934.

Goddard, Pliny Earle and Kew, Della. *Indian Art and Culture of the Northwest Coast*. Saanichton: Hancock House, 1974.

Gunther, Erna. *Indian Life on the Northwest Coast of North America, As Seen by the Earliest Explorers and Fur Traders During the Last Decades of the Eighteenth Century*. Chicago: University of Chicago Press, 1972.

Gunther, Erna and Haeberlin, Hermann. *The Indians of Puget Sound*. Seattle: University of Washington Press, 1930.

Haig-Brown, Roderick. *The Whale People*. Toronto: Collins, 1962.

Harris, Kenneth B. in collaboration with Frances Robinson. *Visitors Who Never Left: The Origin of the People of Damelahamid*. Vancouver: University of British Columbia Press, 1974.

Harrison, Charles. *Ancient Warriors of the North Pacific*. London: H. F. & G. Witherby, 1925.

Hawthorn, Audrey. *Art of the Kwakiutl Indians and Other Northwest Coast Tribes*. Seattle: University of Washington Press, 1967.

———. *People of the Potlatch*. Vancouver: Vancouver Art Gallery, 1956.

Hawthorn, H. B., ed. *A Survey of the Contemporary Indians of Canada*. 2 vols. Ottawa: Indian Affairs, 1966-67.

Hawthorn, H. B.; Belshaw, C. S.; and Jamieson, S. M. *The Indians of British Columbia*. Berkeley: University of California Press, 1958.

Hays, H. R. *Children of the Raven: The Seven Indian Nations of the Northwest Coast*. New York: McGraw-Hill, 1975.

Heyerdahl, Thor. *American Indians in the Pacific*. London: Allen and Unwin, 1952.

Hill, Beth and Hill, Ray. *Indian Petroglyphs of the Pacific*

Northwest. Saanichton: Hancock House, 1974.

Holm, Bill. *The Crooked Beak of Heaven.* Seattle: University of Washington Press, 1972.

_____. *Northwest Coast Indian Art.* Seattle: University of Washington Press, 1965.

Inverarity, R. B. *Art of the Northwest Coast Indians.* Berkeley: University of California Press, 1950.

Jenness, Diamond. *The Faith of a Coast Salish Indian.* Victoria: B.C. Provincial Museum, 1955.

_____. *Indians of Canada.* Ottawa: Queen's Printer, 1955.

Jewitt, John R. *A Narrative of the Adventures of John R. Jewitt.* Edinburgh: Constable, 1824.

Kane, Paul. *Paul Kane's Frontier* edited by J. Russell Harper. Toronto: University of Toronto Press, 1974.

_____. *Wanderings of an Artist Among the Indians of North America.* London: Longmans, 1859.

Keithahn, Edward L. *Monuments in Cedar.* Seattle: Superior Publishing Co., 1963.

Krause, Aurel. *The Tlingit Indians,* translated by Erna Gunther. Seattle: University of Washington Press, 1956.

La Barre, Weston. *The Ghost Dance: Origins of Religion.* New York: Doubleday, 1970.

La Violette, F. E. *The Struggle for Survival: Indian Cultures and the Protestant Ethic in British Columbia.* Toronto: University of Toronto Press, 1961.

Ledyard, John. *John Ledyard's Journal of Captain Cook's Last Voyage,* edited by James Kenneth Mumford. Corvallis: Oregon State University Press, 1963.

Leland, Charles G. *Fusang: The Discovery of America by Chinese Buddhist Priests in the Fifteenth Century.* London: Curzon Press, 1875.

Lewis, Claudia. *Indian Families of the Northwest Coast: The Impact of Change.* Chicago: University of Chicago Press, 1970.

Locher, G. W. *The Serpent in Kwakiutl Religion.* Leyden: Brill, 1932.

Lord, John K. *The Naturalist in Vancouver Island and British Columbia.* 2 vols. London: R. Bentley, 1866.

McFeat, Tom, ed. *Indians of the North Pacific Coast.* Toronto: McClelland and Stewart, 1966.

McIlwraith, Thomas F. *The Bella Coola Indians.* Toronto: University of Toronto Press, 1948.

McKechnie, Robert E. *Strong Medicine.* Vancouver: J. J. Douglas, 1972.

Mackenzie, Alexander. *Voyages from Montreal, on the River St. Laurence, Through the Continent of North America to the Frozen and Pacific Oceans in 1789 and 1793.* London: W. Davies, 1801.

Marchand, Etienne. *A Voyage Round the World.* London: T. N. Longman, 1801.

Mayne, R. C. *Four Years in British Columbia and Vancouver Island.* London: John Murray, 1862.

Meade, Edward. *Indian Rock Carvings of the Pacific Northwest.* Sidney, B.C.: Gray's Publishing, 1971.

Meares, John. *Voyages made in the years 1788 to 1789, from China to the Northwest Coast of America.* London: Logographic Press, 1791.

Miles, Charles. *Indian and Eskimo Artifacts of North America.* New York: 1963.

Morice, A. G. *The History of the Northern Interior of British Columbia.* Toronto: Briggs, 1905.

Newton, Norman. *Fire in the Raven's Nest.* Toronto: New Press, 1973.

Niblack, A. P. *The Coast Indians of Southern Alaska and Northern British Columbia.* Washington, 1890.

Oberg, Kalvero. *The Social Economy of the Tlingit Indians.* Vancouver: J. J. Douglas, 1973.

Patterson, Nancy-Lou. *Canadian Native Art.* Don Mills: Collier-Macmillan, 1973.

Portlock, Nathaniel. *A Voyage Round the World; But More Particularly to the North-West Coast of America. . . .* London: John Stockdale, 1789.

Ravenhill, Alice. *The Native Tribes of British Columbia.* Victoria: C. R. Banfield, 1938.

Rich, E. E. *The Fur Trade and the Northwest to 1857.* Toronto: McClelland and Stewart, 1967.

_____. *The Hudson's Bay Company.* 3 vols. London: 1959.

Robin, Martin. *The Bad and the Lonely.* Toronto: James Lorimer, 1976.

Rohner, Ronald P. *The People of Gilford: A Contemporary Kwakiutl Village.* Ottawa: National Museum of Canada, 1967.

Rohner, Ronald P. and Rohner, Evelyn C. *The Kwakiutl: Indians of British Columbia.* New York: Holt, Rinehart and Winston, 1970.

Smith, Marian, ed. *Indians of the Urban Northwest.* New York: Columbia University Press, 1949.

Smyly, John and Smyly, Carolyn. *Those Born at Koona.* Saanichton: Hancock House, 1973.

Sound Heritage. Special issue: "Skeena Country." Victoria, 1976.

Spradley, James P., ed. *Guests Never Leave Hungry: The Autobiography of James Sewid, a Kwakiutl Indian.* New Haven: Yale University Press, 1969.

_____. "The Kwakiutl Indian Guardian Spirit Quest." Unpublished M. A. Thesis, University of Washington, Seattle, 1963.

Sproat, Gilbert Malcolm. *Scenes and Studies of Savage Life.* London: Smith, Elder & Co., 1868.

Stewart, Hilary. *Artifacts of the Northwest Coast Indians.* Saanichton: Hancock House, 1973.

Stott, Margaret A. *Bella Coola Ceremony and Art.* Ottawa: National Museums of Canada, 1975.

Suttles, Wayne. *Katzie Ethnographic Notes.* Victoria: B.C. Provincial Museum, 1955.

Swan, James G. *The Haidah Indians of Queen Charlotte's Islands.* Washington: Smithsonian Institution, 1874.

Swanton, J. R. *Haida Texts and Myths.* Washington: Government Printing Office, 1909.

Thornton, Mildred Valley. *Indian Lives and Legends.* Vancouver: Mitchell Press, 1966.

Underhill, Ruth. *Indians of the Pacific Northwest.* Washington, D.C.: Government Printing Office, 1944.

Usher, Jean. *William Duncan of Metlakatla.* Ottawa: National Museums of Canada, 1974.

Vancouver, George. *A Voyage of Discovery to the North Pacific Ocean and Round the World.* London: G. G. & J. Robinson, 1798.

Wagner, Henry R. *Spanish Explorations in the Strait of Juan de Fuca.* Santa Anna: Fine Arts Press, 1933.

Wellcome, Henry S. *The Story of Metlakatla.* London: Saxon & Co., 1887.

Wherry, Joseph H. *Indian Masks and Myths of the West.* New York: Funk and Wagnalls, 1969.

_____. *The Totem Pole Indians.* New York: W. Funk, 1964.

Wingert, Paul. *Primitive Art: Its Traditions and Styles.* New York: Oxford University Press, 1962.

Wolcott, Harry F. *A Kwakiutl Village and School.* New York: Holt, Rinehart and Winston, 1967.

Acknowledgements

First, let me thank the editors of the following journals who over the years have encouraged me to write on the peoples of the Coast: *Saturday Night, Arts, Artscanada, The Geographical Magazine,* and the *Burlington Magazine.* Ideas and even passages from the articles I wrote for them, and also from radio talks I prepared for the Canadian Broadcasting Corporation, have been incorporated here and there into this book. I would also thank the Canada Council, which gave me a Senior Arts grant for a period of six months that enabled me to make two research trips and to do in peace a great deal of necessary reading.

It is hard to list, or even to remember, all the people who over the past twenty-eight years during which I have lived in British Columbia have contributed to my appreciation and understanding of the Coast Indian cultures. But the following names must be included. In some cases I am in debt for a single highly illuminating conversation; in other cases there was help over a longer period and in a more material way, such as the obtaining of illustrations, the tracking down of information, the arrangement of introductions, the provision of timely hospitality:

Michael Ames, James Banham, Betty and Cyril Belshaw, A. N. Blicq, Laurenda Daniells, Wilson Duff, Audrey Goodfriend, Colin Graham, Audrey Hawthorn, H. B. Hawthorn, Willard E. Ireland, Della Kew, Michael Kew, David Koven, Lynn Maranda, Carol Meyer, Norman Newton, Kim and Jonathan Phillips, Bill Reid, Doris

Shadbolt, Audrey Shane, Richard Simmins, Hilary Stewart, Elizabeth Virolainen, Gloria Webster.

I would also like to thank the following institutions and their staffs for help in research and in obtaining illustrations, and in the cases where photographs are listed in the Picture Credits to thank them for the courtesy with which they have allowed these to be reproduced: The Public Archives of Canada, the Provincial Archives of British Columbia, the Special Collections branch of the University of British Columbia Library, the Vancouver Public Library, the University of British Columbia Information Services, the National Museum of Man (National Museums of Canada), the British Columbia Provincial Museum, the Vancouver Centennial Museum, the Museum of Anthropology at the University of British Columbia, the Metropolitan Museum of Art, the Philadelphia University Museum, the American Museum of Natural History, the Vancouver Art Gallery, the Art Gallery of Greater Victoria.

I would like also to thank Carlotta Lemieux for her excellent editorial work, and finally, to thank my wife, Ingeborg Woodcock, who has accompanied and helped me in my researches and has provided many of the photographs which illustrate this and other books on the Pacific Coast of Canada.

G.W.

219

Picture Credits

Index

222

223